A Victorian Quartet:

Four Forgotten Women Writers

A Victorian Quartet:

Four Forgotten Women Writers

Liz Thiel
Elaine Lomax
Bridget Carrington
Mary Sebag Montefiore

Pied Piper Publishing

First published 2008 by:

Pied Piper Publishing Ltd.
80 Birmingham Road
Shenstone
Lichfield
Staffordshire
WS14 0JU

www.piedpiperpublishing.com

British Library Cataloguing in Publication
A catalogue record for this book is available from the British Library.

*Every attempt has been made by the authors to trace the copyright of
material used in this book, but in some cases this has proved impossible to
ascertain. We would be pleased to receive information from copyright
holders where material remains unattributed.*

Cover illustration © Jordan Carslaw

ISBN 978 0 9552106 5 5   10 digit - 0 9552106 5 8

Contents

List of Illustrations

Introduction

Kimberley Reynolds

Introduction

Kimberley Reynolds

One of the best ways to visit another epoch is through its fiction. While it is impossible not to read from the perspective of the present, literature of earlier eras, unlike, say, historical reconstructions, draws readers into a world created for its own time. A.S. Byatt's popular novel, *Possession* (1990), takes this phenomenon as its theme, looking at the complex interplay between literary scholars and their subjects, and the way fiction brings minds from past and present together. Byatt's novel, with its central story about reconstructing the life and work of a forgotten Victorian woman writer, compares interestingly with this volume, though her lost poet wrote for an audience of adults while the four women whose work features in *A Victorian Quartet* have come to be regarded as writers for children.

Writing for children, with its emphasis on story and its tendency to include visual images, is a particularly valuable portal to the past – not least because most writers for the young are conscious that their readers are relatively new to the world and need to have its workings explained to them. With this in mind, it is surprising that historians have rarely recognised fiction for children as a primary resource for information about the daily lives of earlier generations. The four contributors to this volume do precisely this. Unlike Byatt's novel, which invents its writer, Christabel LaMotte, and her poems, this study recalls to life the work of four actual women writers whose books have been neglected for approximately a century. Like Byatt, however, the contributors show how these books open windows onto the past, though moving well beyond the literary and romantic preoccupations of *Possession*. The different parts of this work provide vivid glimpses into everything from the mending of streets, preparations for a holiday, Irish politics, and the life of immigrants in Britain's cities, to the writers' business negotiations and their rapid acquisition of professional acumen.

The women whose work is discussed here -'Brenda', Mrs. Molesworth, Flora Shaw and Hesba Stretton – have little in common with the entrapped and pinioned Christabel LaMotte, a figure overly familiar from the Victorian adult fiction on which Byatt based her character. Instead, they are highly effective, managing homes, families, financial vicissitudes, social niceties and Herculean workloads. More importantly, where Christabel LaMotte was virtually unknown, the women featured in the following pages were enormously popular and influential in their day: Hesba Stretton's work, for instance, was hailed by reviewers as 'in the foremost rank of living authoresses' [12], while her obituary credits her with reaching 'millions of readers', and she was a tireless campaigner for the rights of women and children. Like Byatt's poet, however, they have been forgotten, or remembered in a way that distorts how they were known and valued in their day. Each, for instance, was read by adults as well as children, but now they tend to be dismissed as outdated nursery fare.

Just how wrong this perception can be is demonstrated in Elaine Lomax's section on Stretton, who not only worked for social change, but eventually became involved with London-based Russian revolutionaries. The view of the world conjured up in the pages of her fictions is often far removed from the Victorian/Edwardian nursery, too. Many of her subjects live in the poorest parts of the metropolis and witness scenes of vice, violence and degradation. As Lomax observes, Stretton is concerned with 'the overcrowded city inferno, with its suffocating, light-starved courts and labyrinthine alleys, its grim lodging houses … and its flaring gin palaces'. [25] Modern readers may also be surprised by her detailed accounts of the miserable lives led by children of the poor. *An Acrobat's Girlhood* (1889), for instance, is no Noel Streatfeild celebration of aspiring performers but an exposé of the way children's bodies were damaged and their lives risked by the work they were required to do. This kind of critique of the social problems and injustices she observed and her willingness to take the point of view of the outcast – whether a criminal, gypsy, Jew, or vagrant child – mean that the windows Hesba Stretton opens on to Victorian life are often surprising and moving.

At first glance the work of Mary Louisa Molesworth seems more conventional, but Mary Sebag-Montefiore quickly establishes her too as a writer whose accounts of everyday life challenge stereotypes about the Victorian family. At the same time, her books also provide detailed accounts about how middle-class children were raised. Molesworth goes behind the scenes of her families, showing both tenderness and tension between parents and children, inadequate parents, unlovable children, misunderstandings, and psychic wounds. Such a list makes Molesworth's books sound gloomy; in fact, they are lively and engaging, and though realistic, always end optimistically. To modern readers what seems particularly striking is the sympathetic way she writes about angry children, and her ability both to show rage as legitimate and to make it clear that ultimately it is an unhelpful and inadequate response. Her angry characters eventually find more effective ways of expressing and managing themselves and in doing so offer readers strategies for negotiating the power-dynamics of Victorian culture.

The section on Molesworth also invites us to look at that other crucial behind-the-scene aspect of middle-class life in a Victorian household – the world of the servant. Because she is normally seeing the servants through the eyes of her child characters, Molesworth's take on servants is unusually positive. Her pages are filled with loved nurses who are often wiser than parents and intimate scenes between servants and children, who often occupy the same domestic spaces. Her servants, unlike her child characters, are models of rectitude and fortitude; they understand children's inner worlds and their own social positions, and this understanding helps them heal damaged families and prepare their charges to make their way in the world. Where much early children's literature presents servants as the source of corruption in the child's world, Sebag-Montefiore argues that Molesworth's show the nurse in particular as an exaggerated form of the 'angel-in-the-house', an image normally reserved for middle and upper-class women.

Equally radical in Molesworth's work are her child characters – no angels these, but clearly based on observation and knowledge of real children. Over the years critics have tended to focus too much on what has been presented as Molesworth's unfortunate tendency to render childish speech through the use of lisps and twee phraseology; here, by contrast, we are directed to the way she creates fully embodied children in all their aspects. As Sebag-Montefiore observes,

> Molesworth's books ring with hitting, crying, kicking, and squeezed out tears falling down hot cheeks. There is wriggling, pouting, flouncing; streaming, untidy hair, grimy faces, clothes flung pell-mell out of drawers, dressing, undressing, breaking things, hugging, stroking, eating. She creates a very physical sense of childhood. [112]

It is not only children and servants whose lives are set out sympathetically. Bemused and clumsy fathers are explained on her pages and she is especially concerned to legitimise those women who find themselves – as she did herself – forced to work to support their families. In the hands of many Victorian writers this inevitably means loss of caste by becoming a governess or milliner, but Molesworth's working women always remain gentle, and they are admired rather than disgraced.

iii

Exactly this fate befell 'Brenda', the third member of this quartet, who moved from a large house in London to the relative obscurity of Lyme Regis when the family fortunes declined. Liz Thiel's introduction to her subject is strongly reminiscent of the detective work at the heart of *Possession*. Like Byatt's scholars, she visited relatives, read private correspondence, studied images, handled artefacts and gradually reconstructed many aspects of this forgotten writer. That she should have dropped so completely from literary memory is surprising given that in her day she was a much-loved writer, read across the social spectrum.

Like Hesba Stretton, 'Brenda' is usually remembered as a writer of waif fiction and primarily for one book, her powerful story about two orphan brothers, *Froggy's Little Brother*. Thiel concentrates on her domestic fiction which, unlike *Froggy*, features middle-class families at home and on holiday in terrains made up of 'leafy London squares, shopping bazaars, seaside resorts...a secure, comfortable and caring world replete with kindly servants and benevolent relatives.' [187] Of all the work discussed in this volume, these offer the most detailed vignette's of every day life, from descriptions of favourite toys and birthday parties through the early morning noise of the parish steam-roller, the arrival of the cab that comes to the door to be loaded up with the paraphernalia needed for travelling to an account of a bathing-machine and the demolishing of siblings' sandcastles on holiday beaches. The account of children playing at being mothers in Chapter 12 holds the mirror up to adult behaviour in a most interesting and telling way, while the child's-eye view of London (Madame Tussaud's, Westminster Abbey, the Zoological Gardens) shows how much continuity between then and now there is. This London world is not always celebrated, however, and several of the passages quoted deplore its parched and regimented lifestyle for children in ways familiar from E. Nesbit and described in such detail that a mental picture instantly comes to mind:

> ...the Square garden was just like all the other Square gardens in Bayswater; iron railings all round, a stiff gravel path running from end to end...a patch of burnt-up trodden grass in the middle, a black-trunked tree or two, and underneath a rustic seat or wooden bench, and at the gates a shabby notice board stuck up to say 'No dogs admitted,' (and some said the dogs did not miss much!). [195]

This kind of evocation of a time past is what makes these books so valuable as evidence of everyday life in the Victorian period and alone justify the efforts made to recover these women's work, though as each of the sections shows, the writers' lives too are interesting and frequently surprising.

'Surprising' is as good a way as any of describing the last member of this quartet, Flora Shaw, novelist, 'brilliant colonial editor of *The Times*,' [229] colonial historian, Dame of the British Empire – and almost entirely forgotten. Bridget Carrington's account of Shaw's life and activities is an antidote to the widespread tendency to view the Victorian period as a time in which women were debarred from publicly active lives, while her publishing history of Shaw's best-known work, *Castle Blair* tells us a great deal about audiences, publishing practices, and the way long-lived books changed place and appearance over time.

Castle Blair itself is interesting for the version of nineteenth-century Irish politics, with its emphasis on the iniquities of the Anglo-Irish relationship, it offers. Perhaps more significant in a work that deals with children's writers, is its contribution to the development of children's literature. For Carrington, its child characters 'represent a significant, though little recognized, step in the movement towards the modern children's novel, in which the young protagonists operate with an autonomy largely denied to child characters before Shaw.' [243] Nevertheless, Shaw's grasp of the dynamics of colonial rule means that *Castle Blair*'s readers are given an entertaining but insightful – and because it is for children a well explained – look at how the situation was understood by someone in the middle of the nineteenth century. Although in some ways very different from the way the other works discussed in this book bring together past and present, *Castle Blair* too looks at children's lives and the way they experience the world.

Evoking the way children experience the world was to become a hallmark of the modernist sensibility. While in this Introduction I have concentrated on the main enterprise of this book, which is reminding us of forgotten writers and their work with a view to enlarging our understanding of the Victorian world, it is important not to forget that these popular, admired and influential writers inevitably had an effect on those who read them in childhood and went on to write themselves. It is undoubtedly the case that Virginia Woolf, James Joyce and Kenneth Grahame, for instance, would have read at least some of the works discussed in this volume and that some of their ideas about how to evoke childhood sensibilities on the page were drawn from them. Together the lives and work of Stretton, Molesworth, 'Brenda' and Shaw provides us with detailed accounts of every day life, insights into the lives of professional women writers, political analysis, social commentary, and the stirrings of modernism. How profligate of earlier generations to have discarded them; how welcome this enterprise.

Writing Other Lives

The Outcast Narratives of Hesba Stretton

Elaine Lomax

HESBA STRETTON (Sarah Smith) 1832-1911

… 'who by her pen reached millions of readers', reads the caption accompanying the cover portrait for the December 1911 edition of the Religious Tract Society magazine, *Seed Time and Harvest*, following the death of the writer Hesba Stretton. During the second half of the nineteenth century, and, indeed, well into the twentieth, Stretton's status was legendary. Today, the author of bestselling 'waif' titles such as *Jessica's First Prayer* (1867), *Little Meg's Children* (1868) and *Alone in London* (1869) – published by the Religious Tract Society and once familiar in countless homes in England and abroad – is all but forgotten. Held in high esteem by readers and respected by critics and commentators of the day, her considerable and broad-ranging body of work – which, despite a reputation which associates her first and foremost with the juvenile, evangelical market, includes secular stories, articles and full-length novels for older audiences (many texts occupying a place on the boundary of adult-child literature) – is virtually unknown to today's reader.

Whilst acknowledging her influence on the 'street-Arab' genre, modern critics have tended to dismiss Stretton's writings as outdated, overly religious, didactic and sentimental – a view passed on often without examination of the texts[1]. However, her contemporary significance – and, indeed, the resonance of her themes for us today – merits broader recognition; there are ample grounds for recovering and reassessing her work as a whole. Fresh scrutiny reveals her writings to be less sentimental and sermonising, more open, layered and thought-provoking than might be anticipated – a hybrid generic blend rooted in the material but embracing matters psychological and emotional as well as spiritual. These narratives, moreover, engage with some of the most pressing social, cultural and political concerns of the mid- to late-Victorian era, and address unexpectedly complex moral and philosophical dilemmas.

Socially aware and politically engaged, Stretton campaigned vigorously for the rights of others. Embracing an essentially conservative morality, she was at the same time forward-thinking and practical, advocating social change and identifying the progressive potential of Christian teaching. Admitting early in life to an incipient republicanism (a stance which did not preclude her from feeling very sorry for the Queen on the death of Prince Albert, according to her diary on 15 December 1861), and later proclaiming herself, in a letter to [Mr.] Pattison (c.1886) 'thoroughly a

Radical, ... even a Republican', Stretton directed her energies towards radical causes, associating, during the 1890s, with prominent Russian anarchists exiled in London.

Investigation into Stretton's oeuvre exposes its overarching preoccupation with the figure of the child (especially the socially or emotionally deprived child), with the woman and mother, and with the outsider or outcast of all kinds. The product of particular historical circumstances, and caught up in a network of overlapping contemporary discourses, her writings reflect, expose and challenge a range of dominant nineteenth-century anxieties, prejudices and inequalities, intervening in key debates. At the same time, they remind us today of our failure, despite seeming advances, to resolve persistent, albeit differently configured, issues of poverty, oppression, delinquency and division, and of the continued significance of relations of power and abuses of authority across private and public spheres. Tapping into an intermingled fascination with, and fear of, the 'other', which resonates deep within the psyche, Stretton's narratives speak to us of complex and pervasive attitudes – then, but also now – towards the marginalised, and those whom we perceive to be unlike ourselves, underlining a seemingly unremitting need to construct and perpetuate notions of difference – to apply, wittingly and unwittingly, the kind of 'binary branding' and strategies of exclusion identified by cultural theorist Michel Foucault (1979).[2]

Renewed examination of Stretton's life and multifaceted writings against a backdrop of the social, cultural and literary landscape of the period foregrounds the intertextuality of key themes and motifs across this matrix, shedding light on this intriguing woman and illuminating the appeal and significance of not only those works with which she has been readily associated but also countless others of which we know less today, but which were once familiar family reading. Retrieval of this neglected body of work proves an enlightening and enriching undertaking.

Notes

1. More balanced studies include Cutt (1979), Bratton (1981) and Rickard (1996).

2. See *Discipline and Punish*, 1979: 199.

Chapter 1

'I am a woman, and I will act for myself' (Stretton, *Cobwebs and Cables*, 1881)

Private and public arenas

A woman of complexity

The face of the older Hesba Stretton which looks up at us from the Memoirs of 1911 is that of an upright and rather austere personage – an image which accords with the legend which had by then grown up around her, and which she did little to dispel. However, insights offered by Stretton's diaries and other personal material, together with an irrepressible current which runs through her writings, afford glimpses of a less conservative, more playful and irreverent spirit, in many respects undiminished by age. What seems certain is that, as woman and as writer, Stretton was far more complex and less conventional than the myth handed down to us suggests. Unmarried, independent and assertive, often provocative and boundary-crossing in her writings, business and other activities – indeed, displaying, in some respects, a proto-typical feminism – she would doubtless have joined with the protagonist of *Cobwebs and Cables* in declaring: 'I am a woman, and I will act for myself' (1881/n.d.: 128, Ch.18).

Stretton was born, Sarah Smith, in Wellington, Shropshire, into a loving, committed Wesleyan family. As the offspring of a bookseller (and bookworm), formerly apprenticed to the prominent provincial publisher John Houlston, who had produced many of the books of Mrs. Sherwood and Mrs. Cameron and the early work of Harriet Martineau, the siblings – four girls and a boy – grew up surrounded by books of all kinds. Health problems meant that Stretton's formal schooling was irregular, but the range of influences available in the home environment provided an education of the kind which Stretton later endorsed as the 'calling out of all our faculties … rather than the accumulating of a mass of information' ('A Talk with Hesba Stretton', 1896: 165)[1]. Like her protagonist Hester (*Hester Morley's Promise*, 1873/1898: 22, Ch.3), she was permitted to listen quietly to the discussions attended by neighbourhood intellectuals, where all manner of religious and political questions were aired. This early exposure stimulated an interest in diverse areas of prominent debate, and a thirst for both practical and theoretical knowledge. As a young woman, she frequented the Jail and Assize Courts, attended public

HESBA STRETTON
Born 1832
Passed away after a long, happy, useful, and noble life
on October 8, 1911

Illustration 1: Portrait of Hesba Stretton from 1911 Memoir, *The Sunday at Home*
Courtesy of Shropshire Archives & Lutterworth Press

lectures on topics such as Positive Philosophy, and visited museums, galleries, and, occasionally, the theatre. Reviewers of her books later noted the breadth of her views; literary allusions ranging from Plato to Malthus, through Shakespeare, Byron, Scott, Austen, Carlyle and other prominent writers, testify to her engagement with a spectrum of intellectual, cultural, theological and socially-oriented material. Many of Stretton's preoccupations overlap with those of Dickens, and there are numerous correspondences between the themes, motifs and sentiments of her writings and those of Mrs. Gaskell.[2]

The siblings exercised their imaginative faculties in sometimes dark fantasy worlds of their own creation. The hills and valleys formed by the nearby slag-heaps provided 'distant countries' to be explored with a 'delicious' sense of peril; in winter, the children played in the mysterious semi-darkness of a barn, or listened to farm-servants' talk of ghosts, howling dogs and strange noises, half-anticipating, with 'fearful pleasure', the appearance of some supernatural being. These childish imaginings engendered a lingering and ambivalent fascination with the uncanny – embodied in the alluring, yet fearsome 'hobgoblins' of earlier times (*Hester Morley's Promise*, 91) – a preoccupation which, in tension with an evangelical stance, feeds into gothic elements in Stretton's narratives. It surfaces in the dark settings of the two-volume *David Lloyd's Last Will* (1869), and in *Michel Lorio's Cross*, in which a child's secret meetings with the outcast village 'diable' hold a terror-laden charm (1876/inscr.1888: 25).

Stretton's mother – acknowledged as a major influence on the development of her character and her sympathy for humanity – died when the child was not yet ten; the enduring significance of this loss is beyond question. The diary entry for 11 June 1863 records the twenty-first anniversary of her mother's death; the 'dream of [a] lost mother' (*David Lloyd's Last Will*, 1869: 118, Vol.1, Ch.10) is, in various forms, a recurring motif in her writings, which are infused with memory and longing. Her father was also Postmaster at Wellington, and the girls assisted in the office from an early age; later, as his health deteriorated, they handled much of the business organisation, but failed, seemingly as a consequence of gender discrimination, to secure backing to run the office on Benjamin Smith's retirement. In this environment, they were, like the protagonists of 'A Provincial Post-Office' (1863), privy to all the local gossip regarding romantic attachments, indiscretions and petty scandals, which were to provide a rich source of material for Stretton's particular blend of popular, social and spiritual themes.

She maintained a close – perhaps substitute maternal – relationship with her sister Lizzie – a bond which was to endure to the end of their lives; they shared various homes, Sara(h)[3] writing and, for brief periods, teaching, while Lizzie worked as a governess and shouldered the burden of domestic chores. During Lizzie's absences, Sara felt herself a 'widow' (19.12.1863), a perception which reflects the strength and completeness of their attachment – surpassing, according to a note by her niece appended to the *Sunday at Home* Memoir, 'the most devoted companionship of husband and wife' (Webb, 1911: 125). In 1860 the sisters embarked upon a diary in which they charted family activities, events and travels, together with reactions and comments.[4] This more or less regular, if somewhat terse and, at times, enigmatic record (in Hesba Stretton's hand only, after initial entries, and chiefly from her perspective) provides some insight into day-to-day experiences, frustrations, attitudes and relationships, in both private and public spheres. It also reveals areas of apparent overlap, as well as disjunction, between actual and textual preoccupations and themes, which serve, in conjunction with cautious conjecture, to advance our understanding of both the author and her works, the latter perhaps affording a veil for deeper reflection and self-examination than that displayed in the journal, which offers immediate and casual, if telling, responses, rather than introspection.[5]

The diaries evidence a persistent battle with the overwhelming effects of boredom or what Stretton calls 'monotony within the ark' (18.9.1862); they reveal an abhorrence of all forms of containment or enslavement – a terror shared by many of her protagonists, who resist being confined, encaged or institutionalised, literally and metaphorically. Although she sometimes found life in the country tedious and stultifying, and appreciated the vitality of city life, Stretton's love of open spaces reflects a fundamental desire for freedom, both mental and physical, which permeates diary and texts alike; walking, often alone, on the hills and moorlands of her native Shropshire (and, later, in the mountains of Europe), she experienced, like Oliver in *Alone in London*, who yearns to be 'a-top of the Wrekin', rather than in the stifling city (1869/inscr.1872: 11), the sensuality of the landscape and a concomitant liberation of body and spirit.

Journal entries in the diaries reveal a distaste for the mundane and domestic; Stretton playfully mocked overt domesticity in others, but also recognised the value of such attributes, not least – here displaying a certain class-based ambivalence – in terms of their usefulness 'at home or in the colonies', in young girls of the lower classes ('Ragged School

Union Conferences', 1883: 268). Although the myth – which family members and, later, commentators, allowed to persist – constructed her as a reserved individual who denied herself the pleasure of fashion or frivolity, her journals bear witness to a young woman, who, despite a tendency to be intolerant of life's irritations and abrasively critical of those in her circle who disappointed her expectation of unfailingly stimulating company, appreciated 'fun and frolic' in acquaintances and frequently wearied herself with laughter.[6] Stretton recounts practical jokes, party games and festive fooleries; she enjoyed an 'old-fashioned gossip' (16.6.1862) – often at the expense of local personalities, whom she likens to characters in Dickens's novels – and regularly enlivened dull social gatherings with acute, sometimes playful, observation of participants' behaviour, rendered into sardonic commentary in her diaries, which also appreciatively record purchases of clothes as well as outings to local entertainments and performances such as the Christy Minstrels.

Church gatherings and bible studies provided not only spiritual food, but further diversion; the sisters regularly found amusement in appraising sermons or, with an eye to physical attributes, making sport of preachers. According to diary entries – which often carry an ironic tone – they were, for a period in the early 1860s, much exercised with the 'matrimonial question'; as Lizzie was approaching thirty without 'prospects', they embarked, somewhat playfully, on a quest to find an eligible partner for at least one of the three sisters who remained unmarried. Scrutiny of possible candidates yielded chiefly dissatisfaction, and, in the diaries, scepticism regarding the marital state sits alongside romantic aspirations (which are perhaps displaced into textual themes), with Stretton nonetheless articulating the desire for a young man 'on high days and holidays', if only to appear 'more like other people' (25.12.1861). She was, however, determined to mark out her own path, to be – like a number of her protagonists – 'mistress and arbitress' of her actions (*Hester Morley's Promise*, 177, Ch.25). Stretton abhorred the idea of being under authority, and, despite occasionally – and somewhat sardonically – 'lamenting over the carriage in which we might have ridden' (Log Book: 6-9.1863), would not have relished being one of those women whose fate it is, under patriarchy, 'to do as she is ordered' (*The Highway of Sorrow*, 1894/1897, 173, Ch.14).

If Stretton, in texts and campaigning, identified the home as women's sphere of influence, she personally enjoyed the freedom to travel extensively at home and abroad, without the trammels of conventional domesticity. She was at liberty to venture, as it was increasingly acceptable for women philanthropists to do, into the 'miserable slums' of Manchester and London, gaining an insight at first-hand into the 'tragic reality of the lives of the poor' (Webb, 1964: 11) and the 'horrible cruelty practised on little children' ('The Origin of the London SPCC', 1908). She visited Ragged Schools, poor homes, slums and 'low' lodging houses, and spent time in orphanages, infirmaries, refuges and shelters. Her response to these experiences, and her commitment to social amelioration and consciousness-raising, finds expression in her writings, fictional and non-fictional, and in the key role she played in campaigning for the formation of the London Society for the Prevention of Cruelty to Children (later the NSPCC), of which she became a founder member in 1884.[7] A natural extension of her affinity with the young and her longstanding interest in the plight of disadvantaged children, rescue work and child protection became a major preoccupation during the 1880s, this 'maternal' mission further informing her literary project.

The tendency towards anti-authoritarianism permeates all aspects of Stretton's private and public life, her resistance extending to diverse forms of established institutional authority, including the organised Church. Deeply influenced by her mother's early example, Stretton developed a strong, compassionate and practical faith, but later regarded aspects of established religion (and, indeed, of society in general), with a critical, often satirical eye, her caricatures of other-worldliness on occasion provoking complaints from publishers.[8] Religion, as she implies in *Hester Morley*, can be too solemn, conduct too unbending; the protagonist of *David Lloyd's Last Will* urges her over-earnest companion to 'do something dreadfully wrong, just for a change' (Vol.1, Ch.2, 20). Along with her sisters, Stretton was intrigued by, and alternately derisive and supportive of the activities of preachers and Church community during a series of Revivalist meetings during 1861. Broadly evangelical in outlook, but eschewing narrow dogmatism, she condemned inflexibility, exclusivity, hypocrisy and 'humbug' in others[9]; whilst pointing to God's love and forgiveness, her writings call into question unthinking platitudes and examine doubt. Texts such as *Max Kromer* (1871), *Left Alone* (1876) and the longer *In the Hollow of His Hand* (1897) focus on the pernicious consequences of division and sectarianism, and the inability of people to respect different standpoints on religion, which should not consist in 'the observance of forms' (*Half Brothers*, 1892/n.d.: 94, Ch.14).

Comfortably settled in London during the last decade of the century, Stretton turned to overtly political matters, engaging – as, in fact, did many seemingly unlikely individuals – in the cause of leading Russian revolutionists based in London. This group included Prince Kropotkin, co-founder of the anarchist-communist monthly *Freedom*, and Sergei Kravchinsky, known as Stepniak, rumoured to have been implicated in the assassination of the Russian state official, Mezentev. In collaboration with Stepniak, Stretton produced *The Highway of Sorrow* (1894), a text which focuses on the persecution by the Orthodox Church of the dissident Russian Stundists, and highlights abuses of power by the autocratic Tsarist regime. Like the similarly-themed *In the Hollow of His Hand* (1897), the narrative interweaves romantic, spiritual and political soul-searching with an exposé of brutality and coercion matched by loyalty and resilience. In London, Stepniak, like his fellow Russians, associated with radical and liberal intellectuals, publishing articles and books, and lecturing on conditions in Russia.[10] Although atheist, he often exploited New Testament themes in his propaganda, and also sought to bring his theories to the public in popular form, an aim which his collaboration with Stretton no doubt furthered. In *The Highway of Sorrow*, atheist, revolutionary ideas are openly explored, evangelical premises interrogated as well as endorsed, common ground identified. Projects such as these chimed with Stretton's abiding concern for the dispossessed, and with her wider preoccupations. They also provided an outlet for the interests of the other, more anarchic Stretton: even in later life, this rebellious, action-seeking spirit jostles with the persona of the sensible old maiden lady originally contemplated in *David Lloyd's Last Will*, and which usefully served aspects of her multifaceted agenda.

'The making of many books'

Although the diaries cover the period of her growing acclaim, they contain only brief insights into the process of writing; entries during 1860 allude, for example, to 'idea' for, or 'progress' in, the 'big book', and others note simply 'second child's story finished' (9/10.2.1864) or 'begin my third novel' (29.1.1867). They chart the vicissitudes of a writer's life ('author like a barometer', 7.7.1861), recording a sense of rivalry or jealousy in the face of early peer successes. The trials of the profession are perhaps more keenly expressed by the writer-protagonist of the late, full-length novel *Cobwebs and Cables*, who, despite showing an assertiveness in business negotiations characteristic of Stretton's own dealings with publishers, talks of petty enmities, intermittent creative difficulties and periods of self-doubt, with 'vexation of spirit' accompanying 'weariness of the flesh' in the 'making of many books' (275, Ch.40). As journalist Hulda Friederichs discovered in 1894, Stretton remained guarded on the subject of writing methods; however, declaring herself a rapid but careful writer, she confessed to having rewritten *Hester Morley* three times before it met with her satisfaction, and revealed that she did not devise the plot or the actions of her characters – who often behaved in unexpected ways – before starting a story (1894: 331-332).

The 1860s journals (the first simply a list of early submissions and payments) evidence Stretton's persistence in presenting articles of journalism and light fiction to periodicals including Dickens's *Household Words* and *All The Year Round*, the latter becoming a regular destination for her work. Stories are often referred to by the names of their protagonists; they 'journey' and find their 'home[s]' with publishers,[11] suggesting not only their place as substitute offspring, but also the nomadic and waif-like quality of their struggle for acceptance; a writer's thoughts, moreover – which are 'like children' – must not, as the author-protagonist of *Cobwebs and Cables* emphasises, be sent out 'ragged and uncouth' (133, Ch.19), to be shamed and ridiculed.

Journal entries chart progress and allude to critical reviews of her early novels for an adult market; *The Clives of Burcot*, published in 1867 by Tinsley, was, at a moment when 'lady-novelists' were 'legion', acclaimed one of the season's 'soundest and healthiest novels', containing portrayals worthy of George Eliot (*The Standard*, 30.8.1867)); its author was considered by the *Morning Star* (14.1.1867) to be 'in the foremost rank of living authoresses', its popular success deemed certain (*The Observer*, 6.1.1867).[12] By the time of its appearance, Stretton had begun to publish the fiction which was to establish her in the juvenile market, but over the course of her career she continued to produce full-length novels – many of which embrace melodramatic and morally complex themes of bigamy, murder, fraud, exchanges of identity and 'actual adultery' (*The Athenaeum*, 6.9.1873, on *Hester Morley*) as well as social and spiritual preoccupations – alongside shorter and mid-length, *ostensibly* juvenile-oriented narratives. The relationship between these writings is significant, the borders, in many respects, precarious.

The potential of Stretton's writings to reach a wide and varied audience is, in part, a product of the multiple and intersecting agendas of both author and publishing establishment – programmes influenced in turn by personal, social and political considerations. The long-term (although interrupted) association with the Religious Tract Society, established through a family connection, is highly significant, supplying a vital foothold within the literary establishment, from which she could build her reputation. Not only would the relationship forged with publishers and readers – enhanced in many instances by the loyalty generated by initial serialisation – pave the way for Stretton's ongoing social and political project, but it would also provide a vehicle for the expression of her wider agenda as a writer of popular fiction, and for the articulation of an independent female voice.[13]

The Society took up in book form several of her early 'child' narratives, including *Fern's Hollow* (1864), *The Children of Cloverley* (1865) and *Enoch Roden's Training* (1865), all set in working-class rural communities. The originality of her works – which greatly exceeded the customary average (Executive Committee Minutes H8501, 21.6.1864) – was commended by the RTS 'Readers'; the vividly-rendered 'adventures and dangers' (H8501, 27.3.1866) of *The Fishers of Derby Haven* (1866) suited their quest, amidst competition from a growing secular market, for more lively material. It was, however, the sensitively crafted 'waif' story *Jessica's First Prayer*, first serialised in the *Sunday at Home* in 1866, and published by the RTS in volume form in 1867, following 'urgent requests' (H8501, 4.12.1866), which was to bring her name to the attention of a wide reading public and confirm her commercial potential. By the time that *Pilgrim Street*, which centres on the experiences of a young Manchester street-boy, was recommended for publication in 1867, the RTS were identifying her as a 'popular author' (H8501, 26.2.1867) and, emboldened by a growing confidence in her position, Stretton began to dictate her owns terms within the male-dominated world of publishing, a challenge to established authority which she continued to exercise, albeit with a degree of compromise, throughout her career.

Approaching the Tract Society in 1868 with the *Little Meg's Children*, a 'graphically-told' story of childhood adversity deemed to exceed *Jessica* in pathos and power (H8501, 21.4.1868), Stretton was now aware of her ability to command significantly more than the seemingly 'capital pay' (thirty-five guineas) paid for *Enoch Roden* (Log Book: 24.6.1864), and consequently determined not to repeat the mistake she had made with *Jessica* of selling the copyright outright for a low figure. Indignant at the Society's initial offer of £50 for *Little Meg*, and intent on requesting 'so much a thousand' (Log Book: 28.3.1868), she proceeded to play several publishers off against each other – a tactic later deplored by the struggling writer-protagonist of *Cobwebs* and *Cables*, who is constrained to offer a manuscript 'as so much merchandise from house to house', for sale to the highest bidder (*Cobwebs and Cables*, 132, Ch.19). A convoluted – and in terms of her initial demands, not wholly successful – sequence of negotiations (involving bids from publishers Nisbet and Houlston and

Wright) resulted in her reluctant acceptance of £6.5s. for each subsequent thousand from the RTS, an outcome logged in her diary (along with her frustrations over higher offers made and subsequently withdrawn) during April 1868, and noted in Society Minutes, which confirm a sum of £25 for the first thousand rather than the £50 sought by Stretton.[14]

The relationship was highly beneficial to both sides. By November 1868 sales of *Little Meg*, predicted at the outset to be a success by the RTS Readers, had reached 10,000 (Log Book: 19.11.1868); by summer 1869 another 14,000 had been sold, and continuing popularity ensured considerable sums in royalties. When the street-Arab story *Alone in London* was recommended for volume publication in 1869 – again following 'much attention' during serialisation (H8501, 17.8.1869) – the RTS was already acutely aware not only of the evangelical power of her narratives but of her financial importance to the Society. Alert to the 'prominent' fact that her books now accounted for over one-third of the new books, and more than one-fifth of their circulation, they were keen to capitalise on her evident popularity by securing 'another book by her this Christmas' (H8502, 15.7.1869). Her titles were set to become household names, and over the course of time she was to publish her work with firms such H.S. King, Nisbet, Isbister, Hodder and Stoughton and Cassell.

'A child's book truly …'? Crossing the boundaries of age, class, gender and genre

It is perhaps useful to consider Hesba Stretton's oeuvre in terms of family literature – a range of books for different audiences and, at the same time, a range of audiences for individual texts. Stretton may have thought of early works such as *Fern's Hollow* and *The Children of Cloverley* as belonging to the genre of the 'child's story', but there are ample grounds for problematising such categorisation. The Tract Society identified the latter text as likely to 'interest adults as well as the young' (H8501, 3.10.1865); their Minutes refer to books 'for all classes', sometimes adding 'especially for the young' (as with Stretton's short narrative about the Siege of Strasbourg, *Max Kromer* (H8501, 24.1.1871), or targeting those of little education or 'humble condition' (whose conduct in *The Fishers of Derby Haven* they commended). Such relatively fluid categorisation formed part of a multiple agenda which saw publishers intent on profiting commercially from the expanding market for children's literature (and, more perversely and precariously, the contemporary taste for sensation fiction), on raising middle-class awareness of poverty and deprivation, and on implementing a programme of social, moral and spiritual instruction for lower-class adults as well as the young, the ready conflation of 'children' and 'the poor' highlighting a process of subordination and infantilisation relating not only to chronological age, but also social status.[15] Adults might take on board particular messages whilst reading these stories for themselves or to young people, but increased literacy among working-class children meant that they might instead be reading to older family members, in many cases sharing texts purchased for, and not by, their readers, and awarded as Prizes for attendance at Ragged, Sunday, or later, Board Schools – such material constituting perhaps the most readily available reading matter in homes with limited means.

Translated into more than fifteen languages, *Jessica* 'stirred … hearts of old and young' alike (Green, 1899: 79), eventually selling over one-and-a-half million copies in different formats (ranging, as with other Stretton texts, from the Penny Books and the Shilling 'Gift' series to more costly versions directed at middle-class readers), and, allegedly, making grown men weep. The *Sunday at Home* Memoir reported comments that it was 'a child's book truly … but its effect on sailors was marvellous' (1911: 123). Textual lists of works frequently display Stretton's books as general, rather than children's, stories; narratives such as *Carola* (1884) and *Under the Old Roof* (1882) appear alongside full-length novels (the latter title sometimes advertised under 'approved stories for Boys and Girls'). According to surveys conducted by Edward Salmon during the mid-1880s, girls ranked Stretton among their favourite authors, but her work undoubtedly also found its way into the hands of boy readers, offering them not only a degree of incident and adventure – the narrative impetus often stimulated by the demands of serialisation – but a rare source of affective engagement, even if it was not deemed manly to admit to the fact.

The dividing line in terms of adult-child audiences – in any case less rigid in the nineteenth century than today – is blurred in terms not only of targeted reader or thematic content, but also other aspects of reader positioning, including tone and mode of address. Numerous texts revolve around the experiences of juvenile protagonists; however, as with the deceptively simple *Jessica's First Prayer*, attention is also given to the perspective and interests of adult characters – and implicitly, readers, with different levels of engagement invited. All ages are considered equally significant subjects or addressees, their concerns given equal weight; all are invited to engage with relatively mature and introspective concerns. Even the shorter books are less readily identifiable as juvenile texts than those of Mrs. Walton or Mrs. Molesworth. The writing generally displays little obvious accommodation of a child audience in terms of language and register (and might thus be *less* appealing to the young); the tone is not self-consciously maternal or intimate, the authorial presence seldom conspicuous or intrusive, and, unlike Mrs. Castle Smith, Stretton does not directly address a 'little' reader. Although the apparent simplicity of texts such as the popular *Alone in London, Little Meg's Children* and *Lost Gip* might suggest a less sophisticated readership, these layered and nuanced narratives encode darker social and psychological subtexts.

Whilst the density of the full-length novels points to an adult or young adult audience, capable of more abstract understanding, many stories occupy an ambiguous position, with the narratives *Bede's Charity* (1872) and *The Storm of Life* (1876), for example, focusing respectively on the experiences of an 'outcast' mother and a mature spinster, as well as on the plight of the child. *The King's Servants* (1873) deals, to the disgust of *The Athenaeum* (13.12.1873), with the theme of 'fallen girls'; regretting, in this instance, the inevitable attraction of her name, their reviewer deemed its subject matter unsuitable for 'entertaining reading', and, in particular, for the juvenile market. Stretton's treatment of themes becomes rather less child-reader friendly as time goes on, with the stark materiality of child exploitation and abuse in stories such as *The Lord's Pursebearers* dominating myth or sentiment. Nonetheless, the hybrid nature of Stretton's approach and subject matter, with issues transcending age, class and generic barriers, renders her work attractive to diverse audiences and places her narratives, not on one side or another of a binary divide, but within a continuum – part of a single world – in which adult and children's literatures merge, intersect and overlap, usefully illuminating attitudes and concerns which traverse the genres.[16]

This multifaceted, cross-generational appeal is an important factor in understanding the success of not only the very famous titles, but of many other stories. Not only were texts including *Jessica, Little Meg* and *Alone in London* bestsellers (the latter two reaching combined sales of three-quarters of a million, according to the *Sunday at Home* Memoir, 123), but narratives such as *Lost Gip* (1873), *The King's Servants* (1873), *Cassy* (1874) and *The Storm of Life* (1876) – all originally published by H.S. King during a break in Stretton's relations with the RTS, but later reissued by the Society after a resumption of the connection – also sold in large numbers.[17] Whilst evidence of actual reader response is limited – confined, for the most part, to brief allusions (positive and negative) in middle-class autobiographical writings – if we turn to the stories themselves we can posit an appeal beyond that which prompted their selection for moral or didactic purposes, readers across classes potentially appropriating those elements which engaged with particular interests or needs.

At an emotional and psychological level Stretton's focus on the outsider resonates with a sense of isolation and exclusion across classes and circumstances; it interacts with the orphan trope in wider literary fiction, both exposing the child as victim and, as we shall see, empowering him. Her compelling and personalised narratives contribute to the wider project of social reform. The concerns which drive her stories overlap with the preoccupations of social novels, and with contemporary debates on issues of poverty, health, housing, legal and human rights, where fact and fiction intermingle in different configurations within and across overlapping fictive and non-fictive forms.

Just as the fancies which young Hester entertains are a blend of religious and romantic ideas (*Hester Morley*, 97, Ch.15), so the fusion of these elements is a pervasive characteristic of Stretton's oeuvre. The juxtaposition of romance, fairy tale and religion, sometimes intended to highlight the tensions between these realms or the failure of real-life experience to deliver fantasies of fortunes or princes, also brings into focus the proximity of these media, each concerned to varying degrees with desires, adversities and relational ties – and often entailing comparable acts of intervention, leaps of faith and the suspension of rational understanding. Interwoven into Stretton's treatment of material experiences are familiar fairy-tale patterns and allusions – implied and overt – ranging from symbolic dark forests and abandoned or abused children to motifs of Bluebeard or the wicked stepmother, the concrete and the archetypal coalescing to engage with both conscious and unconscious drives. The ingredients of popular sensation which mark Stretton's early magazine stories and many of the longer novels also find their way into other narratives, where romantic relationships, heroic rescues and melodramatic portrayals again mingle with serious social and spiritual concerns.

Different in context, but not unrelated to this emphasis on sensation is the window which many of the texts open onto a different, often sordid, world - one which is at once undesirably and fascinatingly 'other'. Focusing on themes of vice, immorality, violence and degradation – and, significantly, treading a successful line between acceptable innuendo and unacceptable exposition as far as publishers and sensitive readers were concerned –

they incorporate elements of the very otherness which they seek to suppress, generating both compassionate and prurient interest.[18] Their preoccupation with the 'underworld' intersects with the concerns of contemporary novelists, artists, photographers, journalists and social explorers, and with a general curiosity on the part of the public regarding the outcast or alien – at home or abroad: like the social investigator George Sims (1889/1976), who compared the wild 'races' and 'tribes' of the English dark continent to the inhabitants of newly-explored lands, the philanthropist of Stretton's full-length *Half Brothers* (1892) finds the lives of the poor a diverting interest, and the unexplored sights of the City as intriguingly strange as those of foreign countries (58, Ch.8). This obsession with the city and its characters feeds into contemporary stage melodramas such as Boucicault's 'The Streets of London' (a performance of which Stretton attended in 1866); it fuels the author's often sensationalised depictions of a labyrinthine metropolis which ensnares protagonists into its web, such elements satisfying a pre-existing fascination with urban images and, at the same time, potentially broadening the reach of her project.

Such considerations call into question the modern dismissal of Stretton's texts as unremittingly dull, sentimental and pious – as nothing more than thinly-veiled evangelical tracts, their emphasis moralising and regulatory. In fact, much of her writing is surprisingly tough and down-to-earth in its penetrating, frequently satirical, social critique. Indeed, journalist Hulda Friederichs (1894: 332) found no trace of 'mawkishness' or 'weak sentimentality' in her narratives. Whilst there is evidence that the excessive piety of certain protagonists which is unpalatable today was rejected by some contemporary readers, many – including Lord Shaftesbury (letter to the *Record*, 20.11.1867) – were profoundly affected by the sincerity, simplicity and pathetic qualities of her work. We should not, moreover, underestimate the power of sentiment and pathos in terms of their potential to contribute to social change.

Unsurprisingly, these narratives – driven, at least in part, by evangelical imperatives – generally follow a moral and spiritual trajectory. The particular object of *The Children of Cloverley*, according to RTS Minutes, was to enforce submission to God's will (H8501, 3.10.1865) and phrases such as 'self-conquest', 'overcome temptation' and 'moral degradation' accompany the endorsement of texts including *Pilgrim Street* (H8501, 26.2.1867). Religious themes play a prominent part in all but the very early works, often drawing directly or – as with much classic literature of the period – indirectly, on bible doctrines, narratives such as the 'Prodigal

Son' (*Enoch Roden's Training*) or texts such as Bunyan's *Pilgrim's Progress* (*Cassy*). Certain chapter titles – for example, 'A Troubled Conscience' (*A Thorny Path*) – betray moral intent, but others convey social polemic, as with 'A Shameful Verdict' in that text, displaying didacticism of a different kind. Indeed, if publishers intended to inculcate in the lower classes a spirit of contentment with their lot, Stretton, like Gaskell, who demonstrates in *Mary Barton* (1848/1987: 437) that the Bible might be perceived as a 'sham' imposed upon the poor, highlights an acute awareness on the part of the deprived or lawless protagonist that religion – an 'old woman's tale' – is cynically harnessed by the hypocritical better-off, to 'keep [the poor folks] down' (*The Storm of Life*, label 1910: 107, Ch.12). Similarly, in *David Lloyd* (229, Vol.1, Ch.20), religious platitudes are received with scepticism by those who have seen the lives of loved ones extinguished 'like a snuff of a candle' through poverty and disease. Many narratives evidence a refusal to promote the language of forgiveness and acceptance at the expense of critiquing social wrongs and class inequalities.

Seeing otherwise

Although the assessment that these texts carry 'too heavy a weight of religious moralizing' for modern audiences (Cutt, 1979: 154) might have had resonance for some even in Stretton's day, the adoption of an active and selective, rather than passive, reading position potentially frees up alternative emphases and makes other interpretations possible. Readers are at liberty to bypass religious structuring and moral content in favour of different elements, and to engage, for example, with the currents of resistance which, as we shall see, act as a counterforce in texts such as *Carola*, cutting across didactic intention. The latter short novel centres on the susceptibility to moral contagion of a wayward, but ultimately spiritually redeemable adolescent; yet, with its romantic interest (juxtaposed with an assertion of female independence), its exposure of class prejudice, its examination of the destructive misperceptions surrounding different religions, and its focus on substitute parenting by an elderly man, the book is clearly concerned with much more than straightforward moralising. Recognition of ambiguity permeates Stretton's writing, her thought-provoking exploration of moral complexities and soul-searching choices competing with and unsettling instructive frameworks.

Such relative openness is in part the product of a narrative strategy which offers diverse, often competing, perspectives and voices, creating a dialogic element in texts often assumed to be rigidly univocal. Whilst authorial/narratorial endorsement or condemnation of behaviour and attitudes is frequently indicated, shifting focalisation permits a wider, sometimes contradictory perspective, the narrative voice at times merging with the viewpoint of characters and exposing different thought processes and motivations. In her magazine stories, Stretton experimented with alternative voices and forms, adopting a male persona ('No Bribery', 1869) or chronicling the maturation of a character through the use of a diary format ('Not to be Taken for Granted', 1865). She continued to develop such devices to effect: in *Bede's Charity*, a different first-person narrator intrudes at a point when the voice and identity of the narrator-protagonist is temporarily obliterated through physical and mental breakdown. Changes in narration from first to third-person (*Half Brothers*), or the juxtaposition of an omniscient third-person narrative with epistolary chapters (*Hester Morley's Promise*), evidence a willingness to question unilateral perspectives. In *The Doctor's Dilemma*, alternate first-person male and female versions of events reflect a very modern recognition of the instability of viewpoints. Explicitly calling into question the reliability or 'fidelity' of individual accounts, the male narrator's 'postscript' points to the selective nature of memory; no rendering of events can be definitive, and the act of interpretation involves only second-hand impressions (1872: 264, Vol. 3, Part 3, Ch.27). Throughout her writing, Stretton was conscious of the importance – and the difficulty – of putting oneself in another's place and seeing the world with his or her eyes (*Hester Morley*, 243, Ch.35), a capacity which she endeavoured to exercise – with some success, despite the potential prejudices and limitations of an adult, broadly middle-class, evangelical perspective – in her representation of very diverse lives and experiences.

Notes

1. This and subsequent childhood recollections are from 'A Talk with Hesba Stretton', *Sunday Hours*, 1896, Vol.1, No.7 (Anon).

2. *Pilgrim Street* (1867), 'A Story of Manchester Life', carries echoes of Mrs. Gaskell's *Mary Barton* (1848), 'A Tale of Manchester Life', amongst them a mill fire incident. Many settings, including the river scene in *Carola* (1884), evoke the atmosphere of Dickens's novels. Although Stretton attended readings by Dickens, had regular contact with his sub-editor, W.H. Wills, and lunched with Mrs. Charles Dickens, the journal indicates that, contrary to received accounts of a friendship, she failed to secure a meeting with the author.

3. The spellings 'Sarah' and, as in the diary, 'Sara', were apparently used interchangeably. Early in her career she adopted the name 'Hesba Stretton', combining the initials of her siblings with the Shropshire village where the family owned property. Relatives including her sister Lizzie adopted the surname.

4. Notebooks covering 1858-71 and 1875 survive, but although a commentary compiled by her great-nephew (Webb, 1964) cites additional diaries, these appear untraceable.

5. Certain entries reappear as fictional incidents, as with the account of the unsolicited parcel to be discussed in Chapter 4.

6. Log Book: 2.4.1862; 2.1.1867.

7. Stretton's handwritten 'The Origin of the London SPCC' (1908) records her part in bringing together those involved in the formation of the Society. Impressed by the work of Mr. Agnew, founder of a society in Liverpool, she appealed through *The Times* for the establishment of a London Society, and sought the support of prominent persons including Florence Davenport Hill and Baroness Burdett-Coutts (the latter abandoning a personal project in favour of the scheme). Stretton turned to influential contacts, among them Benjamin Waugh, then editor of the *Sunday Magazine*, to locate London premises. She claims credit for urging use of the Mansion House's Egyptian Hall for the public meeting at which the first Committee was formed, and for securing Lord Shaftesbury as President. Stretton participated in practical work and the drafting of legislation until her reluctant resignation in 1894, when the withholding of financial information to the Executive rendered liability without control untenable (Letter to Lord Ancaster, 15.12.1894).

8. As with the response (Log Book: 11.12.1868) from the RTS to *David Lloyd's Last Will*, serialised in their *Leisure Hour* magazine but published with Tubbs and Brook/Sampson Low, Marston.

9. In *Cobwebs and Cables* (1881), Stretton sardonically exposes the overcrowded evangelical mission-field as a 'park for hunting sinners in' (203, Ch.30).

10. The émigrés were well received in London socialist circles, many having some idea of, but perhaps choosing to accommodate, the rumours surrounding Stepniak. Stretton attended a lecture by Kropotkin, and met Felix Volkhovsky (sub-editor of *Free Russia*), taking an interest in his motherless young daughter, Vera. Her involvement with The Society of Friends of Russian Freedom, and with the writer/lecturer George Kennan, whose work *Siberia and the Exile System* (1891) informed *In the Hollow of His Hand*, was probably established through contacts such as T. Fisher Unwin, a member of the SFRF. The revoking of the earlier order, issued by Tsar Alexander II, for *Jessica's First Prayer* to be placed in all Russian schools (Memoir, *The Sunday at Home*, 1911: 123) was probably a consequence of her association with the anarchists.

11. 'Rhoda' (*The Clives of Burcot*) was first 'launched into London' in 1861; the much-travelled 'Alice Gilbert' ('Alice Gilbert's Confession') found her 'home' with *Temple Bar* in March 1862.

12. *The Doctor's Dilemma* (1872) and *Hester Morley's Promise* (1873) were both reviewed under 'Novels of the Week' by the *Athenaeum*, the former as best novel (15.2.1873; 6.9.1873).

13. Although Stretton successfully negotiated the mores of the publishing establishment to fulfil these aspirations, the association with religious publishing houses, and with the historically devalued realm of children's literature, may have limited audiences for her more adult-oriented fiction.

14. In the case of *Little Meg*, Copyright Sub-Committee Minutes (H8502, 21.5.1868) note a restriction of 10 years. *Alone in London* was agreed 'on the same scale of payment as "Little Meg"' (H8502, 16.12.1869). The RTS made additional small payments for texts including *Jessica* and *Pilgrim Street*, with later bonuses for *Jessica* and other successful works which had received only 'ordinary payment' (H8502, Finance Sub-Committee, 17.7.1873). Demands for new terms during negotiations for *Max Kromer*, including 'no limitation in time of the royalty' (16.2.1871) and the printing of the numbers of each thousand copies on the title page, resulted in compromise.

15. The narrator of Dickens's *Bleak House* highlights the 'favourite device' of addressing the poor as children (1853/1996: 711).

16. For example, *Hester Morley's Promise* sheds light on class issues, concepts of childhood and matters relating to women; it also contains a literal echo of the famous *Alone in London* in a chapter sharing that title.

17. Following the disagreements with the RTS, publication with King presented certain advantages. In contrast to RTS policy, they regularly displayed numbers of texts sold; Stretton perhaps also envisaged greater scope for her longer works, of which several were initially published with them.

18. The Society demanded modification by some authors of material deemed sensational or unsuitable for children. Stretton's carefully nuanced texts did not generally overstep the mark, although small additions to the religious content were sometimes required

Chapter 2

'... faces of childhood' (Stretton, 1893: 10)

From Hesba Stretton's earliest short stories for the adult market, the author's insistent concern for the child figure – in particular, the lost or abandoned child, across classes – makes its presence felt.[1] Such sensitivities reflect, and engage with, diverse facets of society's ever-growing investment in the child; intersecting with a range of mutually-constituted, materially and symbolically inflected discourses of childhood permeating literary and non-literary forms, these textual representations circulate within a complex network of ideas, meanings and lived experiences which encompass the personal, the psychological, the social and the political. The late Mitzi Myers (1995: 3) identifies the child as a 'historically constituted signifier' – an 'evocative, contradictory, and ideologically weighted verbal image'. Concepts of 'the child', childhood and family are not fixed or neutral; subject, in part, to the preoccupations and anxieties of society at particular moments and in specific material circumstances, they operate within the broader cultural matrix as transmitters of prevailing social, moral and political values and imperatives.

The Victorian 'ideal' child and childhood innocence

For Stretton, as for Victorians generally, dominant perceptions of childhood are measured in terms of notions of what childhood *should* be, an ideal linked to Rousseau's theories of uninterrupted play and freedom from anxiety as the *natural* state of the child.[2] In Stretton's writings, 'unbroken childish happiness' (*The Lord's Pursebearers*, 1883/n.d.: 248, Ch.19) is assumed to be a right, and, in its 'proper' state, her child bears the normative rosy, 'merry [face] of childhood' (Stretton, 1893: 10). Such ideals are embodied in the Edenic pastoral space, with its connotations of prelapsarian childhood innocence – associations encapsulated in the assertion that in the 'sunshine and bracing air of the fields', one is 'as far from murder or any other sin as a child is' (*Hester Morley's Promise*, 1873/1898: 152, Ch.22).

This state of innocent ignorance carries multiple symbolic and cultural charge. It is enmeshed with the Romantic vision of the child as uncontaminated, uncorrupted and possessing heightened perceptive and redemptive powers – a concept which took root in the cultural

24

consciousness, feeding into countless literary and visual representations and continuing to influence present-day notions of childhood. Such innocence represents in part a projection by the adult, reflecting a nostalgia for the child he or she once was – a yearning for that which has been lost – and at the same time, an investment in a potentially unblemished future located in the child.

The conflation of the child with innocence means that even the presence of a child is perceived to constitute a restraining influence, keeping immorality at bay, as in *The Lord's Pursebearers*, 239, Ch.15. In an era of doubt and questioning, the child figure provides both a focus, and, paradoxically, a substitute, for religious sensibilities. Blending the Romantic spirituality and the intercessory, Christ-like purity of the child, many Stretton narratives contain cameos of the blond, blue-eyed infant[3], with 'pure and heavenly expression', as depicted in *The Children of Cloverley* (1865), in which the 'cluster of the faces of angel-children' (label 1876: 9) in a family painting suggests the configuration of artistic representations such as Joshua Reynolds' 'Angels' Heads' (1787). In *Max Kromer* (1871/n.d.), the golden-haired, angel-like Elsie sits at the window, with nothing 'save the deep blue sky' beyond her (17, Ch.2), her proximity to heaven implicit.

Other faces of childhood

The ideal childhood environment is enclosed, nurturing and protected, such images reflecting a predominantly middle-class perspective (although, indeed, they may not be representative of that child's experience). Other kinds of childhood, and other children, are seen to be lacking by reference to the ideal – a deficiency which is often, though not always, related to class/social environment.

In many Stretton stories, that environment is the antithesis of the tranquil countryside with its lark-filled meadows and cleansing rivers, and a far cry from the protected home or community in which the child is 'encircled' from the knowledge and sorrows of the world ('Not to be Taken for Granted', 7.12.1865: 20). The setting is often the overcrowded city inferno, with its suffocating, light-starved courts and labyrinthine alleys, its grim lodging houses which hold 'not a sound of play or laughter' (*Pursebearers*, 36, Ch.2) and its flaring gin palaces – characterised not by regenerative and redemptive qualities, but by misery, vice and deprivation.[4]

Such a picture confounds the dominant understanding of a 'proper' childhood; child misery is deemed 'unnatural, an indictment of somebody: parent, institution, nation' (Kincaid, 1992: 80). As the nineteenth-century progresses, we find the symbolic investment in the ideal child juxtaposed and elided with an acknowledgement of, and concern regarding, the concomitant material oppression and exploitation of a different child – a preoccupation apparent from the 1830s, but increasingly evident in later decades, and repeated not only in social accounts but across cultural forms. Literary and artistic movements, whilst endorsing constructions of idealised, angelic perfection, simultaneously tap into both a heightened sense of compassion and a voyeuristic fascination with the alterity of the lower-class child and his surroundings, generating images of sentimentalised poverty and representations of exoticised or threatening otherness.[5]

Accounts of children wandering the streets, dying of cold and starvation litter the pages of newspapers such as the *Morning Star* (4/5.1.1867). From Dickens's earlier evocation of 'heaps of children' (*Oliver Twist*, 1838/1985: 103), through the ubiquitous 'ragged' and 'sickly' subjects of Henry Mayhew's social studies (1861-2/1985: 120), to reformer Benjamin Waugh's 'swarming' juveniles (1873/1984: 73), impressions of 'thousands and thousands of poor children … everywhere (*Pursebearers*, 87, Ch.4) abound. The true wretchedness of the 'dwarfed, ugly, and famished' infants who crowd the narrow alleys defies description' (*Bede's Charity*, 1872/c.1890: 163, Ch. 21). In her short narrative *Left Alone*, Stretton invokes the sentiments of 'a great French writer' to establish that the 'misery of a child' eclipses all miseries experienced by man or woman (1876/n.d.: 25). This suffering not only demands attention, but is made to stand in for wider anxieties. Discussing the pervasive fascination with victimised children, critic Laura Berry (1999) argues that nineteenth-century novels and reform writings 'reorganize ideas of self and society as narratives of childhood distress' (3), the child occupying a homogenising place; social anxieties are mediated by the transformation of 'powerful adult appetites' into the 'pitiable needs of an innocent (and therefore socially pure) victim' (4-5).

The child – perhaps by virtue of its 'incompleteness' – inhabits, in one sense, a particular space beyond class or situation. At the same time, it is enlisted to reinforce borders – defined not only as 'other' to the adult, but subject to complex processes of 'othering' which operate within the state of childhood. Emblematic of its environment, the orphan, urchin or poor child from a deprived or dysfunctional family represents the polar opposite of that ideal, carefree infant; for 'cherished' and 'nurtured', as were the 'nestlings' of Stretton's own family (1875: xiv), we can substitute 'unwanted' and 'unnurtured' – neglected, abused, abandoned and excluded.

Foregrounding the complexities which underlie society's interest in, and ambivalence towards, this figure, Stretton's writings explore different faces of childhood, alternative versions of the child. The existence of waifs such as Tony (*Alone in London*, 1869) is characterised by an absence of laughter and play; ten-year-old Meg – a 'stunted girl of London growth', with dark-circled eyes, wrinkled brow and weary, unchildlike gait (*Little Meg's Children*, 1868/label 1889: 13-14, Ch.1) is, like Dickens's Little Nell, Mayhew's 'Watercress Girl', or Thomas Barnardo's 'City Waif'[6], perceived as prematurely burdened, possessing an untimely 'womanliness', the absence of a maternal figure robbing her of identity *as a child*.

'Oh! if mother hadn't died.' Such is the heartfelt cry of forest-girl Cassy (*Cassy*, 1874/c.1888: 14, Ch.1). Motifs of loss and separation permeate Stretton's work, tapping into archetypal fears and anxieties deeply embedded in the individual and collective psyche, which find expression in early myths and resurface in oral stories and fairy tales. Currents of maternal longing promote conscious and unconscious engagement between writer and reader, mother and child. Sharing with many of her protagonists the devastating loss of the maternal figure, Stretton could begin to identify with the 'loneliness', 'desertion' and 'dumb sufferings' of forlorn and desolate children who experience the trauma of abandonment (*Hester Morley's Promise*, 381, Ch.54), whether as a result of maternal death – as with protagonists Meg, Cassy and middle-class Hester, or through neglect and desertion – the fate of Jessica (whose mother would gladly pawn her along with her other belongings); of Dot in *A Thorny Path* (abandoned, in desperation, in the disorienting mist); and Sandy of *Lost Gip* (left to fend for himself and his infant sister by an inebriate mother, whose occasional presence is, at best, parasitic).

Stretton's contemporary, Henrietta Synnot, in an article on institutions/orphanages, poses the question: 'What is to make up for the mother's kiss every night?' (1875: 493). The primary need for maternal love is deeply experienced through the pages of Stretton's narratives, whether, as in Gaskell's *Mary Barton*, it manifests itself in the longing for the restorative maternal kiss (*Alone in London*), the imagined voice as a child drifts into sleep (*An Acrobat's Girlhood*), or the tactile comfort derived from a mother's faded dress (*Cassy*). Key to the impact of her narratives is Stretton's engagement with the intensity of childhood experience. Sensory images and responses – drawn from intimate observation and a retained understanding of what it is to be a child in terms of vulnerability and pain – convey an immediacy charged with both fear and a sense multiple deprivation, a longing for warmth, nurture and comfort. Jessica's gaze, as hungry as that of a mouse 'driven by famine into a trap', is intensified through its refinement to 'a pair of very bright dark eyes', which gleam hungrily; she smacks her lips as though 'in fancy she was tasting the warm and fragrant coffee (*Jessica's First Prayer*, 1867/n.d.: 11-12, Ch.1). The child's feet – lifted 'first one and then the other' and laid 'one over another' for momentary respite from the damp pavement – are acutely observed, the impressions of emotional and physical chill and ill-usage united in the doubly telling image of Jessica's blue-black limbs.

The orphanhood or virtual orphanhood of these protagonists resonates with a wider sense of isolation and displacement, raising issues of identity, social validity and self-worth. Young Don of A *Thorny Path* – his 'proper' identity lost before memory – appropriates the name of a dog because 'folks kept callin' me anythin' they liked, till I didn't even know who I was' (1879/c.1882: 17-18, Ch.2); unwanted, and casually 'sold' by her natural father, Cassy refuses to belief herself worth the ten shillings paid for her (*Cassy*, 117, Ch.13). The sense of 'not belonging' attached to the actual or apparent *filius nullius*, or 'nobody's child', is palpable: others dismiss the disappearance of Dot (*A Thorny Path*) since 'she didn't belong to nobody' (99, Ch.12); for Don and the small child, the surrogate sibling relationship alone offers a yearned-for sense of connection – each has only the other (112-13, Ch.13). Accentuating the rootlessness of the street-child, Tony (*Alone in London*), who 'never had any father' (22, Ch.2), identifies himself as from 'nowhere particular' (21, Ch.2), and Sandy (*Lost Gip*) – repeatedly moved on, like Dickens's Jo (*Bleak House*) – is painfully aware, when ordered to go about his business, that he 'ain't likely to have no bis'ness anywheres' (1873/1878: 13, Ch.2).

If parental absence or neglect figures prominently, the threat of violence forms a constant undercurrent, perhaps reaching beyond the narrative setting to articulate anxieties which, although not alien, remain unspoken in middle-class homes; these fictional children embody not only difference, but, potentially, a displaced sameness. The anticipation of a father's – and sometimes a mother's – return inspires dread, as in *Pilgrim Street* and *Lost Gip*; Cassy, fearing a beating when the fire will not burn,

Illustration 2: *Jessica's First Prayer* (edition n.d.) Frontispiece, A.W. Bayes/Butterworth and Heath

flees in panic through the darkening forest with its menacing fairy-tale topography (14, Ch.1). In *Alone in London*, the 'bruise about [the] eye' of a mother indicates to young Tony that 'somebody had been fighting with her' (18, Ch.2) – such matter-of-factness pointing up the internalised acceptance of abuse as a prerogative of (often male) authority. The paternal figure is frequently the 'worst foe' (Stretton, 1875: xii), a sentiment which chimes with Stretton's exposure and condemnation of tyrannical patriarchy across classes, with its cultural perversion of biblical models of fatherhood.

Resistant childhoods and alternative family patterns

From a contrasting perspective, whilst the orphan trope serves as an expression of alienation and uncertainty – both at an individual and, increasingly, a societal level, the attendant necessity for independence in decision-making and 'negotiating the world', as Reynolds and Humble (1993: 27) confirm, offers writers and readers – particularly women – the potential to transgress the norms of accepted conduct. Likewise, the apparent autonomy and licence of street-life might appear enviable to the reader of either sex who is constrained by a more protected upbringing, where freedom and responsibility are circumscribed and transgression contained. Stretton's narratives disturb expectations, providing encounters with different kinds of childhood which, as well as eliciting concern and sympathy, may evoke a more complex response. Such confrontations embody a conflict between that which is known and secure, yet tedious and constraining, and that which is unhomely, dangerous and exciting – tensions between freedom and containment, safety and stimulation, which are identifiable throughout Stretton's life and writings.[7]

Like Thomas Barnardo, who acknowledged the waif's 'bold independence' and love of the 'adventure-life' ('A City Waif', 1885/6: 17, Ch.2; 9, Ch.1), Stretton comprehends the reluctance of the street-child to relinquish the 'change and stir' of an unfettered out-of-door existence. In *Carola* (1884/inscr.1898), which integrates elements of the social novel, the orphan story, the tract, and romantic fiction, the protagonist exists like a 'wild creature' (11, Ch.1), refusing to 'brook any restraint' (57, Ch.5); she 'shakes off' the 'shackles' of the school-room (18, Ch.2), and remains 'free as air'. Despite Carola's gradual reformation, telling linguistic choices betray Stretton's covert, perhaps unconscious, identification with the defiant protagonist, reflecting a consistently fierce defence of her own independence and an abhorrence of containment: she was, as we have seen, deeply frustrated by periods of monotony or 'stagnation' and rejected the idea of being 'in bondage' to anyone (Log Book: 19.8.1868). In tension with the social and moral imperatives of the narrative, a half-implied empathy with Carola's refusal of physical and social constraints contributes – as in other texts – to an undertow of rebellion, potentially promoting engagement with audience resistance to authority and discipline, at a time when the new 'adventurousness' of girls of all classes was the subject of fierce debate, and Stretton was herself expressing anxiety about the consequent threat to their future maternal abilities (Letter to *The Times*, 8.1.1884).

In many Stretton texts, surrogate roles confirm the positive potential of alternative relational configurations. The assumption of adult responsibilities by Stretton's young protagonists challenges perceptions regarding appropriate social codes/patterns. Set against the vulnerability and seeming impotence of Meg, Cassy, Jessica and others, is a resourcefulness and resilience born of enforced independence, which is empowering as well as burdensome; as Mayhew and Barnardo discovered, the idea of working for one's bread carries prestige. Stretton's Cassy takes charge of household affairs following her employer's flight; Little Meg assumes responsibility for the economic, physical and emotional welfare of her siblings, pragmatically devising survival strategies for the benefit of 'her' children. Likewise, Don (*A Thorny Path*) adopts the maternal role in respect of his infant companion, sacrificing his own nourishment – as does Mrs. Castle Smith's Froggy – to feed his 'little gel' (112).[8] Alliances of the disenfranchised traverse family and generational borders, with protagonists such as Tony (*Alone in London*) ably protecting the interests of an old man whose business capabilities are failing, as well as taking care of the young grandchild; Cor, of *Bede's Charity*, practically and emotionally supports the spinster Margery, who has fallen on hard times. Stretton's young males emerge as protective and nurturing; in a world where the emotional sensitivity and domestic capabilities are feminised, these narratives subvert conventional gender paradigms, offering alternative models of masculinity to readers whose needs are perhaps not met through traditional reading and other forms of enculturation for boys.

The critique of authority and exposure of inequities through the sometimes naïve voice of young characters might be judged exploitative, but Stretton's protagonists are, arguably, elevated rather than devalued by the authorial strategy. Her children demonstrate agency and independent judgement; possessing a forthright openness and a clear-sightedness which lays bare society's flaws, they participate in an empowering discourse which has the potential to impart practical, rather than merely compensatory, confidence to the reader. Pointing up, through her frankness, the condemnatory attitudes of adulthood, Hester Morley presents an astute critique of guilt-inducing indoctrination (51, Ch.7); protagonists Jessica and Sandy likewise expose adult bigotry and hypocrisy, usurping conventional spiritual or social authority, and acting as Romantic agents of transformation and instruments for societal change. Jessica subverts other-worldly notions of Judgement Day by her deflationary understanding of a 'reckoning day' in its bread-and-butter context (*Jessica's First Prayer*, 62, Ch.7), and her identification of church as fairy-land conveys not only her sense of awe, but the theatricality of organised religion. Similarly, Cassy's matter-of-fact recognition of male brutality and lack of commitment – the forest men were always 'run[ning] away a-purpose' and 'it wasn't nice' for families when they were forced to return (*Cassy*, 74, Ch.9) – together with her unwitting analysis of the normalisation of gender inequality (see my discussion in Chapter 3) underline the cultural marginalisation and oppression of the child-as-woman. Here, as in *Lost Gip*, in which young Sandy is instrumental in promoting a more egalitarian relationship between his surrogate mother and her husband, religion is revealed as potentially emancipatory.

The child as victim

In line with society's growing recognition of the extreme vulnerability of the child of all classes (and concomitant drive towards closer protection and containment of that child), the tone of Stretton's narratives becomes, over time, increasingly dark. Anger permeates novels such as *A Thorny Path*, in which the verdict of death by starvation – so common it fails to shock – prompts a tirade about structural inequalities and the failings of the system (Ch.19). In *The Lord's Pursebearers*, Stretton vents her fury at those who trade 'on the agony of babies' (227, Ch.11). The diminutive begging companion, lightly appropriated as pathetic attraction in *Alone in London*, is now uncompromisingly exposed as victim. Stretton uncovers the grotesque form of theatre practised by fraudulent begging communities, in which the remnants of fractured families are harnessed to create counterfeit units. The 'paternal' role is cynically assumed and readily discarded; relationships are enacted to serve economic purposes, a ploy which evokes Mayhew's identification of the 'ingenuity' of the beggar in judging/adapting to the bent of popular sympathy (Mayhew/Neuburg (ed.), 1985: 505). The narrative exposes the predatory nature of the vicious Mrs. Moss – a 'wicked-stepmother' figure, who holds dependent children in her 'power' (a situation reminiscent of Barnardo's 'Kidnapped' (1885/6) in which Mother Brown incarcerates deliberately half-starved children and hires them out as begging attractions). As Mrs. Moss's 'clemmed' victim 'Lucky' bluntly concedes when her young companion talks of a life without hunger, 'I shouldn't be little Lucky then ... If I grew fat and big, rich folks wouldn't be so sorry for me' (85, Ch.3). In this tale, the skeletal Fidge – less a human being than a 'living mass of misery' (227, Ch.11) – is paraded under the gaslights for begging purposes, exploited to the point of death.[9] Stretton starkly describes the discovery of the child's body by his young companion: 'the sunken cheek with no flesh in it, and the strained muscles showing clearly under the parchment skin ... cold as the coldest day in winter (228, Ch.11). His 'owner', fearing detection, arranges to have the dead child – always merely an 'object', but now valueless – 'chuck[ed] over a garding wall' (238, Ch.15). Through such narratives, the author points up the child's need for protection, and society's failure, despite changing attitudes, to intervene in crimes relating, not to material possessions, but only to the lives of uncared-for children whose interests remain unprotected (247, Ch.19).

Claiming, by the mid-1880s, a twenty-year-long interest 'in the condition of the children of the poor', Stretton was actively pressing for the means to 'deliver us as a nation from the curse and crime, the shame and sin of neglected and oppressed childhood (Letter to *The Times*, 8.1.1884). Her narratives interact with an intensified concern, at individual and societal level, with 'lift[ing]'children from the 'pit', and placing them in 'safe and happy' homes (*Pursebearers*, 177, Ch.8). Engaging, later in the decade, with a heightened focus on the exploitation and abuse of young performers, and with a parallel emphasis on the physical development of the child, *An Acrobat's Girlhood*, narrated through the voice of the protagonist's sister, centres on the maltreatment and commodification of children in the arena of public spectacle.[10] Like other Stretton characters, motherless Trixy is high-spirited and strong-willed, challenging conventions of feminine propriety in her overt, boyish physicality. Her father is lured by the promise of financial reward to relinquish his burdensome daughter to a circus troupe, to be trained as an acrobat. The prospect of the circus environment initially proves enticing to Trixy, as, indeed, it might to the reader attracted by the seemingly anarchic and exotic otherness embodied in its energy, glitter and cheering crowds. However, now in the 'possession' (49) of the tyrannical managers, these young workers, their bodies exposed under blazing light to the shame-inducing gaze of the voyeur, are driven to the point of injury, exhaustion and fatal collapse – put on the 'rack' for the amusement of complicit audiences. There are no sentimentalised or sanitised descriptions here: the bodily twisting and writhing results in contortion and overstraining, dislocation of joints and tearing of sinews (71, Ch.4).

The young 'criminal': 'deviant' childhoods and the potential for criminality

Set against notions of childhood innocence, which override yet intersect with Calvinist notions of the child's innate depravity, is the idea of his potential corruptibility. The condition of childhood is ambiguous, a Lockean *tabula ras*a and a battle site between good and evil. Alongside more sanitised and romanticised portraits of the street-boy or crossing-sweeper, images of the street Arab's alterity carry a more negative charge. Stretton's texts underline the association of the city and its streets with deviance and crime. Exposed to the contaminating criminal world – and, as Samuel Green reports, spurred on by the 'pernicious literature circulated among our lads' (1899: 127) – the boy of the streets is deemed likely to fall prey to malign influences.

Anxiety about juvenile lawlessness – perceived as emanating from the poorer classes – was, as Pearson (1983) and Cunningham (1991) demonstrate, entangled with fears of social unrest. As the century progresses, this fear *of* the delinquent is juxtaposed with increasing concern for his welfare, reflecting the gradual application of ideas of childhood dependency and need for protection to those outside the middle and upper classes. It forms part of a gradual move to a more humanitarian, reformative approach to deviance – 'We cannot take these lads out of streets, but we can try to make them very different' (*Pilgrim Street*, 1867/c.1890: 28, Ch.3) – and a progression towards a separate juvenile justice system. Shifting attitudes reflect religious influences, liberal thought, developments in education, and the expansion of social Darwinist/imperialist policies. Stretton recognises that the nation's future depends on 'what the children of the present decade are' (1893: 12); identifying rescued street-children, with their evident capacity to survive, as the 'very individuals whom nature has selected for existence' (1875: xiv), she presents as an intrinsically (though not exclusively) 'patriotic project' (xv) the mission to raise them from their circumstances.

Stretton's narrative concerns reflect and address society's often contradictory responses. She does not shy away from the world of crime and immorality, although her protagonists are often balanced precariously on the margins of deviance, set slightly apart from their environment, and, frequently, of 'better stock'. Blending an essentially conservative morality with a progressive vision, the author interrogates attitudes towards deviance, engaging with the experiences of the young offender (or potential offender), and making it clear through the development of the story that, although wrongful behaviour is not to be condoned, it is, in many instances, the approach of authority figures which is wanting.

These stories expose society's preconceptions about the street child's criminal propensities – assumptions based, in part, on material evidence, but entangled with constructions or perceptions of deviance which have their roots in class-related prejudices, determining the responses of society and the justice system – as, sadly, remains the case today. The child who is effectively homeless or unanchored – at liberty to roam the neighbourhood at will (*Bede's Charity*, 108, Ch.14) and subject to what Waugh terms the 'wild energy' of the streets – is perceived as untamed, lacking in restraint. Such juveniles, often unmothered (and thus unsocialised/uncivilised and beyond control) betoken disorder and pose a threat to society.

Hesba Stretton demonstrates that the 'common boy' of the streets is, in the public perception, '*no doubt*' (my italics) a rogue, a thief or a pickpocket (*Alone in London*; *Lost Gip*). Authority figures base judgements on such preconceptions, labelling street youths as 'born and bred' lawbreakers (*Pilgrim Street*, 16, Ch.2); '*this sort*' (my italics) are 'slippery as eels' (*Lost Gip*, 50, Ch.7). In common with novelists such as Dickens and Gaskell, social commentators including Mayhew and contemporary illustrators such as Gustave Doré, Stretton highlights issues of control and surveillance, alluding to the deep-rooted instinct of the City Arab to escape from authority (*Pilgrim Street*, 76, Ch.9); the outcast is forced into dark recesses 'out of the beat of the too busy policeman' (*Cassy*, 32, Ch.4). There exists among these protagonists a predetermined sense of destiny; hounded unremittingly under the piercing searchlight of authority, most come to see jail as an inevitable fate.

'Other' bodies

If the fact that the waif roams the streets indicates his potential for criminality, his appearance confirms it. It becomes abundantly clear that the 'othering' of the poor child (and, indeed, the outcast in all his guises) operates in/through discourses of the body – a crucial site, according to Foucault (1979), of social control.[11] The social and moral decline of protagonists such as David (*Prison*, 151) is symbolised by bodily filth, which renders them untouchable and reinforces their exclusion. Not only does the street-urchin's place amongst the 'dregs' of the polluted 'nether regions' associate him with refuse or effluent, but his dark, matted or tangled hair, unwashed face and bare feet also indicate an unmistakeable potential for deviance – an assumption evidenced, for example, in Dickens's 'The Chimes' (1844/1995: 83), in which an absence of shoes and stockings is associated with 'grow[ing] up bad', and necessitates summary 'Put[ting] … Down'. Similarly, when Stretton's 'bare-footed and bare-headed' Ben (*The Children of Cloverley*) is caught trespassing, no-one credits his respectable background; his appearance confirms him as rascal, vagabond and thief, fit only for jail (Ch.11). In an echo of such prejudices, Aunt Charlotte of *Alone in London* (whose snobbery, the chapter title 'Highly Respectable' sardonically affirms, is reprehensible) is horrified to find an ignorant 'common boy', without boots or cap, in the company of her young relation.

Such discourses further intersect with the rhetoric of reform and, significantly, of colonialism. The relationship between childhood and savagery pervades the writings of explorers, colonisers, social investigators and reformers alike. Embodying crucial issues of power and subordination which have their counterpart in patriarchal family structures, the association of the as yet unformed child with the primitive of race and society – underpins Victorian imperialist perceptions; the bare, mud-black feet of waifs such as Tony (*Alone in London*) or the 'negroish' sweep's child (Barnardo's '"God's Little Girl"') reflect the complex interplay of discourses of physical and moral filth, spiritual or intellectual darkness and racially-inflected notions of the 'other'. On the one hand valorised, the natural wildness of the Rousseauesque noble savage also carries a negative – and, literally, darker – charge, making the 'uncivilised' wild child or the Arab/savage-identified street-urchin the object of fascinated disgust – a scapegoat for society's failures and a candidate for redirection.[12]

Who Rocks the Cradle?

Hesba Stretton exposes the harsh realities which flow from these processes of 'othering'. She brings into sharp focus the arbitrary nature of justice based on class prejudices, and the concomitant powerlessness of the juvenile accused, who has no voice: no-one believes him and no time is allocated to proper investigation. To Tom, in *Pilgrim Street*, there appears no point in *not* pleading 'Guilty' (19, Ch.2). If such texts testified to a belief in the need for change, *In Prison and Out: Facts on a Thread of Fiction* (1880) conveys the by now acute urgency for reform. Whereas

Benjamin Waugh, like Barnardo, intersperses his polemic with illustrative anecdotes, Stretton weaves factually-based themes – the foundations of which are clearly recognisable in Waugh's 1873 *The Gaol Cradle: Who Rocks it?* – into her 'thread of fiction', constructing a narrative which convincingly draws the reader into the individual circumstances of the young offender. She exposes the inadequacies of existing social and legal systems, highlighting issues of labelling, branding and internalisation, and the problems of contamination and recidivism: 'if you send him to gaol, he'll grow up a thief' (112, Ch.12) – a prophecy tragically fulfilled in her protagonist, David.

Like Waugh, Stretton exposes the failure of the law to take into account the circumstances of the crime: David begs in order to feed his sick mother and fights to uphold her rights. The street boy is 'cast into a gulf' for misdemeanours which, in other classes, are interpreted as 'heroic' or, at worst, minor day-to-day trespasses. Directly invoking the 'scrapes' and offences committed by the protagonists of the popular *Tom Brown's Schooldays* (1857), Stretton contends that, if subject to the justice accorded to the lower-class offender, many a present-day gentleman would now find himself a 'greyhaired convict in penal servitude' (*Prison*, 125, Ch.14). Definitions of, and responses to, transgression – and also, significantly, the very boundaries of childhood – are, demonstrably, fluid and class-determined: the egg-stealing for which Ishmael (*No Place Like Home*) is imprisoned is but 'a lad's trick'; in 'happier homes', these youths would be 'reckoned among the children', and treated leniently (*No Place*, 1881/inscr. 1904: 63, Ch.5; *Prison*, 140, Ch.16). In Stretton's *A Man of His Word* (1876), a magistrate faced with the dilemma of whether to convict his errant grandson in accordance with his unflinching treatment of other young offenders, suddenly recognises the incongruity of incarcerating frightened urchins in conditions suited to the 'blackest criminals' (Ch.5). The use of repeated prison sentences as a 'fitting penalty for childish faults' (*Prison*, 190, Ch.22) is exposed as ineffective and counterproductive. Directing the reader to Waugh's text, Stretton highlights both communal and individual responsibility, suggesting, in answer to the question 'Who Rocks [the Gaol Cradle?]', that it is indeed 'You and I' (208).

The 'waif's female counterpart': sexual signposts

If juvenile delinquency, with its accompanying physical/sartorial signifiers, is associated primarily with the 'perils' of boyhood, there are,

"He met with rebuffs, and felt downcast."

Illustration 3: *In Prison and Out* (edition 1880) 'He met with rebuffs, and felt downcast' 11, Ch.2, R. Barnes

for pubescent girls like Stretton's Bess, 'untold' dangers; on the streets, she stands little chance (*Prison*, 58, Ch.6; 145, Ch.16). The discourse which colours representations of the prematurely knowing street-girl – privy to a brand of knowledge incompatible with home-embodied, feminine propriety – is subtly, but unmistakeably, sexualised. Coded or ambiguous signifiers and lightly-veiled subtexts break through the surface silence, engaging, at the same time, with unspoken fears that uncontained sexuality might spill over into the impulses of the (supposedly a-sexual) middle-class child, whose safety and purity depend on the poor, untamed 'other,' who symbolically, and literally, stands in for her.

Her 'sex alone' deemed her 'crowning misfortune', the 'waif's female counterpart'[13] or the street-seller of flowers and fuses is separated by a thread from, and readily elided with, the seller of her body. Barnardo's Tracts suggest that, of the many street-women living a 'life of shame', numbers 'have been drawn from the ranks of wretched little children' ('A City Waif', 27, Ch.3), some as young as ten.[14] Like that of Barnardo's Bridget, or of Mayhew's 'loose' girls (1985: 86), the portrait of Stretton's Jessica – similarly enticed by the fragrant warmth of her benefactor's coffee – confirms the waif as object of an ambiguous and potentially predatory gaze. The image of the scantily-clad girl, her 'tattered' frock 'slipping down' over her shoulders (*Jessica's First Prayer*, 12, Ch.1), or the 'overgrown' Joan of *The Lord's Pursebearers* – whose far-too-short dress, inappropriately exposed legs and 'promise of beauty' signal imminent profitability (37, Ch.2) – embodies both innocence and awareness/availability, the border between childhood and adulthood rendered doubly ambiguous. Intersecting with a multi-nuanced discourse which, in turn, infuses complex class-inflected images such as Lewis Carroll's 'Alice Liddell as "The Beggar Maid"' (c.1859), these charged representations encode much more than material deprivation.[15]

As in *An Acrobat's Girlhood*, which points not only to immodesty but to lost virtue – the protagonist has *only* forfeited her life – Stretton's narratives are constantly on the point of articulating sexual issues. The innocence, but emergent sexuality, of Little Meg is highlighted by her moral distance from, yet implicit proximity to, the errant Kitty, who claims to have grown up 'bad', and, significantly, can 'never … be good again' (*Little Meg's Children*, 62, Ch.6). The fact that Kitty is from a respectable family underlines the danger for all girls. Yet, Stretton's treatment is sympathetic; in contrast to the tendency in contemporary novels and reportage to present the prostitute as an empty stereotype signalling the 'limits of the socially tolerable' (Reynolds and Humble,

1993: 47), she gives identity/voice to the fallen Kitty, who seeks to protect Meg from a similar fate, and is subsequently redeemed and lovingly rehabilitated into the family. If the growing child's sexuality forms a persistent undercurrent, the promiscuity of Kitty, and, to an even greater degree, the 'wild eyed', 'painted-faced' girls of Stretton's *The King's Servants* (1873/label 1911: 135, Part 3, Ch.7), their 'dingy', shoulder-revealing finery recalling that worn by street-walkers such as Gaskell's Esther (*Mary Barton*), constitute prominent, if unnamed, surface themes – to the extent that, in the case of *The King's Servants*, the reviewer for *The Athenaeum* (13.12.1873) judged the book unfit to be put into the hands of young people, the revelation of such mind-darkening 'knowledge' deemed a 'grave error' on Stretton's part.[16]

The shadow of undesirable or burdensome knowledge is clearly perceived to compromise the innocence and tender sensibilities of the reader. Yet Stretton does not flinch from the disclosure of young lives which are alien or 'other' in diverse ways, at home and abroad. She sets up, but continually explodes, normative myths of childhood innocence and freedom from care. Resonating still today, texts such as *Max Kromer*, *Left Alone* and *In the Hollow of His Hand* foreground the physical and emotional plight of children caught up in violent warfare and religious division, or harnessed as pawns in sectarian persecution – consequences of the 'crimes and mistakes of men'.[17] Illuminating the faceted discourses at work in the conscious and unwitting construction of distinctions and divisions, she harnesses the fictional child as mirror and messenger, mediator and interrogatory or subversive force, in a mission to speak on behalf of the 'real' child, and to convey both his vulnerability and his potential.

Notes

1. See, for example, 'Felicia Crompton' (1863).

2. Mrs. Castle Smith also emphasises play as a childhood necessity (*Froggy's Little Brother*, 1875, Ch.3).

3. The link between blue eyes and a heavenly provenance recurs across literary/cultural forms, as in MacDonald's *At the Back of the North Wind* (1871/1966: 246).

4. Social investigator Henry Mayhew notes the 'extraordinary licentiousness' of street-children (1861-2/1985:181); urban explorer

Andrew Mearns labels the slums 'hotbeds of vice and disease' where 'all kinds of depravity have ... their schools' (1883/1976: 99).

5. The art market, as Leslie Williams (1994: 127) notes, was particularly eager to consume pictures of poor children. The nineteenth-century author Silas Hocking confirms the 'deep and ... growing interest in the lives of the poorer classes'; the sale of street-life stories continued unabated, with one hundred and fifty thousand volumes disposed of over the preceding five years (Preface to *Dick's Fairy*, 1883).

6. Dickens *The Old Curiosity Shop* (1841); Mayhew *London Labour and The London Poor* (1861-2); Barnardo 'A City Waif' (1885/6).

7. See also Hollindale (2001: 30) and Nodelman (2000: 9) regarding competing/confrontational patterns of childhood.

8. In Barnardo's *Taken Out of the Gutter*, the little brother receives the 'best and choicest morsels' (1881: 12, Ch.1).

9. According to the 1900 postscript to the preface, Fidge is based on a child Stretton encountered when visiting 'low' lodging houses in Spitalfields.

10. Texts including Mrs. Walton's *A Peep Behind the Scenes* (1877) had highlighted, in less graphic terms, the dangers of circus life; Silas Hocking's *Dick's Fairy* (1883) concerns an orphaned child performer. Prominent figures including Lord Shaftesbury campaigned to expose the inadequacies of legislation in this area; articles appeared in the press and medical journals and consciousness-raising narratives such as E.M. Barlee's *Pantomime Waifs* (1884) were published. Deficiencies in earlier legislation were addressed in the Prevention of Cruelty Acts of 1889 and 1894. For further discussion, see Steedman (1995), especially Chapter 6.

11. For Foucault (1979), the body becomes 'object and target of power' (136); 'power relations have an immediate hold upon it; they invest it, mark it, train it, torture it, force it to carry out tasks, to perform ceremonies, to emit signs' (25). See also Kristeva (1982) on ideas of 'abjection' and the necessary expulsion of that which defiles, and Butler (2004: 107) for a discussion, drawing on Mary Douglas's work, of the body as synecdoche for the social system, with social and bodily margins linked as sites of transgression.

12. Lindsay Smith (1996), discussing Victorian photography, childhood, class and ethnicity, identifies the child as a 'reduced form of the ethnic other' (29), the 'street Arab' signifying a 'knowable other interposed between self and absolute other' (31). See also Cunningham (1991) regarding the intersecting discourses of primitivism, savagery and the nineteenth-century waif/delinquent, and my further discussion in Chapter 4.

13. Pike, *Children Reclaimed for Life* (1875: 155).

14. Barnardo's accounts, with their language of 'fishing' and 'baiting the hook', betray an uncomfortable relation to the discourse of seduction.

15. Although we should be wary of too readily assuming sexual connotations, particular markers are associated with prostitution or sexual availability across Victorian discourse.

16. Sales of *The King's Servants* had nonetheless reached thirty-six thousand by 1877, according to textual advertisements.

17. Preface to *Max Kromer*. Stretton speaks of 'softening down, rather than heightening' the horrors of the siege of Strasbourg, the effects of which she witnessed whilst travelling through the Rhine valley (n.d.: 6).

Chapter 3

'Where women have their rights …' (Stretton, 1893: 4)

Second only to Stretton's preoccupation with the child figure is her concern for the woman and mother. Reflecting the perception of a world divided into, on the one hand, 'men', and on the other, 'women and children' (1893: 4), her writings emphasise the deep bond, the intersecting concerns and shared marginalisation of woman and child; as their omission from the listed village population (*In the Hollow of His Hand*, 152) illustrates, their rights as citizens – indeed, their very existence – are often denied. The motif of the outcast mother and her child threads through her writing, intersecting with a plethora of contemporary literary and artistic representations, including Mrs. Gaskell's *Ruth* (1853), Eliot's *Adam Bede* (1859) and paintings by, amongst others, Frederick Walker and Richard Redgrave.[1] Crucially, as Stretton recognises in 'Women's Work for Children', the happiness of children depends on women being in possession of their rights (1893: 4).

If the idealised image of childhood is juxtaposed in Stretton's writings with alternative representations of the child and adolescent, so paradigms of the ideal wife and mother are set alongside 'deviant' patterns of female and maternal identity. Marriage and motherhood are in some instances portrayed as empowering and a source of unparalleled joy and fulfilment (*The Clives of Burcot*, n.d.: 188, Ch.26), the role of wife and mother meriting iconic status. Elsewhere, the marital state is represented as a lesser evil, a 'yoke' (*The Highway of Sorrow*, 176), or a form of subjection which constrains and stultifies (*The Doctor's Dilemma*, *Hester Morley's Promise*); maternity is marked by material hardship, by onerous and restrictive cultural or familial expectations, and by physical and emotional sacrifice. Oppression is often class-related, but, in numerous cases, cuts across class lines.

Born to be 'masters and tyrants'

Despite Stretton's portrayal of certain male protagonists as gentle, protective and nurturing (among them, Matthias in *Carola*), a competing theme is men's natural tendency towards despotism, in both public and private spheres.[2] The experience of young Cassy is such that she already understands the male sex to be the inevitable 'masters and tyrants of the race' (*Cassy*, 75, Ch.9); women and children are destined, self-evidently, to submit to men's whims and drunken violence (64, Ch.8). That this represents a distortion of biblical patterns is subsequently driven home by Cassy's innocently surprised observation – overlaid with barbed authorial irony – that Jesus treated the female sex, 'as if they were almost as good as men!' (138, Ch.16).

Across texts, the exposure of male selfishness and tyranny chimes with attitudes expressed in Stretton's diaries, in which men are described variously as demanding, foolish, unfathomable and dishonest. In *A Thorny Path*, the alien presence of a man in the house troubles the elderly protagonist, who 'can't abide to have aught to do with men' (21, Ch.2), and initially likens her visitor to a wild beast from the zoo (44, Ch.6). Male privilege within the domestic hierarchy, and the concomitant limitation of female space, are evidenced in this and other narratives by the appropriation of the comfortable chair and entire fireside area by the male, while the woman 'make[s] herself as small as possible' (45, Ch.6; *Lost Gip*, 59, Ch.8).[3] The opinion of Colonel Cleveland (*Half Brothers*, 40, Ch.5) that women should remain obediently at home, like their Eastern counterparts, rather than 'go gadding about in public, blocking up the streets, and hindering business' (a view which clearly demands the reader's condemnation) reflects Stretton's longstanding recognition of men's determination to exclude women from the affairs of the world. Her narratives consistently underline, yet often seek to bridge, the gulf 'betwixt men and women' (*A Thorny Path*, 59, Ch.7); it transpires that the disapproving attitude of *Bede's Charity's* Uncle Simister towards women – who, he complains, need regulating like a watch, make a dust wherever they go, and have a tendency to go into 'hysterics' – stems from his unfamiliarity with, and deep-rooted misunderstanding of, the opposite sex (55, Ch.7; 67, Ch.9).[4]

A distrust of men and the mysteries of marriage is often encoded in gothic allusions such as the Bluebeard motif ('The Lucky Leg'; *The Doctor's Dilemma*) – an image commonly harnessed by women writers as a subversive emblem of the female condition. There is, perhaps, also a hint that the prospect of a safe, companionate marriage, with 'no Bluebeard's Chamber', might be devoid of the frisson engendered by the unknown and feared (*The Doctor's Dilemma*, 165, Part 2, Ch.10). In common with prominent contemporary commentators such as John Stuart Mill, Frances Power Cobbe and Annie Besant, Stretton draws on the master-slave analogy in her critique of relations between the sexes, suggesting marriage as a form of bondage more cruel and degrading than slavery itself. Stretton's own rejection of the domestic role, as evidenced in diary comments on domestic slavery, add fuel to her critique, with personal and wider grievances often expressed through the mouths of characters; women, to their chagrin, bear the brunt of household management, exercising prudence in the face of men's failure to manage their affairs, and recognising, despite biblical injunctions to the contrary, the necessity of worrying about 'the morrow', 'or how 'ud the work get done'? (*Two Secrets* (1882/inscr.1901: 26).

Inequalities in the domestic sphere are pointedly addressed in *Lost Gip*, in which the awakening of Mr. Shafto's religious conscience (through the agency of young Sandy) prompts interrogation and revision of the male's assumed right to the lion's share of comfort and nourishment, and overturns a blind acceptance of the woman's duty to place her husband's needs first: 'she had cleaned [his] boots for him every day ever since they were married, even when her work was very pressing' (85, Ch.11). Here again, religion is harnessed to progressive and emancipatory ends. Engaging with proto-feminist expressions of discontent, and with sentiments common in contemporary popular novels, Stretton's narratives comment on the subjection and exploitation of women across classes, exposing woman's status as passive ornament (*The Clives of Burcot*), and as the property or chattel of self-regarding men: 'she bore his name, and belonged to him' (*Hester Morley*, 77, Ch.12) – a denial of a woman's identity and self-ownership which the narrative vigorously contests. The young protagonist of *the Doctor's Dilemma*, confined under the 'authority' of a husband intent on enforcing submission to his will, and perceiving herself as much a captive as the howling dog who strains at its shackles, opts to escape, friendless, from this 'bitter slavery', to take her chance in the world (60, Part 1, Ch.6).[5] The relationship between economic dependence and subjection is made clear in texts such as *Carola*, where an independent livelihood permits greater autonomy and choice. By contrast, children like Jessica and Cassy are rescued from poverty, isolation and exploitation to be integrated into more comfortable (albeit not always conventional) homes and families, but, significantly, as willing servants to their benefactors.

The question of women's rights under law comes under close scrutiny in Stretton's *Under the Old Roof* – a text designed, according to the preface, to demonstrate the injustices suffered by women prior to the Married Women's Property Acts, and to highlight equalities now secured. Its publication coinciding with the 1882 amendment (passed after twenty years of campaigning, legislation and reform, supported by prominent figures such as Mill and Barbara Leigh Smith Bodichon), the text underlines the economic, social and legal oppression of women, despite their material contribution – in this case the fruit of bodily labour. Abigail, as chief breadwinner, is less dependent on her husband than most women. She works 'like a man' to reclaim cottages once owned by her family, but her leading role and ownership of property is resented by her stepson, who promises never to set foot in 'a house where a woman was the master' (n.d.: 28, Ch.2). In delineating earlier grievances, including the married woman's status as 'nobody' under law (49, Ch.4.), the narrative interrogates ongoing prejudices surrounding women's position and rights within marriage. Such questions were widely aired in the contemporary press, and Stretton, as an avid reader of journals, is likely to have followed these debates; she perhaps read articles on the subject such as that published in 1882 by the campaigner Annie Besant, which deals with many of the concerns addressed by Stretton.[6]

'Natural' motherhood

Society's investment in the woman as mother reflects the underlying presence, in dominant constructions of motherhood, of the religious iconography of the Madonna and Child – an image which pervades all cultural forms. Highlighted in contemporary paintings such as Mulready's 'The Lesson' (1859) and evoked in texts including Stretton's *The Children of Cloverley*, it is specifically cited in her 1893 article 'Women's Work for Children' and implicit throughout her work in representations of the ideal mother and child relation. Stretton's writings, at one level, endorse motherhood as essential to a woman's identity, the 'guardianship of a child of [one's] own' ('The Lucky Leg', 375) deemed by certain protagonists to be crucial to women's self-completion and sense of self-worth. The idea that the child's dependence makes a woman 'precious to [her]self' (375) reflects not only a widespread cultural belief, but, perhaps, a personal sense of lack; a devoted aunt, how much, indeed, did Stretton yearn for children of her own, and, perhaps subconsciously, to reproduce through a child the lost union of the mother-child relation?[7]

These narratives emphasise the fundamental importance not only of the mother to the child, but of the child to the mother, the disconnection of this bond, for whatever reason, constituting the severest of ruptures; no-one can love a child like its mother does (*Hester Morley*, 444). If, for the child, the glimpsed folds of an old gown evoke the expectation of, and a yearning for, the accompanying maternal face ('Not to be Taken for Granted'), and a beloved armchair affords something of the solace once provided by a mother's lap (*Hester Morley*), the loss of, or separation from, a child entails, for the mother, pain beyond endurance. Such suffering is palpable in early texts such as *The Clives of Burcot*, in which the mother's union with the child is all-consuming; the sense of attachment and commitment is crucial to the narrative in *The Storm of Life* and other stories, and recurs, undiminished, in *In the Hollow of His Hand*, where maternal love is cynically exploited as a lever – the most effective in the authorities' armoury – to enforce compliance with dominant religious norms, the severance of child from mother driving women to total distraction. The intensity of the maternal relationship permeates Stretton's narratives; significantly, in terms of audience engagement, currents in her writing express, in their fluid, oceanic rhythms and their enactment of the womb-associated mutuality and continuity between mother and child, a sense of yearning for reunion or pre-oedipal fusion, which offers a powerful, and arguably subversive, sense of connection, both on the surface and below the level of the text, potentially tapping into unconscious drives and primal desires in writer and reader and dissolving boundaries between self and other.[8]

If motherhood is seen to be important *to the woman* at a personal and emotional level, its cultural status also reflects society's designation of, and dependence on, the mother as preserver of order, stability and civilised values; her absence signals a lack or malfunction in the fundamental framework of society. The expression of longing for the mother's presence, echoed by the motherless narrator of *An Acrobat's Girlhood* [1889], and reinforced in the recognition that there is 'no loss like that loss to girls like us' (7), underscores the role of the mother, not only as primal shelter from the terrors of the world, but as crucial formative influence – conveyer of moral instruction, guardian of virtue, and restraining hand (sometimes, as in *The Children of Cloverley*, even in death). The widely-held belief that a child's character is 'formed … in great measure by the influence of the home, and above all, by the mother', is voiced by Stretton's contemporary, Mrs. Sumner (1893: 67), who suggests that only a mother can exert a softening influence on boys growing up under difficult conditions. Just as writer Charlotte Yonge (1876: 264) identifies homemaking as the most essential duty of 'womankind', Stretton emphasises the importance of mother and home for children such as Ishmael (*No Place Like Home*), as they face the dangers of adolescence; in the narrative *In Prison and Out*, it is David's love and respect for his mother which sets him apart from the rest of the criminal fraternity, and mediates his response to his imprisonment.

In an echo of Gaskell's recognition of the wife and mother as humanising influence (*Mary Barton*, 22), Stretton identifies the lack of such restraining ties as the root of a father's profligacy, recourse to drink and lack of parental concern (*An Acrobat's Girlhood*); in the case of Cassy's father, only her mother's influence had ensured a degree of decency in his conduct (*Cassy*, 25, Ch.3). When it comes to the matter of growing girls, a mother's guidance is paramount. In common with Gaskell's Mary, whose 'pitiful loss' means that she lacks maternal direction of matters of propriety (383), the motherless girls of Stretton's early 'The Postmaster's Daughter' are compelled to be particularly 'careful in their conduct', 5.11.1859: 40); similarly, adolescents such as the eponymous Carola are seen to be more vulnerable because of the lack of a maternal mentor. The central role played by the mother in answering a daughter's questions, emphasised by Stretton's friend, Henrietta Synnot (1875: 497), was clearly appreciated by the author herself. Continually mindful of her own, pivotal early experience, and her subsequent lack, at a crucial age, of maternal instruction and guidance, Stretton stresses the need to equip young girls, in their turn, for the vital task of patient and gentle motherhood (*The Times*, 8.1.1884) – concerns echoed at a societal (and eugenics-inflected) level by critics such as Edward Salmon (1886), in his call for juvenile reading matter likely to build up women as 'future wives and mothers of [the] race' (526).

'Othered' mothers and wayward women

The fact that ideal womanhood is located in maternity, with loving motherhood the 'natural' state of woman, means that those who deviate from the norm of the 'good' maternal figure are not only subject to society's opprobrium, but also defined as inhuman – monstrous, barbaric and an affront to nature. Furthermore, the concomitant conflation of the domestic and the moral or virtuous means that the slatternly, neglectful or unloving wife or mother is regarded as akin to the 'fallen woman', and similarly categorised as 'bad' and 'other'. Stretton can be seen to reproduce such assumptions: her belief that women's wholehearted involvement with children (in whatever capacity) is 'as natural as that the sun should shine' (1893: 4), coupled with an internalisation of circulating images of the deviant mother, leads her ostensibly to portray such women negatively (albeit often as *perceived* by others), in terms which evoke descriptions by social reformers, commentators and novelists including Dickens, and which once again evidence the harnessing of discourses of the body in the construction of otherness. Like the outcast child stumbled upon as a 'something', rather than a 'somebody' (Barnardo's 'A City Waif', 5), these 'tattered and wretched', irresponsible and often gin-sodden 'creatures' are objectified, mistaken for 'heap[s] of rags' *Lost Gip,* 136, Ch.18; *Jessica's Mother,* label 1925:34, Ch.3).

Concern for the child means that its welfare may be in conflict with the interests of the biological mother: Jessica's benefactor rejoices that his charge of the young waif is unhindered by 'interfere[nce]' in the shape of her mother (*Jessica's First Prayer,* 91, Ch.10) – a situation which in part reflects a growing tendency for society to intervene in families perceived as defective, to the extent of withdrawing the child in order to place him or her into the care of others, sometimes as part of the officially sanctioned emigration projects which were becoming increasingly popular. In order to fulfil the moral agenda, the child character may be accorded agency which operates to the detriment of the unsatisfactory parent, as happens in *Jessica's Mother* when the child, appropriating the adult, instructive role, reprimands her inebriate mother for her improper conduct and rejects her request to shelter under benefactor Daniel's roof (59-60, Ch.5). Stretton's ambivalent attempt to reinstate the mother who is absent in the first 'Jessica' story, and to reconstitute her as subject in this melodramatic sequel, ultimately ends with the social and textual ejection of the unfortunate maternal character, who does not 'belong' and continues effectively to be excluded, despite her title role.[9]

At the same time, an understanding of errant mothers and transgressive women threads through her narratives, which often explore the material and emotional circumstances that influence women's responses, moral decisions and actions. If oppression affects women of all classes, Stretton recognises that the rights of those living in conditions of extreme poverty and hardship, often with responsibility for several generations, are even more severely compromised. The comparatively light-hearted satire which sometimes accompanies the exposure of inequalities is markedly absent in more extreme settings. Worn down by hardship and sacrifice, the terminally-ill, widowed mother of *In Prison and Out* suffers cruelly because the allotted dole is insufficient to meet both her needs and those of her family: unable to afford adequate nourishment, she experiences raging hunger, 'as if a wolf was gnawing' at me' (1880: 6). This woman's conduct is without fault, but even those who transgress accepted norms of maternal or moral behaviour as a consequence of material or social pressures are not denied compassion and understanding.

Engaging not only with the issue of infant mortality, but also with contemporary debates surrounding the erosion of 'natural' mothering instincts, Stretton sheds light on the manner in which material conditions

49

may shatter ideals. As narrator, she describes in *Lost Gip* the apparent sense of relief which may follow the death of a child in the courts of the East End, where infant funerals are so frequent that they escape notice. Here, mothers have seemingly 'lost their natural love for their little ones, and are glad to be rid of a care which would have made their lives a still heavier burden to them (2-3, Ch.1).[10] The text goes on to reflect widespread anxieties regarding the growing incidence of infanticide: when little Gip disappears, gossiping neighbours hint that 'maybe she had been made away with as a trouble' (20, Ch.3). Stretton displays an awareness of the extent to which conditions of hardship brutalise parents: decrying, in a later letter to *The Times* (8.1.1885), the uncontrolled violence meted out, as chastisement, to orphaned girls by a so-called 'sister of charity', she points to the understandably greater difficulty in terms of self-control experienced by poverty-stricken and degraded families whose children have come to represent a 'burden and a hindrance'.

In foregrounding the mother who deserts her own children, Stretton's stories arguably tap into, not only the universal terror of abandonment, but also a deep-seated, perhaps unconscious, fear on the part of women of finding themselves the instigator of such a separation – of being, for whatever reason, the one who deserts. In the narrative *A Thorny Path*, the widowed Hagar – plunged into despair by weight of her 'burden' – abandons her responsibilities only after 'slaving' for her family and denying her own needs until she is physically and mentally at breaking point (Ch.1). *Left Alone* (1876) takes as its theme the dilemma of a woman, who, as sole breadwinner, must leave her child alone while she labours to provide for her, a material situation encountered by Stretton during rescue activities recounted in 'Women's Work', in which she writes of working women who are obliged to lock up their offspring without warmth or nourishment in order to provide bread and a roof to shelter them (1893: 7).

The writer L.T. Meade alludes, in the waif story *Scamp and I*, to the tendency for drink to kill all other love in a woman's breast, blighting homes, ruining children and spreading destruction (1877/label 1916: 78-79, Ch.9). Likewise, an unmistakeable temperance message underlies numerous Stretton narratives, including *Lost Gip* and *Jessica's Mother*. However, in common with Barnardo and, later, social commentator Charles Booth, she recognises that starvation, misery and childbearing often cause women to take to gin and vice. Whilst the mother who drinks (and sometimes plies her child with the same poison) has clearly, in Stretton's eyes, betrayed her natural calling, there is an awareness of the

SHELTERLESS,

Illustration 4: *A Thorny Path* (edition c.1882) 'Shelterless' 25, Ch.3 (illustrator unknown)

pressures which may lead women to this path. Jessica's mother has been 'driven' to it, and although there is less apparent authorial sympathy here than in some Stretton texts, the narrative ensures that Daniel's judgemental attitude towards her undergoes revision. In the later *Carola*, Stretton plainly acknowledges the fact that, for those living in squalor and deprivation, there is an inevitable temptation to drink as compensation for boredom and a lack of material comforts.

Similarly, an understanding of the circumstances which lead to transgression finds its way into Stretton's treatment of the 'fallen' woman, whether in circumstances of material necessity or exploitation, or of moral weakness. Condemnation and compassion are sometimes in tension, but it is perhaps the acknowledgement of the susceptibility of all, including herself, to such weakness or temptation – a recognition voiced in the early story 'Alice Gilbert's Confession' (1862) – which allows Stretton, as narrator, to present this predicament, at least in part, from the perspective of the errant or vulnerable woman, a stance earlier adopted by Mrs. Gaskell in *Ruth* and by Stretton's acquaintance, Mrs. Henry Wood, in *East Lynne* (1861), and which is in conflict with the social and moral assumptions which drive the narrative. She recognises the stark options facing women under certain conditions, with numbers driven to suicide; the river is perceived by many outcast girls as the ultimate solution – an escape attempted by the rescued 'painted-faced' girl of *The King's Servants*, contemplated by Rachel (*The Storm of Life*) and, for Cassy, perceived as the 'best' fate (*Cassy*, 26, Ch.3). The likely career of Jessica's mother (consistent with her theatrical background and associated moral decline) is only hinted at, but the woman's melodramatic fall from the river bridge reinforces implied elision with the figure of the prostitute, whose river death is the subject of countless contemporary literary and artistic images.[11]

In *Cassy*, the feckless Mrs. Tilly's conduct is shown to be understandable as well as reprehensible; her romantic illusions, and the concrete actions inspired by her novel-reading are plainly irresponsible, yet criticism is accompanied by a comprehension of the woman's desire to escape from a reality marked by poverty, monotony and abuse, into a book-world filled with fantasies of a better life: 'Why should she not be admired as much as the heroines she read of?' (73, Ch.9). Her imagination stimulated by her consumption of 'high-flown romances', Mrs. Tilly eventually takes flight, in a manner which seems to her mysterious and 'almost romantic' – a 'novel-like event' (94), leaving the child Cassy to manage the household and arrange the grandfather's funeral. Juxtaposing the serious and the near-playful, this narrative – which, given Stretton's own novelistic aspirations and incorporation of themes of romance and murder, can be considered to exhibit an element of ironic self-reflexivity – represents both a warning against, and a concrete demonstration of, the power of books to inspire action and change, however morally dubious the consequences.

Ambivalence towards, and understanding of, the aberrant conduct of protagonists extends on occasion beyond settings of poverty and physical deprivation. In the full-length *Hester Morley's Promise*, the lively young Rose – trapped, like a butterfly unable to spread its wings, in a gloomy, middle-class marriage – is not spared the consequences of her adultery (outcast and destitute, she is separated from her child, and later dies). However, Stretton's treatment is sympathetic, reflecting insight and comprehension rather than narrow judgement; the constraints and temptations which lead to Rose's misconduct are fully recognised. Moreover, the double-standard which allows the man to retain his home and place in society, while the woman is condemned and cast out, is brought under scrutiny: Robert continues to live in luxury, repenting with 'a comfortable penitence, which left him free for many pleasures', despite the fact that '[Rose's] poverty-stricken, ill-clad, friendless, dying misery' is, as the narrator makes clear, the result of a sin of which both were guilty (276).

In life, Stretton was not always patient or forgiving with members of her own sex; she did not suffer fools gladly, and, particularly in her youth, expressed contempt for those who were 'meek', 'silly' or 'empty'. Those assessed in her diaries as overly domineering and exacting, or, like the participants of the hated local Dorcas sewing group, 'stone-eyed', are equally subject to criticism, and pomposity or hypocrisy meet with little leniency. Later in life, and perhaps including herself in the evaluation, she pointed to the tendency for women to be provocative, with 'nothing so bitter as a woman's tongue' (*The Times*, 30.6.1884).

Many of the women who feature in Stretton's fictional narratives are strong-minded and independent – perhaps her personal ideal; others are vain, frivolous, materially-inclined, and often misguided, meeting variously with censure and empathy in the narrative tone. There are numerous examples of the scheming and capricious stepmother or mother-in-law figure, portrayals fuelled perhaps by fears of the archetypal fairy-tale figure – a fictional trope which inspires terror of the real in the young Hester Morley, and which is implicit in Stretton's depiction of the evil and bullying Matoushka of *In The Hollow of His Hand*, who imprisons the young protagonist in a windowless closet and treats her as a drudge. At another level, such characterisation is perhaps also a product of Stretton's antipathy towards acquaintances such as Mrs. Henry Wood, who displayed the kind of negative '"mother" influence' (Log Book: 25.10.1867) which is manifested in the possessive and interfering Mrs. Arnold in *Carola*, or the manipulative Mrs. Ashworth, to whose authority the protagonist of *The Clives of Burcot* submits. The envious and controlling Miss Waldron of *Hester Morley's Promise* – a bitter spinster figure, 'infallible and autocratic' as a 'domestic pope' (112, Ch.17) – is, as a consequence of the constraints on her sex, a frustrated theologian, whose natural forum is the pulpit. This sardonic portrait, no doubt drawn from experience and intended as an indictment of the self-righteous, domineering woman, also gives voice to a wider resentment of the limitations on women's involvement in the public sphere and, at the same time, despite Stretton's ambivalence towards marriage (and her awareness of the freedoms offered by an independent, unencumbered state), a consciousness of the single woman who has let opportunities pass by (*Bede's Charity*) and who faces the potential 'empty' lot of the spinster (*The Doctor's Dilemma*, 279, Part 2, Ch.20). Nonetheless, in the late *The Soul of Honour* – written during a decade in which Stretton had already demonstrated her engagement with the much-debated 'Woman' question (Friederichs, 1894: 329) – the author, in the guise of first-person narrator, underlines the realisation by modern-spirited girls that 'marriage with a good settlement' need not, as their elders had given them to understand, be the 'aim and end' of a woman's life (84, Ch.8).

Hesba Stretton's narratives contain diverse models of womanhood and motherhood, or, indeed, substitute maternity (a role fulfilled by Stretton, as by many contemporary women philanthropists, through a child-centred mission, in this case both practical and literary).[12] Undeniably, her representations are underpinned by normative paradigms, and sustained by prevailing binaries which construct and reinforce difference; at the same time, contradiction and ambivalence, coupled with the overt exploration of moral complexities, serve to complicate, interrogate and destabilise these images. Throughout her work, the denial of women's rights, and the attendant personal and societal ramifications, are abiding concerns, whether the author's crusade relates to the entitlement to material necessities of food, shelter and support; to freedom from abuse, fear or exploitation; to education, property and the product of female labour; or, crucially, to equality, autonomy and self-determination – a fundamental emancipation identified so plainly by the protagonist of *The Doctor's Dilemma* as a woman's 'right to [her]self' (106, Part 3, Ch.10).

Notes

1. See, for example, Walker's 'The Lost Path' (1863) and Redgrave's 'The Outcast' (1851). See also the photography of Julia Margaret Cameron (1815-1879) for its emphasis on women and children.

2. Such sentiments match those of campaigners such as Harriet Taylor (who influenced, and in 1851 married, John Stuart Mill). In 'The Enfranchisement of Women' (1850/1995), Taylor asserts that a man who believes himself 'first in law and in opinion – that to will is his part, and hers to submit' will undoubtedly become 'either the conscious or unconscious despot of his household' (30).

3. In Foucauldian terms, such divisions reflect a 'language of subordination', in which women's 'spatiality' is restricted and men 'expand into the available space' (Bartky, 1988: 73; 66-67).

4. Simister also dislikes the idea of heaven if all the angels are women, as implied by the way they are depicted with curls and trailing gowns (69, Ch. 9).

5. Stretton's language coincides with Mill's rhetoric in 'The Subjection of Women' (1869/1998) regarding men's intolerance of domestic equality, and their desire that wives should be willing slaves; Mill discusses the emphasis in women's upbringing on submission, abnegation of self and yielding to the control of others, and stresses the personal/social benefits of liberating women from a life of subjection to the will of others.

6. Besant, in 'Marriage: As It Was, As It Is, and As It Should Be' (1882/1987) cites the application of the master-slave analogy to the marital state; she also invokes the comments of the early feminist Mary Wollstonecraft in order to identify (as does Stretton) married women as amongst those 'in subjection to the power of others' (412/3).

7. See psycho-social theorist Nancy Chodorow's discussion of women's desire to return to the symbiotic relationship with their mothers through oneness with a child (1978: 212).

8. The sense of the mother and child being totally immersed in each other, as conveyed by passages in *The Clives of Burcot*, *The Storm of Life* and *Half Brothers*, is suggestive of the potentially subversive energies (operating partly at a level beyond conventional male-ordered language and rational understanding) discussed by psychoanalytical theorists such as Julia Kristeva ('Revolution in Poetic Language', 1986).

9. This story first appeared in 1867 in the *Sunday at Home*, but proposals for its issue as a separate volume in 1870 were rejected – without explanation, but perhaps because of its more sensational tone and content. Although it was included in the RTS Penny Tales for the People series before 1900, and was issued by the Bible Institute Colportage Association, Chicago, as Part II of the complete 'Jessica' story [1897], it is thought that a separate-volume hardback edition did not appear until early in the twentieth century. (See also Alderson and Garrett, 1999: 22-23.)

10. The acceptance of bereavement by deprived families as, at all events, a lessening of expenditure is echoed in contemporary newspaper and journal articles on the subject of infant mortality (see Matus, 1995: 166).

11. Contemporary depictions of river suicides include Gustave Doré's 1878 illustration to Thomas Hood's 'The Bridge of Sighs' and W. Gray's 'Found' which appeared in Hayward's *London by Night* (c.1870).

12. The rescued 'lost' girls of *The King's Servants* are in need of someone to call 'mother' (144, Part 3, Ch.8).

Chapter 4

Representing others

Repeatedly, these narratives seek to take the part of the dispossessed and the outsider, giving him a voice and a story, whether his marginalisation stems from his material circumstances, his social status, his age, race or religion. At the same time, there are clearly problems involved in any project which aims to speak on behalf of others – to represent particular groups or individual figures from the inherently voyeuristic stance of outside observer or spectator, rescuer or socialising agent. Whilst Stretton plainly sets out to expose and counter inequalities, social injustices and systemic failures, in so doing she participates to some extent in prevailing discourses of alterity which encode deeply embedded assumptions and stereotypes. In the process of assessing the strengths and shortcomings of her project, in examining her representations of the outcast in his/her various manifestations, we come face to face with many of the prejudices and related discursive practices which reflect the preconceptions of her times, and we also glimpse something of the aspirations, uncertainties and ambivalence which inform her personal perspective.

'Poverty and cotton gloves'

Stretton's protagonist Hester Morley, daughter of a 'poor' bookseller, and regarded by some in the community as inferior, defends her trade-class background; refusing the status of 'lady', she unashamedly claims to 'belong quite to the working-class' (*Hester Morley's Promise*, 294, Ch.42). Perhaps, in part, by virtue of their own trade-class origins, Stretton and her sisters sometimes felt themselves to be outsiders – even 'natural curiosities' – in the eyes of Wellington society (Log Book: 19.12.1860). Such a perception, despite the tone of amused indignation (tinged, no doubt, with a certain pleasure in failing to conform), embodies a sense of not quite belonging which arguably feeds into Stretton's understanding of those on the fringes of society. By the same token, this impression of difference potentially gives rise to tensions and insecurities which are reflected in her writing, surfacing in empathy with the rejected, but also, perhaps, in a partial identification with the very expressions of pride and superiority which she seeks to condemn. Diary entries (ironic, but telling) declare the sisters, by their own assessment, 'not fitted for society' (23.4.1867); at the same time, they evidence a distaste for the 'vulgar' or 'common' (a label applied to the neighbourhood of their lodgings in October 1864 – 'not altogether our proper sphere yet'), and a

perception of being fit for a somewhat better world (20.1.1866). The dread
of being regarded as a charity case is palpable in the 1864 entry which
records the receipt by the sisters of a parcel of less than desirable cast-off
clothing from a local resident – an incident perceived as an unmitigated
insult, and recycled (perhaps as retribution and catharsis) almost a decade
later in *Hester Morley's Promise* (Ch.43), a text which, like numerous
others, raises issues of poverty and inferiority. The fact that many of
Stretton's outcast protagonists are of somewhat higher origin or 'naturally
refined' (not an uncommon pattern in contemporary novels) betrays an
urge to distance innate respectability or 'decent' poverty (a term also used
by Mrs. Gaskell) from 'low' and degraded conditions or lifestyles.

Decline in fortune or position, or the fear of such a fall, is a recurring
theme in Stretton's work, reflecting anxieties – shared by wider society –
regarding the precariousness of economic and social boundaries.
Condemning the pretentiousness of newly affluent friends (Log Book:
3.7.1869), but also acknowledging in fiction the pleasure of spending
'without counting the pence' ('Eleven Hundred Pounds', 1864: 17),
Stretton appreciated her growing financial security; she noted with great
rejoicing in early 1870 the banking of £375 from the RTS (for
copyrights), and, as the eventual holder of a substantial portfolio, patently
recognised the importance of prudent investment – not to be confused
with the miserly hoarding practised by certain protagonists. Her narratives
warn of the dangers of increasing materialism, of the rush to engage in
financial speculation and the undue importance given to 'Getting and
spending' (*The Soul of Honour*, 100, Ch.10). However, she doubtless also
relished the peace of mind afforded by having 'ample means at [her]
disposal' (*Soul*, 249, Ch.27), and the consequent freedom to *choose* (as
does the protagonist of that text) to work among the poor and outcast – an
undertaking confirmed nonetheless as 'no easy task', and one which
ideally requires an intimate experience of real poverty rather than the
insights gained only in the course of 'playing at it' (248, Ch.27).

In *Bede's Charity*, the fall in status experienced by the elderly Margery
permits changes of material perspective, offering engagement across
classes with experiences of hardship and exclusion; it also serves to
interrogate prominent contemporary issues of social mobility and
affluence in relation to notions of breeding and gentility. Importantly,
Stretton examines the effects of changes in economic and class
positioning upon the perceptions of others and, crucially, upon individual
identity. Given unstinting support in her dramatically reduced
circumstances by her young street-waif companion, Cor, Margery –

originally from a respectable farming family – is rejected by her own brother, whose social advancement (following emigration) leaves him unable on his return to contemplate – for himself or his family – association with someone of such degraded appearance and status.[1] When, despite his attempts to prevent the slightest physical contact, she is befriended, and, as yet unidentified, eagerly accepted by her young niece, the directness of the child is harnessed to expose the hypocrisy of a father who advocates being 'kind and good to all poor people' (117, Ch.15), but shuns his own flesh and blood. Such openness also serves to explore the question (implicit throughout the narrative and extending to the concept of 'gentleman') of what 'makes a woman a lady?' (155, Ch.20). In the same text, Stretton presents us with a satirical portrait of Margery's acquaintance, Mrs. Moss, who, unable to reconcile herself to the loss of her genteel status, regards the 'common' people with scorn and rejects the idea of her daughter going into service, protesting that 'nobody belonging to me has ever been a servant' (171, Ch.22).

Awareness of gradation and difference between and within classes is apparent in the assumptions of superiority held by the 'respectable poor' regarding the rough savageness of the population of the 'low' parts (*Enoch Roden's Training*, Ch.1). Here, the aspirations, pride and insecurities of the respectable cottagers are manifested in their anxiousness to conceal the extent of their poverty from their neighbours (a concern also evidenced in middle-class settings, as in *David Lloyd's Last Will* (Vol.1, 279-280, Ch.23) where the move to a smaller residence might betray reduced circumstances), and in their desire to learn to conduct themselves in the manner of gentlefolk in the presence of the well-to-do of the area.[2] In *Lost Gip*, Stretton draws attention to waif Sandy's perception that his better-clad working-class friend appears 'almost a gentleman' (32, Ch.4); the narrative exposes the intra-class bigotry inherent in the initial hesitation by his working-class rescuers as to whether such a child is fit to share the comforts of their house. It also pinpoints Sandy's internalised assumptions of his own inferiority, and of his status as, indeed, 'unfit for such a place' (77, Ch.10) – a perception which is contested through the interrogation and revision of attitudes, with Sandy becoming (after a little brushing-up) a substitute son. The young-adult novel *Carola* presses home the need for the city girl to escape her 'black' background; at the same time, its condemnation of those who are anxious to preserve their good name from the stigma of association is unmistakeable, and in this text arrogant fears concerning class contamination and marrying beneath one's station are shown to be unattractive and misplaced.

Echoing sentiments expressed by writers such as Mrs. Gaskell, Stretton mocks the snobbery of those for whom being reduced to 'poverty and cotton gloves' – at a time when the poor of Manchester were dying in vast numbers of starvation (*David Lloyd's Last Will*, Vol.2, 164, Ch.14) – represents unthinkable privation. Her narratives emphasise the construction of physical and psychological barriers, bringing into sharp focus the proximity of, but gulf between, rich and poor within the metropolis – itself a vast, disorientating network of noisome streets which represents the embodiment of alienation, chaos and confusion, and in which 'strangers have been lost for ever' (*Bede's Charity*, 105, Ch.14). The adjacent worlds, each with its unknown, 'foreign' ways, are separated by a 'sea deeper than the ocean'; the wealthy inhabitants of the fashionable West – the cost of whose fine dresses would have 'fed and clothed many a poor child for years' – are resolutely blind to the existence and sufferings of those living but a stone's throw away (141, Ch.18). Such unimaginable poverty and squalor inspires 'loathing and horror' in those 'too refined and sensitive' to contemplate these sights (*David Lloyd's Last Will*, Vol.1, 54, Ch.5); the emaciated Fidge of *The Lord's Pursebearers*, valuable as he is in begging terms, is, likewise, too grim a spectacle for West End sensibilities (38).

Stretton's anger is directed in no uncertain terms at society's failure to address the situation of the poor. She brings before the reader the ease with which it is possible to gratify emotional pity or pacify the conscience by merely dropping a few coins into the outstretched hands of a begging child, and to pass by this 'painful object' without consideration of the need to take practical steps to ameliorate his individual situation, or to tackle poverty at the level of official government or church action (*In Prison and Out*, 14, Ch.2; *The Lord's Pursebearers*, 88 and 1900 postscript to Preface). The indiscriminate giving of alms is condemned as a misguided evil which only encourages begging, 'pav[ing] the road to ruin' for many (*Pursebearers*, 246), and, in treating effects, not causes, evading the fundamental problem.

'I would not, if I could …': 'dark dens' and the 'dregs' of society

Stretton, like Dickens, plainly does not hesitate to write about the underside of society, often tackling themes generally deemed unsuitable for a woman's pen. If there were some who preferred to ignore its existence, others found in this world, with its cast of outcasts and unfortunates, a rich source of material with which to attract a public obsessed with images, if not the reality, of poverty and the 'darker' regions of the city. Indeed, we might question the morality of exploiting the misery of others to commercial ends, were it not for the clear social imperative and compassion for humanity which accompany Stretton's identification of an appealing context or story-line. The difficulty acknowledged by novelists, journalists and commentators – among them Dickens and Lord Ashley – of adequately expressing the extremes of deprivation – is, as we have seen, shared by Stretton, whose visiting protagonists encounter scenes of 'squalor and degradation such as they had never dreamed of' (*The Lord's Pursebearers*, 181, Ch.9). The desire to shock the reader, or to impress upon him the extent of the misery, coupled in some instances with a reluctance to confront him with its excesses, leads to both avoidance and overemphasis: 'I would not, if I could, describe to you in full …' (*Pursebearers*, 227, Ch.11). The clichéd, sensationalised descriptions, the stereotypes and generalisations which dominate contemporary fiction and non-fiction alike, are drawn from a common discursive arena and come to symbolise a uniform degradation, obscuring particularities and individual identities and reinforcing contemporary perceptions of the poor as an undifferentiated mass.

Whilst her sympathies are undoubtedly with the underdog, Hesba Stretton cannot be exempted entirely from the charge of contributing to dominant mythologies – of reproducing, through the narrator or characters, images which ostensibly depersonalise, stigmatise, objectify and exclude. Furthermore, because it is not always immediately clear whether or not these perceptions are shared by the author, there is a danger that the reader might take on board the values and prejudices which appear to underlie these commonplaces. The 'shrivelled, meagre wretch[es]' (*Pilgrim Street*, 93, Ch.12), the ragged, barefoot urchins, hollow-cheeked men, hysterical 'staggering' women and swarming children who people the 'filthy, crowded alleys' and miserable bare attics (*The Lord's Pursebearers*, *Little Meg's Children*, etc.) replicate those encountered across media forms; Stretton's outcast citizens are similarly branded as 'swine' (*The Lord's Pursebearers*), their living quarters 'styes' (*Lost Gip*). Such images have the *potential* to degrade and dehumanise, stripping the poor of their dignity. Furthermore, the ubiquitous depictions of slum-life risk desensitising the reader, who looks but no longer sees.

Like Benjamin Waugh, however, Stretton is deeply conscious of the 'distance-haze' which conceals the personalities of 'the unhappy' masses from those comfortably seated in power (Waugh, 1873/1984: 170) – a mist which renders them less disturbing; her central purpose is to counteract social blindness and to place those personalities centre-stage.

Despite her participation (and that of her characters) in prevailing forms of labelling, she plainly does not seek to treat the poor or dispossessed figure with condescension, nor to diminish or humiliate him; rather, she is concerned to expose and condemn those who do – often, as with *Jessica's* Daniel or *Carola*'s Mrs. Arnold, endowing them with a revised or transformed perspective. Her narratives bring to life the experiences of individual outcasts (as does Mrs. Castle Smith's *Froggy's Little Brother*), giving them identity and personal significance, so that they stand out convincingly against the background, *most* becoming much more than mere types. Demonstrating the extent to which dominant discursive patterns influence self-perception – those whom society labels as inferior, or as akin to animals, come to perceive themselves as such (*Lost Gip, A Thorny Path* and others) – she aims to restore dignity and self-worth to her protagonists. Moreover, as we have already discovered, although these writings foreground exploitation and suppression, they also affirm the possibility of subversion and answering back.

Across nineteenth-century forms, we find the polarities of language employed to reinforce messages and underwrite value-judgements; such binary imagery, of course, forms a staple element of religious discourse and a common pattern in evangelical narratives. In Stretton's writings, as in many contemporary accounts, the hell-like 'pit' of the city, with its pollution, disease, sin and darkness (*Bede's Charity, The Storm of Life, Carola* and others) is represented as the personification of evil, the antithesis of the heaven-identified, regenerative countryside. The 'dark den' of the East End (*The Lord's Pursebearers* and others) – its fog and gloom reminiscent of Dickens's London – epitomises, and conflates, diverse forms of otherness. Intermingling with discourses of the contaminated body, which, as we have seen, define the outcast and encode attitudes towards him, justifying his exclusion as others physically 'shrink' or 'draw back' from him, the evaluative binaries of good and evil, black and white, dark and light coalesce. Significantly, these texts expose the overlapping, mutually-constituted nature of such metaphors across a range of discursive domains, including, once again, those of social reform, domestic virtue (equated with moral virtue) and colonialism. Stretton exploits the potential of this imagery to multiple effect; she utilises oppositions not only to reinforce associations between physical, spiritual and moral aspects, but to throw into relief the effects of material disadvantage, often undercutting normalised 'black and white' assessments through her social critique, even as she appears, through linguistic choices, to endorse them.

Texts such as *The Storm of Life* juxtapose the language of individual sin and that of physical darkness and dirt, again foregrounding the ambiguous relationship between ideas of depravity and deprivation. The blackness of the light-deprived courts symbolises emotional as well as physical and moral despair and degradation, the dark river prompting thoughts of suicide in the ex-criminal Rachel, before she and her bedraggled offspring find shelter in the white-curtained, white-furnished house – as spotless as possible in the London smoke – of their chimney-sweep benefactor; the darkness of a life marked not only by transgression, but also by hardship and marital oppression, is contrasted with the snow, and with the white covering spread over the dead (and morally uncontaminated) baby who has succumbed to the physical effects of this literally dark and socially-deprived environment. Such multiply-charged imagery recurs in waif texts such as L.T. Meade's *Scamp and I* (1877/label 1916), in which young Flo, accustomed only to the dirt and darkness of the city, and awakening in the pure white bedroom of her benefactor, mistakes her surroundings for heaven (26, Ch.13).[3]

The short story 'Mrs. Burton's Best Bedroom' [1878] – its tone in complete contrast to that of the sad tale of degradation and patriarchal blackmail recounted in *The Storm of Life* – employs such patterning to serious and satirical effect, cleverly encapsulating the diverse, overlapping connotations of black/white, clean/unclean oppositions. Stretton's humorous account of a cross-class encounter in which a drunken intruder makes himself at home in the bedroom of the obsessively house-proud Mrs. Burton, besmirching the spotless white linen of her 'best bed' with his grime (with the result that she will never take pleasure in it again), serves to interrogate, through the interplay of opposites, the perceptions of the inhabitants of very different worlds. Stretton mocks the pretentiousness of those who set excessive store on appearances of respectability and domestic perfection – a particular contemporary preoccupation – but are lacking in their acceptance of others. At the same time, she highlights the failings and misfortunes of those whose lifestyle and living conditions, through both individual fault and the inadequacy of social/institutional care or provision, are sadly lacking in moral or physical decency or cleanliness. Both protagonists ultimately see the error of their ways.

Although Hesba Stretton ventures into the 'black' world of the criminal, exposing the dangers awaiting those drawn into its net, she remains generally detached from the perspective of the worst 'villains'. Notwithstanding her apparent belief, at one level, in the possibility of redemption and rehabilitation for all, certain elements are portrayed as thoroughly bad, irredeemably cruel and vicious; there is no pity for those who lead others, particularly children, astray. However, the author is acutely aware that structural inequalities lead to anger and resentment, which in turn fuel crime and unrest; she uses the criminal protagonist to voice her critique of a system which allows the rich to 'idle' whilst others starve, and to offer a degree of justification, filtered through the criminal consciousness, for crimes which seek to redress the balance: what harm can there be in robbing those who possess unlimited wealth, and who treat others 'like slaves', depriving them of their entitlement? (*The Storm of Life*, 107; 110; 120, Chs.12 and 14). She also demonstrates that felony is not uniquely the province of the underclass; middle-class perpetrators of crimes such as financial fraud (*Cobwebs and Cables* and others) are acknowledged by society as no better than common thieves and find themselves similarly stigmatised, hounded and cast out.

Eternal Outcasts and Civilised Englishmen

Among prominent nineteenth-century social and literary tropes of the outsider, both the Jew and the gypsy feature repeatedly, these characters sharing – literally and mythically – the status of 'eternal' outcast. The East End Jew – a focus of anxiety towards the end of the nineteenth century because of rising numbers in this part of London, is, by virtue of his race and his poverty, doubly or triply marginalised. Subject, like other liminal figures, to the ambivalence inspired by his difference, he is both exoticised and despised, sometimes respected for qualities of sobriety, self-discipline and family loyalty, but often reviled and treated with suspicion as a consequence of the *assumed* characteristics of his race.

Chapter 1 of Stretton's *Carola*, entitled 'An East End Jew', establishes Matthias – who is unpopular with neighbours 'chiefly because he [is] a Jew' (191, Ch.20) – as a central player in her story. Unlike Dickens's damning portrayal of Fagin 'the Jew', Stretton's representation of the elderly resident who assumes guardianship of the rapidly-growing Carola challenges negative preconceptions of the Jewish character, bringing to the fore Matthias's positive qualities and his moral superiority. Despite the fact that people are 'accustomed to think of all Jews as cunning and avaricious' (63, Ch.5), Matthias is not in any respect artful or predatory; he is 'always at work', and earnest in carrying out his job of repairing and selling old shoes to the maximum benefit of his customers. Indeed, many children 'went into that little shop barefoot, and came out shod, without Matthias being a penny the richer' (8, Ch.1). The old man ensures the physical well-being of his high-spirited, increasingly self-willed charge, undertakes careful stewardship of her money, and is protective of her moral and spiritual welfare, regarding her as the apple of his eye and fretting about her waywardness as a mother might worry about a recalcitrant daughter. Clearly, the eventual conversion of Matthias to Christianity forms, for Stretton, part of a missionary enterprise; his faith, and its moral and practical outworking – shown to be superior to that of many who purport to be Christians – provide a starting-point on Carola's road to spiritual maturation, and he too is eventually assimilated into the Christian community. However, in juxtaposing the perspectives of Jew and non-Jew, Stretton takes pains to explore once again the misunderstandings which develop, often with tragic consequences, between people of different religions and communities, and to bring under scrutiny the mythologies and prejudices formed in the process.

The gypsy – that other pervasive signifier of otherness – appears in Stretton's narratives in various guises. Imagined as wild, dangerous and of an alien 'black' race, this figure again embodies contradictions and evokes ambivalence; it embraces romanticised concepts of 'difference' in which the picturesque, the exotic, the unconventional and the undesirable commingle, engendering fear and fascination. Encompassing diverse kinds of itinerant and vagrant, the gypsy figure is subject to the same discourses which label the outcast city-dweller as filth or refuse and reduce him to animal or savage status.[4] In winter months the numbers of urban poor were swelled by the mass movement from country to city of these 'wandering tribes'; hence, Stretton's Gip has the appearance of a 'reg'lar' little black-eyed gypsy (*Lost Gip*, 4 Ch.1). Recalling the dirty, ragged, 'dark … as if … from the devil' 'gipsy brat', Heathcliff, of Bronte's *Wuthering Heights*, 1847/1992: 51), Gip's 'black tangled curl[s]' (51, Ch.7) echo a common motif – present in various forms in the work of novelists including Charlotte Bronte and George Eliot – which intersects with wider discourses of darkness, evil and savagery. With its connotations of non-conformity and the dark 'other' of self and society, the gypsy figure invites, in material and mythological terms, both identification and rejection, distrust and vilification: Stretton's 'strange child – belonging to nobody but gipsies' (*Two Secrets*, 1882/inscr.1901: 18) – is, although needy, initially unwelcome in cottagers' homes. Elsewhere, the author tells of 'talismanic' precautions to 'secure me from gipsies and other baby-stealers' (A Provincial Post Office', 1863:12). Yet the open-air lifestyle, symbolising independence – physical, moral and social – and an escape from conventional routine, holds a certain allure. Perceived as a source of contamination and a threat to civilised values, this emblem of lawlessness also figures as guardian of the simple life in the face of relentless material progress, the lifestyle captured and romanticised by artists and given prominence by writers such as George Borrow, whose *Lavengro* (1851) and *The Romany Rye* (1857) were popular with contemporary audiences.[5]

Regularly attracting attention in newspapers and periodicals, gypsies, like others on the fringe of society, invited curiosity as well as anxiety or philanthropic concern. After visiting a gypsy camp at Christmas 1868, and meeting a group in January 1869, Stretton notes '… a very droll and interesting scene' (Log Book: 3.1.1869). Later that year she published 'Gipsy Glimpses' in *All The Year Round*, which, in charting a visit to the encampment and the attendance by the gypsy community at a reception in their honour, encapsulates the contradictory responses to this figure. Framing gypsies simultaneously as creative agents and objects of interest or fear, it exemplifies ambivalence towards the exotic or marginalised 'other'. The gypsies are presented as colourful, mysterious and slightly disturbing players in an entertaining spectacle, the snarling dog and black-haired child, the baby with shrewd 'fortune-telling face' (539) reinforcing the aura of fear-laden superstition. The exotic crimsons and purples of the tent furnishings, the immense cooking pots and richly-painted china, add to the poetic air of 'luxury and romance' (537). At the same time, the 'vagrant tribe', later described as 'strange guests', demonstrate an unanticipated measure of dignity and civilised conduct at the reception, behaving like 'any other gentlemen' and displaying only minor breaches of etiquette (one announces rather too loudly his discovery of hot buttered cakes). Underlining intra-group distinctions, those of the 'true gipsy race' distance themselves from the Epping Forest community, perceived as a 'mongrel lot' with 'low and dirty habits' (537-9).

Stretton incorporates aspects of these encounters into texts such as *Lost Gip* and *Cassy*. The 'pleasure-parties' enjoyed by Londoners escaping to the unenclosed forest areas are contrasted with the deprivation experienced by the 'strange wandering population', whose rough encampments nonetheless represent a 'free life' for which they yearn during confined winter months (*Cassy*, Chs.1 and 10). The threatening atmosphere of Cassy's mud-engulfed campsite – the fractured contents of her tent symbolising broken, abusive relationships – is juxtaposed with the

See page 100.

Illustration 5: *Cassy* (edition c.1888) Frontispiece, W.S. Stacey/ Whymper

homely, colourful gypsy caravan of her benefactor – a pastoral idyll untainted by darker gypsy powers. In *The Doctor's Dilemma*, the gypsy constitutes a wider signifier of freedom and resistance to socialisation; the protagonist – like a gypsy 'caught, and caged' (Part 3, 231, Ch.22) – finds sophisticated urban life, in the words of the Chapter title, 'Too Highly Civilised'.

In the novel *Half Brothers*, the binaries of civilised/savage, converted/heathen, educated/ignorant, English/foreigner, self/other again intermingle, exposing notions of class and racial superiority and illuminating the power relations embedded in colonialist discourses which harness educational and socio-scientific theories. The narrative has at its centre an altogether wilder gypsy-type: the child of a secret marriage, abandoned among peasants in the remote Italian mountains and less nurtured than the animals, Martino leads a 'savage and uncivilized life' (1892/n.d.: 29, Ch.3). This feral child represents an alter ego, both a personification of his father's errors and a symbol of the bestial, monstrous 'other'. Nearly naked, he springs like a monkey; his hair is matted, his grin 'savage and uncouth' (76-7, Ch.11) – descriptions also habitually applied, as we have seen, to the free-roaming city-Arabs. Even in adulthood, Martino remains an unsocialised 'beast' – an outsider even in his own environment; like Shakespeare's Caliban, he is the 'wild-man' whose habits, lifestyle and very essence pose a threat to civilised society. 'Barely human', he clings to his den 'like an animal', but (in line with customary modes of distancing) displays a particular 'susceptibility inherited from his educated and civilised parentage …' (264-6, Ch.38).

Deemed an ignorant, untrained and potentially ungovernable peasant, Martino is brought to England to be reclaimed and re-educated. He is likened by others to a child, again underlining the shared infantilisation of child and savage. At one level, the text reaffirms through the viewpoint of characters – and their internalised prejudices – a commonsense belief in the superiority of English values and education, perceived as synonymous with civilisation. With identity located, from the family's perspective, uniquely in Englishness and English-speaking, Martino must become Martin. However, in highlighting the importance of communicating with him in his own language, Stretton underlines the interdependence of language and identity, and conveys Martin's sense of exclusion. Like Stretton and many of her protagonists, this stranger resists the 'shackles' of civilisation, the narrative tone and the rendering of the outsider's perspective endorsing the right to freedom rather than the constraints of 'custom and conventionality' (369-70, Ch.53). Frustrated at being held in captivity and under surveillance, he finds solace on the moors which recall his homeland – their wildness evoking both a Rousseauesque, life-sustaining freedom and a state of primitive, heathen savagery such as that applied to outcasts in so many other contexts. Whilst, on the one hand, the text underscores once again the importance of reclamation, education and socialisation, Stretton also raises questions about the family's (and, implicitly, society's) civilising/humanising endeavours, bringing under scrutiny their imposition of cultural norms and the power or right of 'civilisation' and 'civilising missions' to transform the 'other'. In suggesting that ideas of what constitutes civilisation – 'more a fashion than a reality' (282, Ch.40) – are arbitrary and shifting, she demonstrates in this late text, which is by turns uncomfortably racist and markedly sensitive and humane in its discourse, a very modern relativist awareness.

In bringing together these multiple strands of alterity, Stretton's texts illuminate the complex, intersecting discourses of which surround the outsider – whatever the source of his oppression or exclusion; they also foreground his experiences, his pain, his fears, his hopes and his achievements, and, crucially, his rights. Taken as a whole, these narratives afford a lens through which the attitudes and anxieties, preoccupations and obsessions of the period are brought into focus; the complex motivations which underlie the project to rescue, reform, convert and civilise the outcast, and the concomitant investment in positioning him as 'other' are laid bare. Yet, for a reader familiar with the range of Hesba Stretton's work, and acquainted over the considerable period of her career with the spirit of her writings, the abiding impression is arguably one of her humanity; her project to represent – not only in the sense of depicting, but also of promoting the cause of – those whose voice and rights are suppressed resonates throughout, despite recognisable tensions and ambivalence. Tapping into the contemporary mood, and harnessing pathos and melodrama as a political tool, Stretton exploits popular forms both for their own appeal and as a forum through which to discuss prominent issues, ideas, dilemmas and injustices. She explores with humour and sensitivity the conflicts and complexities inherent in the human condition, and, admitting doubt, error and uncertainty, acknowledges the painful choices facing the individual, whether in matters of love, fidelity, morality, integrity, loyalty, duty, or self-fulfilment. Drawing the attention of the reader to matters of both individual and collective responsibility, and evincing a belief in the importance of material as well as spiritual transformation, these texts feed into a strengthened public consciousness of diverse aspects of the 'social question', projecting a distinctive female voice and perspective, and playing, as Samuel Green, writing in 1899 recognised (79), no small part in awakening wider awareness and influencing opinion.[6]

The ability to blend this range of elements, and to encompass diverse facets of life and experience, means that, despite – indeed, often because of – its contradictions and ambivalence, Stretton's writing is, even today, surprisingly absorbing and provocative, its intertextual relationship with the broad circumstances of its production serving to deepen our insight into the author and her times, its striking modern relevance across a range of areas causing us to look more closely at the complex prejudices, mythologies and insecurities which persist in the modern consciousness in respect of those whom society would overlook, indict or exclude on account of their difference, and in whose otherness it finds reflected its own desires and fears.

Notes

1. The sense of mingled pride and resentment in *Bede's Charity* towards the brother who deserts the family in search of material improvement is perhaps a reflection of Stretton's own ambivalence regarding her brother Ben's emigration to Canada.

2. Distinctions between 'rough' and 'respectable' formed an important element in the social hierarchy of the poorer classes; in Stretton's work they also mirror the shades of poverty/respectability which inflect social status further up the class scale, and underline insecurities engendered by society's ready conflation of poverty and class position. The material implications of a financial 'fall' were, of course, also very real, the fear of the workhouse extending beyond the lower classes to those of higher social standing who had unexpectedly fallen upon hard times.

3. This linguistic overlap and ambiguity is also reminiscent of the morally, socially and racially-inflected imagery which characterises Charles Kingsley's *The Water-Babies* (1863).

4. For discussions of nineteenth-century society's preoccupation with the gypsy, see Behlmer (1985) and Nord (1998).

5. Mrs. Ewing's *Lob Lie-by-the-Fire* (reviewed by the *Athenaeum* alongside Stretton's *The King's Servants* in 1873) highlights the misgivings which surround the gypsy. Mrs. Molesworth was also to

draw on various facets of the gypsy image in *Sheila's Mystery* (1895), and later in *The Ruby Ring* (1904), which explores the allure and positive aspects of gypsy life as well as those elements perceived as less desirable.

6. See also Raphael Samuel (1998: 305-7) on the influence of strands of nineteenth-century Nonconformity, and the preparatory role of waif literature, in the promotion of progressive reform.

Bibliography

Works by Hesba Stretton cited in this study

Texts in order of first publication as a volume

Fern's Hollow (n.d.), London: The Religious Tract Society (first published 1864)

Enoch Roden's Training (label 1902), London: The Religious Tract Society (first published 1865)

The Children of Cloverley (label 1876), London: The Religious Tract Society (first published 1865)

The Fishers of Derby Haven (label 1884), London: The Religious Tract Society (first published 1866)

The Clives of Burcot (n.d.), London: Miles and Miles (first published 1867, London: Tinsley

Jessica's First Prayer (n.d.), London: The Religious Tract Society (first published 1867)

Pilgrim Street (inscr.1890), London: The Religious Tract Society (first published 1867)

Little Meg's Children (label 1889), London: The Religious Tract Society (first published 1868)

Alone in London (inscr.1872), London: The Religious Tract Society (first published 1869)

David Lloyd's Last Will (1869), London: Sampson Low, Son and Marston

Max Kromer (n.d.), London: The Religious Tract Society (first published 1871)

Bede's Charity (c.1890), London: The Religious Tract Society (first published 1872)

The Doctor's Dilemma (1872), London: H.S. King

Hester Morley's Promise (1898), London: Hodder and Stoughton (first published 1873, London: H.S. King)

The King's Servants (label 1911), London: H.S. King (first published 1873, London: The Religious Tract Society)

Lost Gip (1878), London: C. Kegan Paul (first published 1873, London: H.S. King)

Cassy (c.1888), London: The Religious Tract Society (first published 1874, London: H.S. King)

Michel Lorio's Cross (inscr. 1888), London: The Religious Tract Society (first published 1876, London: H.S. King)

Left Alone (n.d.), London: The Religious Tract Society (first published 1876, London: H.S. King)

The Storm of Life (label 1910), London: The Religious Tract Society (first published 1876, London: H.S. King)

A Man of His Word (inscr.1901, combined with *Two Secrets*), London: The Religious Tract Society (first published 1878, London: H.S. King)

A Thorny Path (c.1882), London: The Religious Tract Society (first published 1879)

In Prison and Out (1880), London: Isbister.

No Place Like Home (inscr.1904), London: The Religious Tract Society (first published 1881)

Cobwebs and Cables (n.d.), London: The Religious Tract Society (first published 1881)

Under the Old Roof (n.d.), London: The Religious Tract Society (first published 1882)

Two Secrets (inscr.1901), London: The Religious Tract Society (first published 1882)

The Lord's Pursebearers (n.d.) *Day of Rest* (Annual), London: Strahan (first published 1883, London: Nisbet)

Carola (label 1898), London: The Religious Tract Society (first published 1884)

An Acrobat's Girlhood [1889], London: SPCK

Half Brothers (n.d.), London: The Religious Tract Society (first published 1892)

The Highway of Sorrow (1897), London, Paris, Melbourne: Cassell (first published 1894)

In the Hollow of His Hand (inscr. 1912), London: The Religious Tract Society (first published 1897)

The Soul of Honour (label 1905), London: The Religious Tract Society (first published 1898, London: Isbister)

Jessica's Mother (label 1925), London: The Religious Tract Society (first published in single-volume hardback c.1904)

Stories and articles by Hesba Stretton cited

'The Lucky Leg', *Household Words*, 19.3.1859 (p374-380)

'The Postmaster's Daughter', *All The Year Round*, 5.11.1859 (p37-44)

'Alice Gilbert's Confession', *Temple Bar*, May 1862 (p253-267)

'Felicia Crompton', *All The Year Round*, 10.1.1863 (p425-432)

'A Provincial Post Office', *All The Year Round*, 28.2.1863 (p12-16)

'Eleven Hundred Pounds', *All The Year Round*, 13.8.1864 (p15-24)

'Not to be Taken for Granted' in 'Dr. Marigold's Prescription', *All The Year Round*, 7.12.1865 (Extra Christmas Number) (p20-27)

'Gipsy Glimpses', *All The Year Round*, 8.5.1869 (p536-540)

'No Bribery', *All The Year Round*, 23.10.1869 (p493-497)

'Mrs. Burton's Best Bedroom' [1878]/n.d. In *Penny Books for the People*, 2, London: The Religious Tract Society (p2-6)

'Ragged School Union Conferences', *The Sunday at Home*, 7.4.1883 (p266-268)

'Women's Work for Children' (1893). In A. Burdett-Coutts (ed.) *Woman's Mission*, London: Sampson Low, Marston (p4-12)

'The Origin of the London SPCC' (handwritten account dated 4.4.1908, material by permission of Shropshire Archives, Ref.6000/19290)

Log Books 1858-71; 1875 (material by permission of Shropshire Archives, Ref. 6001/5556)

Correspondence

Stretton to *The Times*, 8.1.1884; 30.6.1884; 8.1.1885

Stretton to [Mr.] Pattison, 16.4. [1886] (University of London Archives, AL225)

Stretton to Lord Ancaster, 15.12.1894 (NSPCC Archives)

Other sources cited

Up to and including 1911

Anon. (1896) 'A Talk with Hesba Stretton', *Sunday Hours*, Vol.1, No. 7 (p164-166)

Anon., signed C.H.I (1911) 'Hesba Stretton', *Seed Time and Harvest*, December (p11-12)

Anon. (1911) 'Hesba Stretton – Born 1832', I. Memoir, *The Sunday at Home*, December (p121-124)

Barlee, E.M. (1884) *Pantomime Waifs*, London: Partridge and Company

Barnardo, T.J. (ed.) (1881) *'Taken Out of the Gutter': A True Incident of Child Life on the Streets of London*, London: Haughton and Company

Barnardo, T.J. (ed.) 1885/6 'A City Waif: How I Fished for and Caught Her'. In *Tracts on Dr. Barnardo's Homes*, London: Shaw and Company

Barnardo, T.J. (ed.) (1885/6) 'Kidnapped: A Narrative of Fact'. In *Tracts on Dr. Barnardo's Homes*, London, Shaw and Company

Barnardo, T.J. (ed.) (1885/6) '"God's Little Girl"'. In *Tracts on Dr. Barnardo's Homes,* London: Shaw and Company

Besant, A. (1987) 'Marriage As It Was, As It Is, and As It Should Be' (first published 1882). In S. Jeffreys (ed.) *The Sexuality Debates*, London: Routledge and Kegan Paul (p391-445)

Bronte, E. (1992) *Wuthering Heights* (ed. L. Peterson), Boston: St. Martin's Press (first published 1847)

Castle Smith, Mrs. (1875) *Froggy's Little Brother*, London: Shaw and Company

Dickens, C. (1966) *Oliver Twist* (ed. P. Fairclough), Harmondsworth: Penguin (first published 1838)

Dickens, C. (1995) 'The Chimes'. In *Christmas Books*, Ware: Wordsworth (first published 1844)

Dickens, C. (1996) *Bleak House* (ed. N. Bradbury), Harmondsworth: Penguin (first published 1853)

Friederichs, H. (1894) 'Hesba Stretton at Home', *The Young Woman*, No.22, July (p327-333)

Gaskell, E. (1987) *Mary Barton* (ed. E. Wright), Oxford: Oxford University Press (first published 1848)

Gaskell, E. (1997) *Ruth* (ed. A. Easson), Harmondsworth: Penguin (first published 1853)

Green, S. (1899) *The Story of the Religious Tract Society for One Hundred Years*, London: The Religious Tract Society

Hocking. S. (1883) *Dick's Fairy*, London: Frederick Warne and Company

Hughes, T. (1857) *Tom Brown's Schooldays*, Cambridge: Macmillan

Kennan, G. (1891) *Siberia and the Exile System*, New York: Century

Kingsley, C. (1995) *The Water-Babies*, Harmondsworth: Penguin (first published 1863)

MacDonald, G. (1966) *At the Back of the North Wind*, New York: Airmont (first published 1871)

Mayhew, H (1985) *London Labour and the London Poor* (ed. V. Neuburg), Harmondsworth: Penguin (first published 1861-2)

Meade, L.T. (label 1916) *Scamp and I*, London: Shaw and Company (first published 1877)

Mearns, A. (1976) 'The Bitter Cry of Outcast London' (first published 1883). Extracted in P. Keating (ed.) *Into Unknown England 1866-1913*, Glasgow: Fontana/Collins

Mill, J.S. (1998) *The Subjection of Women*, Oxford: Oxford University Press (first published 1869)

Molesworth, M. (1895) *Sheila's Mystery*, London: Macmillan and Company

Molesworth, M. (1904) *The Ruby Ring*, London: Macmillan and Company

Pike, G. Holden (1875) *Children Reclaimed for Life*, London: Hodder and Stoughton.

Religious Tract Society Minutes: H 8501 (Executive Committee), H8502 (Sub-committees), incorporated in the United Society for Christian Literature Archive, University of London, SOAS

Salmon, E. (1886) 'What Girls Read', *Nineteenth Century*, Vol.20 (p515-529)

Sims, G.R. (1976) 'How the Poor Live' (first published 1889). Extracted in P. Keating (ed.) *Into Unknown England 1866-1913*, Glasgow: Fontana/Collins

Sumner, Mrs. (1893) 'The Responsibilities of Mothers'. In A. Burdett-Coutts (ed.) *Woman's Mission*, London: Sampson Low, Marston (p65-86)

Synnot, H.L. (1875) 'Institutions and Their Inmates', *The Contemporary Review*, Vol.26, (p487-504)

Taylor, H. (1995) 'The Enfranchisement of Women' (first published 1850). In A. Pyle (ed.) *The Subjection of Women: Contemporary Responses to John Stuart Mill*, Bristol: Thoemmes Press (p11-36)

Walton, Mrs. O.F. (1999) *A Peep Behind the Scenes*, Fearn: Christian Focus Publications (first published 1877)

Waugh, B. (1984) *The Gaol Cradle: Who Rocks It?*, New York and London: Garland (first published 1873)

Webb, Hesba D. (1911) II. 'A Personal Note' to Memoir, *The Sunday at Home*, December (p124-125)

Yonge, C.M. (1876) *Womankind*, London: Mozley and Smith

Post-1911

Alderson, B & Garrett, P. (1999) *The Religious Tract Society as a Publisher of Children's Books* (Exhibition Catalogue) Hoddesdon: The Children's Books History Society

Bartky, S. Lee (1988) 'Foucault, Femininity, and the Modernization of Patriarchal Power'. In I. Diamond and L. Quinby (eds.) *Feminism and Foucault*, Boston: Northeastern University Press (p61-86)

Behlmer, G.K. (1985) 'The Gypsy Problem in Victorian England', *Victorian Studies*, Vol.28, Winter (p231-253)

Berry, L. (1999) *The Child, The State, and The Victorian Novel*, Charlottesville and London: University Press of Virginia

Bratton, J.S. (1981) *The Impact of Victorian Children's Fiction*, London: Croom Helm

Briggs, J. (1989) 'Women Writers and Writing for Children: From Sarah Fielding to E. Nesbit'. In G. Avery and J. Briggs (eds.) *Children and*

Their Books: A Celebration of the Work of Iona and Peter Opie, Oxford: Clarendon Press (p221-250)

Butler, J. (2004) *The Judith Butler Reader* (ed. S. Salih with J. Butler), Malden, Oxford, Carlton: Blackwell

Chodorow, N. (1978) *The Reproduction of Mothering*, Berkeley, Los Angeles, London: University of California Press

Cunningham, H. (1991) *The Children of the Poor*, Oxford: Blackwell

Cutt, M.N. (1979) *Ministering Angels*, Wormley: Five Owls Press

Foucault, M. (1979) *Discipline and Punish: The Birth of the Prison* (transl. A. Sheridan), Harmondsworth: Penguin

Hollindale, P. (2001) 'Odysseys: The Childness of Journeying Children', *Signal* 94, January (p29-44)

Kincaid, J. (1992) *Child-Loving: The Erotic Child and Victorian Culture*, New York and London: Routledge

Kristeva, J. (1982) *Powers of Horror: An Essay on Abjection* (transl. L. Rodez), New York: Columbia University Press

Kristeva, J. (1986) 'Revolution in Poetic Language'. In T. Moi (ed.) *The Kristeva Reader*, Oxford: Blackwell (p89-136)

Matus, J.L. (1995) *Unstable Bodies: Victorian Representations of Sexuality and Maternity*, Manchester: Manchester University Press

Myers, M. (1995) 'The Erotics of Pedagogy: Historical Intervention, Literary Representation, the "Gift of Education", and the Agency of Children. In F. Butler et al. *Children's Literature* 23 (Annual), New Haven and London: University of California Press (p1-30)

Nodelman, P. (2000) 'Pleasure and Genre: Speculations on the Characteristics of Children's Fiction'. In E. Lennox Keyser and J. Pfeiffer (eds.) *Children's Literature* 28 (Annual), New Haven and London: Yale University Press (p1-14)

Nord, D. Epstein (1998) '"Marks of Race": Gypsy Figures and Eccentric Femininity in Nineteenth-Century Women's Writing', *Victorian Studies*, Vol.41, No.2 (pp.189-210)

Pearson, G. (1983) *Hooligan: A History of Respectable Fears*, London: Macmillan

Reynolds, K. and Humble, N. (1993) *Victorian Heroines: Representations of Femininity in Nineteenth-century Literature and Art*, New York: New York University Press

Rickard, S. (1996) '"Living by the Pen": Hesba Stretton's Moral Earnings', *Women's History Review*, Vol.5, No.2 (p219-238)

Samuel, R. (1998) *Island Stories: Unravelling Britain – Theatres of Memory* (Vol.2) (eds. Light, Alexander and Stedman Jones), London: Verso

Senese, D. (1987) *S.M. Stepniak-Kravchinskii: The London Years*, Newtonville, Mass.: Oriental Research Partners

Stedman Jones, G. (1984) *Outcast London: A Study in the Relationship Between Classes in Victorian Society*, Harmondsworth: Penguin

Steedman, C. (1995) *Strange Dislocations: Childhood and the Idea of Human Interiority 1790-1930*, London, Virago

Webb, R. (1964) *Notes regarding the life of Hesba Stretton*, held by Shropshire Archives (Ref. BS91 v.f.)

White, J. (1984) 'Further Notes on Children's Best Sellers', *Children's Books History Society Newsletter* No.29, November (p3-4)

Williams, L. (1994) 'The Look of Little Girls: John Everett Millais and the Victorian Art Market'. In C. Nelson and L. Vallone (eds.) *The Girl's Own: Cultural Histories of the Anglo-American Girl 1830-1915*, Athens and London: University of Georgia Press (p124-155).

The Hidden Self

Late Victorian Childhood, Class & Culture in Mrs Molesworth's Books

Mary Sebag-Montefiore

MRS. MOLESWORTH, AUTHOR OF "CARROTS."

Illustration 6: Photograph of Mrs Molesworth

MARY LOUISA MOLESWORTH (1839-1921)

As a child, Molesworth's books took me into an other-world fantasy in which girls with flowing hair, (mine was short) wearing pinafores and party frocks, (I wore boring hand-me-downs from my brother and sister) led charmed, enviable lives with mammas, papas, nurses, governesses, and siblings. They fought fierce battles with their families and feelings, and I identified with them all the way to the satisfactory happy ending, while the sympathetic lessons in the books about the difficulty and importance of *trying* to be good made a deep impression on me. (I must have been an awful prig.)

When I read, years later, dismissive criticism of Molesworth's datedness, snobbishness and sentimentality, it seemed unfair and wrong. Though her fantasy tales have lately received critical attention, her domestic tales have been cast into oblivion. This chapter has grown out of a wish to re-introduce these novels to the historical canon of children's literature, and a hope that new readers might enjoy her books as much as I do. Equally, I want to show how her books provide rich literary evidence of Victorian methods of upbringing. There was a sharp distinction between feeling and behaviour; the latter ruled the former to educe instinctive self-control. Only in understanding the nineteenth-century attitude to emotion and the values inculcated into its young can one appreciate the Victorian frame of mind. Molesworth's insight and realist style reveal a detailed, domestic, social-historical portrait of middle-class childhood.

Between 1870 and 1911 Molesworth wrote a hundred and one books, ranging from nursery-age to late girlhood and marriage. She thus encompasses an entire stretch of girlhood as well as the entire late-Victorian period. She was a highly respected best-seller. She is regularly cited as a favourite author by the child correspondents of *Little Folks*, a popular children's magazine. She contributed articles on behaviour to L.T. Meade's *Atalanta*, a high-quality girl's magazine, and Charlotte M Yonge's *The Monthly Packet*, an erudite Church of England girl's magazine. The *Westminster Budget*, an up-market, intellectual review, describes the children in her books as 'all natural, possible human beings', (Oct 4th, 1893) while Edward Salmon, himself a well-respected reviewer, declared

> Her sympathy with children is unbounded. She loves them with her whole heart while she lays bare their little minds. (*Literature for the Little Ones*, 1887, ed *A Peculiar Gift,* 1976: 61)

On her death *The Times* wrote

> The news will rouse in thousands of minds affectionate thoughts of
> one who during not far short of half a century has given happy
> thoughts to childhood....And though now children's books come
> yearly in hundreds, Mrs Molesworth's have not been superseded,
> and very likely never will be. Indeed, there is only one living writer
> for children - the creator of the Psammead - whose books compete
> with Mrs Molesworth's in the affection of nursery and schoolroom.
> July 22nd, 1921.

Molesworth defines her own credo.

> Writing for children calls for a peculiar gift...It is more than the
> love of children....It is...clothing your own personality with theirs,
> seeing as they see, feeling as they feel, realizing the intensity of
> their hopes and fears, their unutterably pathetic sorrows,
> yet...remaining yourself...never forgetting the marvellous
> impressionableness of the little hearts and minds...never...losing
> sight of what is *good* for them. ('On the Art of Writing Fiction for
> Children,' *Atalanta* May, 1893: 583)

She straddles two worlds, an old and a new, using both Puritan and
psychological approaches to dissect children and families. She is alert to
children's psychological needs, she pleads ardently for love, trust and
security, she passionately defends individuality. She wrote in a time of
rapid change and uncertainty, the result of the industrial revolution, the
political changes engendered by Education Acts, Poor Laws, Reform
Bills, and new thinking after Darwin's unsettling *Origin of Species*.

The effect of uncertainty was to intensify the importance of tradition,
behaviour, and etiquette. As the economy at the end of the nineteenth
century diminished the aristocracy's landed strength and increased
industrialists' fortunes, the class system both expanded and ossified. Its
effect was to make a hedge of prohibitions around middle-class female
upbringing. From it Molesworth extracts the hidden female mind. Her
heroines fight with conformity. Molesworth's sensitivity within strictures,
her liberalism within traditionalism make her as much an oxymoron as
these heroines, who are strong but gentle, autonomous but finally put
family first.

Mary Louisa Molesworth's own life was likewise a paradox. She was a
paradigm of secrets and double standards, though in Victorian eyes

convention and propriety were thus laudably preserved. She was born in Holland, in 1839, to Scottish parents, Charles Augustus Stewart, merchant, and his wife Agnes. Agnes came from a landed, wealthy family; Charles was the illegitimate son of William Stewart, an army officer and Isabel Innis, a girl intended for domestic service. William later became extremely respectable as Governor General of New South Wales, a Major-General, with a wife and legitimate family. Charles was brought up by his mother, a housekeeper. His father ordered him never to regard his half-siblings as relations. He hid his illegitimacy from his own children. Molesworth knew only that his origins were shrouded in mystery, and romanced that he was the illegitimate son of the Duke of Sussex, because both bore the name Augustus. The prosaic servant, not royal, irregularity would have jeopardised any claim to middle-class decency as Charles rapidly grew richer, moving to ever bigger houses, from Manchester to rural Cheshire.

Her marriage in 1861 to Major Richard Molesworth, nephew to the seventh viscount Molesworth, lifted her from trade to aristocracy. Though initially deeply in love, they separated unhappily in 1879. Richard was recklessly extravagant with a violent temper, possibly caused by shrapnel left in a head wound in the Crimean War. Molesworth, her mother and five surviving children (two had died) set up home in France, where Molesworth passed herself off as a widow. Later she moved to London, and for the rest of her life her writing supported her family, 'budgeting carefully, otherwise I do not think they could have lived in the style they did', remembered her cousin. (Lancelyn-Green, 1961: 47) She worked furiously, publishing several stories a year, playing her many publishers off against each other, to make more money. She launched her girls into the London Season and her boys into professions, overcoming with her drive, brains and charm the social obstacles barricading the path of a separated, wage-earning single mother.

Her failed marriage was not her only tragedy. Violet, her adored eldest child, died in 1869 aged seven. Her first son died aged three months. Her other sons predeceased her; Bevil as a young man, and Lionel in 1917, aged 43. '*A very grievous sorrow*,' she told her publisher, Mr Macmillan. 'He quite realised his condition and met death bravely and resignedly.' (Jan 27th, 1917) Her troubles 'soured her… it was many years before the sweetness came back,' said her granddaughter. 'This accounts for her being so stern a mamma and so sweet a grandmother.' (Lancelyn-Green, 36) Her friends, who included Kipling, Swinburne and Watts-Dunton, remembered her for her charm. She was also independent, as a letter to Mr Craik[1], her friend and publisher at Macmillan's shows.

> I *will* remember your kind offer of help to me just at this time, though I do not know of any special direction for it....My sons-in-law & Lionel (her son) are all affectionate and good to me, but they are *all* very busy with their own affairs...As far as possible, I rely on myself. (Oct. 28th, 1902)

An aside to Mr Craik: 'My hand is much better; indeed it only "hurts" now, and I am told not to mind this as it is inevitable,' (April 13th, 1896) is a clue to her fortitude. She forefronts in her texts optimism, endurance and resilience; her heroines battle through vicissitudes. As she wrote in the *Monthly Packet* (1894) 'The sunshine is there...though it is sometimes so veiled to us.'

In 1896 her husband was admitted as a Military Knight to Windsor Castle, an office that gave accommodation and income to ex-soldiers. Molesworth dreaded the appointment for fear it bestowed a real title; a sudden elevation to 'Lady' might have shattered her 'widow' status. Hiding cracks in the edifice still remained essential. After he died she told Mr Craik, 'you, who know the whole,' how she would try to think of him kindly, without anger or disappointment. She never stopped trying to improve herself, just as she constantly strove to improve her readers. The different standards of the new century finally silenced old anxieties on her death. *The Sunday Times* reports the funeral of 'Mrs Mary Louisa Molesworth, the well-known authoress, and widow of the late Major Richard Molesworth of the Royal Dragoons...many literary friends attended'. (July 24th 1921) She had achieved her goals, well kept secrets, financial, literary and social success and happily married children. None of it was without struggle.

Her books examine norms and test boundaries. They illustrate a domestic world in which the tension between ideality and reality, duty and progress, ideology and individuality reflect a profound unease beneath a hope of happiness. I have looked at her domestic children's novels, concentrating on the family, the home, the relationship with servants, and upbringing and behaviour; areas that construct the background - the loves, hatreds, fears, and hopes - of nineteenth-century, middle-class girlhood.

Notes

1. George Craik, husband of novelist Dinah Mulock Craik, was publishing partner at Macmillan, founded in 1834. He also published Charles Dodgson, thus enjoying a unique preview of Victorian children's literature, from *Alice in Wonderland* in 1865, until his death in 1905.

Illustration 7: *Sheila's Mystery* (1895) illus. L. Leslie Brooke, frontispiece, London: Macmillan

Chapter 5

*Un*happy Families

The fetishism of Family is a worse fetishism than that of Sunday.
Because that only rolls its Juggernaut car one day of the week - the
other every day of the week.
Letter from Florence Nightingale to Mary Mohl (Clarkey, 1984:
176)

Nor could a theory entailing dislocation and severance of the
members constituting our human nature, a doctrine assailing the
Divine thought of the family as the centre of all society, ever really
take root or permanently flourish.
Mrs Molesworth, ('English Girlhood' *Studies & Stories*, 1893)

Diverse Inheritance

Molesworth writes constantly about a difficult, unlovable child. The child
causes misery until he, more usually she, learns self-control. The battle is
between a bid for individualism and capitulation to family demands; the
battleground is the daily round of family life. The winner - by a narrow
margin - is the family. Individuality is described with empathy.
Molesworth's polarisation of self and selflessness makes them almost
even contenders, till her heroines subdue themselves in the struggle to be
a happy family. That it *is* a struggle is as much her message as all her
moral teaching.

The Victorian family represented stability in a time of revolutionary
change, of new inventions, new technology, new Reform Bills, and an
unprecedented sense of living at speed from faster communications. It was
seen as a refuge and a reinforcement of Victorian middle-class Christian
concepts. The sanctity of the mother and the power of the father created a
source of virtue against which the evils of the world were impotent. Its
corollary, where the family was unable to provide security for its
members, was the workhouse. This, a nadir of fear, was a shameful plunge
into degradation in which all sense of family was removed.

This family ethos has left a folk-memory of secure middle-class papas and
mammas and their happy children. In unmasking disharmony however,
Molesworth reveals a set of values as uncertain as the background of
current thought. On one hand was a patriarchalism, developed during the
seventeenth and eighteenth centuries as the nuclear family became less

obviously reliant upon state, kinship, and community, which reached a Victorian fruition. The function of the family became the nurture and socialisation of its children, 'the economic, emotional and sexual satisfaction of the husband and wife' (Stone, 1990: 145), while the father's authority was constantly reinforced by Church and state. On the other hand was an eighteenth century inheritance of individualism extolling the uniqueness of all human beings: provided the pursuit of happiness did not prevent another's, each person should seek individual fulfilment.

Stone cites Pope's *Essay on Man* (1733) to illustrate its effect. ' "That reason, passion answer one great aim/ That true self-love and social are the same." Pope drags in God, Nature, Reason, and Passion to support a...transformation of human consciousness...that the egocentric pursuit of self-interest contributed to the public good.' (179) A new ideal of domestic affection, a new prototype of the 'Man of Sentiment', the weakened power of kin, a change in the concepts of duty and obligation, all combined to bring this about.

Victorian middle-class upbringing was built on clashing attitudes. Molesworth's fictional children are reared on a conscience-examining, Puritan seriousness, a Calvinist repression of will, a Lockian reliance on psychology and a Rousseau-like vision of a naturally-good child easily corrupted by society. The mixture curdles. Molesworth frequently contradicts herself. 'Stories about children are not always the healthiest reading for children, because they tend to make them introspective. I never vivisect children.' (*Women at Home*, 1897: 193) Yet of her hundred books published, most are for and about children; in them the authorial voice minutely dissects her characters; her protagonists inwardly examine themselves.

Late-Victorians engendered, as never before, an explosion of child-orientated materiality. A new plethora of toys, books and games filled a gap in the market created by a need to spend money on children. The increasingly child-centred family produced another kind of unease, as Molesworth noted. 'I fancy that the children of today are the victims, not so much of over-indulgence as of over-notice...It has a tendency to make them feel as if they were the centre of the universe.' (*Women at Home* 1897: 193) Fighting through a maze of confliction was confusing. Molesworth shows well-meaning parents making mistakes and children challenging their restraints as she airs doubts about the possibility of family happiness. The explosions of strong personalities in proximity, the frustrations of restricting self-expression and individuality are drawn with painful clarity. Yet over it all, the mirage of the happy family beckons, like the crock of gold at the foot of the rainbow.

In exploring family fragility she concludes that its existence depends on effort made by its members. She shows that the family was not an absolute value but an article of faith, a doctrine of both confirmation and aspiration, implying certainty and uncertainty together. Walter Houghton, in *The Victorian Frame of Mind* (1957) alleges that after 1870, there were no absolute values. 'About that time a number of things converged to suggest the relativity of knowledge and the subjective character of thought.' (14) Science, for instance, now propounded that all things were in a state of constant flux, making truth variable.

> Though the Victorians were certain that truth existed and the mind could discover it, they found themselves involved in two forms of doubt: either what is sometimes called negative skepticism, when the judgement is suspended between alternative conclusions, one of which is considered true; or the affirmation of a belief which they only half believed - and half doubted. (Houghton, 1957: 18)

Likewise the happy family was both an inviolable truth and an illusory mantra. The family was a sanctified icon of togetherness and a cauldron seething with individual passions. Whichever way you looked at it, there were doubts, insecurities, anxieties, fortitude, duty, and idealism. Such a disparate collection of epithets illustrates both the Victorian way of thinking and the diverse inheritance of the Victorian family. Molesworth's frank, radical look at the family asks why it is so hard to be happy, and guides her readers through the difficulties of family life.

The Chasm Explored

Molesworth's first children's novel, *Carrots: Just a Little Boy* (1876), was a best-seller, written uniquely from a realist base. She scoffs any cosy assumptions that all middle-class children are welcomed by their parents.

> The truth was that though of course every one meant to be kind to this new little baby...no-one was particularly glad he had come. His father and mother   felt that five boys and girls were already a good number to bring up well and educate and start in life, not being very rich, you see. (6)

When Carrots is six, his nurse loses a half-sovereign. When questioned Carrots doesn't realise she's lost a coin; a 'sovereign' to him is a monarch; a half-sovereign, therefore, a muddling concept. He has already found and hidden a 'fairy yellow sixpence.' He is afraid of his father's hot temper, and narrowly escapes a paternal whipping for theft.

Molesworth explains poor parenting in a way that is easy for children to understand, contradicting her statement: 'the obtruding or emphasising parental mistakes should surely be avoided when writing *for* the tender little ones.'

> Captain Desart, Carrot's father was...a sailor. If any of you children have a sailor for your father, you must not think I mean to teach you to be disrespectful when I say that sailors *are*...hot and hasty. I do not think they understand much about children...All this was the case with Carrots' father. He had been away so much from his children that he really hardly knew...anything about their childish ways...

> But once he did begin to notice them, though very kind, he was very strict. He had the most decided opinions about the only way of checking their faults... and he could not and would not be troubled with arguing about such matters. One child, according to his ideas, was to be treated exactly like another; why the same offence should deserve severer punishment with self-willed, bold, matter of fact lad, such as Maurice, than with a timid, fanciful, baby-like creature as was his little (Carrots), he could not have understood had he tried.

The half-sovereign episode changes Carrots. 'It gave him his first glimpse...of that saddest of all sad things - the way in which it is possible for our very nearest and dearest to mistake and misunderstand us.' (92)

Moleworth's realism shows children that their integrity remains intact despite crushing patriarchal absolutism; it helps them to understand their parents' inadequacies, reassures the timid, thus encouraging their independent maturity. Like all her books it ends happily. She shows that family relationships *must* succeed if the individual is to be happy, and parents must try as hard as children.

In *The Rectory Children* (1889) Biddy, aged eight, is the youngest of three. Biddy knows she is her mother's least favourite. When her thoughtless behaviour nearly kills her father

> he had a feeling that if he did not recover a sad shadow would be cast over Biddy's life...'It would leave a sore memory in her

mother's heart,' (he) said to himself, 'however much she tried not to let it come between her and the child.'

And I fear it would have done so

The mother admits she doesn't have the 'right way' with Biddy and is described as easily dispirited and excitable. She needs understanding as much as Biddy. Biddy, in becoming aware of her mother's needs, grows up, while her mother tries harder. As Molesworth points out in *Carrots*, children's development depends 'on the people who take care of them as well as themselves.'(11) Relationships, she emphasises, require effort.

> It was not without putting some slight force on herself that Biddy's mother pressed the little hand...In spite of still feeling irritated and sore against cross-grained Biddy, her mother crushed down her own vexation and met the child's better mind more than half-way.
>
> A queer feeling came over the little girl...
>
> "If mamma was always like that *how* good I would be," thought Biddy. (110)

Parenthood, says Molesworth, cannot guarantee parental instinct. Her authorial voice frequently identifies parents' blunders, for instance, 'in treating Biddy thus, I think her mother made a mistake.' (44) Molesworth's parents are not 'better' than their children, making their authoritative status, as she often notes, an onerous responsibility. Mrs Vane, like Biddy, must learn. Her stumbling attempts to be a good mother refute the ivory-calm image of always-right Victorian motherhood. Instead, she and Biddy enact another Victorian edifice - endeavour, echoing the epochal title of Samuel Smiles' *Self-Help, with illustrations of Conduct and Perseverance.* (1859)

Hoodie (1881) describes another uneasy mother-child relationship. Angry Hoodie is five, the second of four children. The book opens with her elder sister, 'a soft-haired, quiet-eyed little girl...and at each side, nestling in beside her, a cherub-faced dot of a boy, listening to the story she was reading aloud.' (3) Hoodie ruins the peace by screaming 'I don't love *any* body...go *away,* go AWAY.' Hoodie's well-meaning mother can't cope with the tantrums. She tries everything from gentle talks to locking Hoodie in her bedroom.

> Hoodie's mother now stood and looked at her, asking herself what *would* be best to do...
>
> "If Hoodie cared about my knowing (of her naughtiness) for fear of it grieving me, I would understand better how to manage her....It is her pride, not her love, that is concerned."
>
> She was right, but wrong too. Hoodie was proud but also intensely loving. She did grieve in her own wild, unreasonable way, at distressing her mother, but most of all she grieved that *she* should be the cause of it. It was the misery of believing herself to be always the cause of the unhappiness that seemed to come back and back upon her, making the very time at which she was "sorriest," the time at which it was hardest to be good.(11)

The authorial voice is more omniscient than the mother, who falls short of the mother-at-home idyll of 'infallibly faithful and wise counsellors' that Ruskin elevated in 'Of Queen's Gardens.' (*Sesame and Lilies,* 1864: 104) Hoodie feels unloved. When she nearly dies of scarlet fever, her mother finally understands. In the text's period sentimentality is an urgent timeless plea: children must know they are loved.

> The fever seemed to have seized her in its strong, cruel arms with so hard a grasp, that often and often it appeared to those about her as if it never again would let her go, but would carry her away out of their sight, without her even being able to bid them good-bye - murmuring ever those sad words which seemed to be burned into her childish brain, about no-body loving her because she wasn't good like Maudie, about having tried in vain to be good...
>
> It was very sad for them all - most sad for Hoodie's mother, whose heart grew sore as she listened to her poor little girl's faint words. It seemed to her that never before had she understood her child and the great longing for love that had been hidden in her nature.
>
> "Oh, Hoodie darling, we do love you - dearly, dearly," she would sometimes say as she bent over her...but the eyes...gazed up without seeing....
>
> "If she dies without knowing us again it will break my heart," said Hoodie's mother. (262)

Hoodie's tantrums were, according to family legend, drawn from Mrs Molesworth's daughter, which may explain the sincerity with which they are described. Once she realises her family love her, she wills herself well;

self-help wins again. But the book's message - make the child *know* he/she is loved – raises the question: why does Hoodie, offspring of a warm, close family - feel in any doubt? Why does she feel 'deep down *somewhere* in her - there was a feeling that...there was a mistake about her somehow, which no-one could understand or ever would, and which it never entered her head to try to explain to anyone'?(8)

The Daughter's Dilemma

Molesworth's most powerful children's books centre on a daughter's longing for family love. Struggling through anger and unhappiness, battling with self and selflessness, she finally achieves self-control, and learns to be *good*, thus earning family appreciation, and the reward of love. Molesworth's exposition of female rage splits pleas for sympathy and self-control.

Girls' upbringing trained them to accept the convoluted view of womanhood. Milton's 'He for God only, she for God in him' (*Paradise Lost*) was reiterated in Patmore's *The Angel in the House* (1854)

> Her will's indomitably bent
> On mere submissiveness to him...

The London Review 1864 (vol 5, 174) amplifies the general hope

> High-minded, noble, delicate, trusting to her instincts ...glad to be the recipient of strength and the giver of purity - grateful for the gracious duties of her home - grateful for the precious burdens of maternity - grateful that her path lies in sheltered ways...loving, giving...

Or, as Virginia Woolf put it: 'She sacrificed herself daily. If there was a draught she sat in it.' (1995) The angel ethos of subjugation, purity, domesticity and fecundity was reinforced, as Nead notes, by definition and regulation in discourses such as medicine, psychiatry and criminal justice. (1988)

Nevertheless nineteenth-century literature fore-fronted rebellious heroines; Jane Eyre, Maggie Tulliver and Dorothea refused to conform. As Reynolds and Humble point out, while 'for the majority of the century these creatures are contained by being taught to ...discover the true joys of love and motherhood...by the end of the century the rebel was appreciated for her own sake'. (*Victorian Heroines,* 1993: 18) Molesworth, as a children's writer, had a different approach. She wanted to reflect and promote stability for her middle-class audience, at a time when feminine consciousness was changing. Her rebels are not appreciated 'for their own sake'; they conform. But she secretes into the text a signpost towards individuality. In emphasising the child-rebel she underlines her significance. Her child readers could relate their own frustrations to Molesworth's heroines' dealings with the contra-flow of capabilities and limitations. They learnt that the cause of rage might be justifiable, but that rage had no place in feminine identity. Hence the daughter's dilemma: conformity versus need and individuality, in which the salve was the reassurance of love. In writing so sympathetically, Molesworth posits the daughter's difficulty in conforming to the ideal female image. The daughter's fierce demand for love shows her doubt of her worth in the impossibility of female ideology.

As a girl Molesworth had revered Charlotte M Yonge, who, as Coleridge notes, made 'trying to be very good...interesting and romantic to thousands of girls'. (1995: 65) Guy Morville, for instance, the hero of *The Heir of Redclyffe*, (1853) typified a medieval-chivalric tradition of loyalty and sacrifice. Houghton observes that Yonge allies Tory politics with Anglican Christianity. (1957: 326) Molesworth, writing a generation later, reiterates Yonge's moral earnestness, while exposing gaps between middle-class Christian ideals and human frailty.

Victorian middle-class life posited an 'utter divorce between practise and profession which has made the entire life of modern England a frightful lie'. (Froude, 1849) Houghton concludes the Victorians created standards of behaviour too high for human nature, hence the legendary Victorian hypocrisy and self-deception. 'The same man who on Sunday was a pious and devout Christian, pillar of the Church, supporter of missions, distributor of Bibles, on Monday was the tough businessman and hard bargainer.' (Houghton, 1957: 405) Similarly attitudes to women were allied to a reverence for religious ideals of suffering, purity, morality and honour. Since this was as impossible for women to accept as for men sincerely to embrace, this perspective engendered yet another - that of believing-while-not-believing; an utterly sincere self-deception. If female ideality were as far from actuality as human identism with Christ's holy perfection, if both were a shrine but also a mirage, then cracks in the edifice were inevitable.

Sheila's Mystery (1895) is an exposé of adolescent female rage brought under control. Sheila Margaret Josselyn is twelve, the brink of adulthood.

Her sister, Sheila Honor, always called Honor, is eleven. Their shared/different names pools, then differentiates girlhood, splitting it into opposites. Sheila is dark, Honor fair, Sheila has a temper, Honor is sunny. Honor is content; Sheila must learn to be happy. The split *must* be sewn together.

Sheila makes a handkerchief-case for Honor's birthday, and discovers her mother has bought Honor a better one, richly embroidered. Furious, Sheila chucks hers out of the window.

Sewing, Michie observes, was the most common occupation of Victorian girls.

> While on the surface it is a safe, dainty and appropriately feminine way of filling up time, ...for heroines like Maggie Tulliver, Caroline Helstone, and Aurora Leigh...sewing represents a way of repressing and controlling the self....It means the sacrifice of the physical self and the repression of bodily urges....sewing is the tiny and fragile channel into which their creativity and their sexual energies must be poured to maintain feminine decorum. (1987: 41)

Sheila's ejection of her sewing is akin to throwing away her femininity and purity. When she reforms she returns the handkerchief-case 'in spite of one or two marks which she could not *quite* remove.' (197) Though her feminine mantle is restored, a faint but ineradicable stain remains, as a warning, of moral jeopardy.

Sheila's temper is her own fault. Mrs Josselyn never knew Sheila was giving Honor the same present, due to the separateness of school-room and drawing-room lives. Molesworth uses this to throw responsibility on to the child. Though the omniscient voice is sympathetic, especially since poor Sheila sewed when she didn't even like it – a character plus point - readers understand that her reaction is wrong. Unfairness, says Molesworth, never excuses bad behaviour.

Having always felt unloved, Sheila now discovers she is adopted. Adoption, a common adolescent fantasy, challenges the parental relationship in reinforcing the search for self. Molesworth twists the adolescent process into an acceptable Victorian answer. Furious Sheila runs away to a humble farmers' family, where she learns self-discipline. Now she learns that Honor, not she, is adopted. Mr and Mrs Josselyn reclaim her, full of love, and tell her the truth.

"We could scarcely bear to do it," said her mother; "to leave you all these weeks under the mistake. But---"

"It was my own doing, mamma. *Nothing* could have taught me as well. And *oh*, the joy of it now !"(196)

The hard lesson taught a vital message. Self-control, family harmony and a girl's femininity were linked in a trinity as inviolable and as fundamental as a religious tenet. There was no room for a girl who broke the rules. Sheila felt unloved, Molesworth implies, because her behaviour put her outside the trinity.

Rosy (1882) explores a frequent Victorian scenario- a family disrupted by the Empire. Rosy, aged eight, having lived with an aunt while her parents were in India, returns home. As the family re-forms, Rosy has difficulty adapting to new family members and a different method of upbringing, which makes her doubt her lovableness. Her sense of being an outsider however applies to a wider base. Daughters everywhere had to struggle for recognition.

Late Victorian girls were still regarded as the inferior sex. Boys were better educated, represented the family by carrying on its name, encouraged to be active, mentally and physically. Too much education was thought to over-stimulate a girl's maturity; too much physical exercise was unladylike or worse. As Molesworth put it, 'The "hoydenishness", to coin a word, degenerates into fastness.' ('Coming out' *Studies and Stories*, 1893: 2) From the 1870s onwards an emerging concept of 'girlhood' gave girls a new culture of their own, distinct from adult expectations. (Mitchell, 1995) Even so, 'they perhaps suspected they could be 'new girls' for only a few brief years before they grew up to be traditional women.' (3) Most girls were brought up to know that their true adult fulfilment lay in marriage and motherhood - if they were lucky enough.

Here lay another *impasse*. Although a girl knew her security lay in her ability to attract a husband, to do so overtly was fast and unladylike. Precepts of upbringing guarded her, making escape difficult, as Gerald Du Maurier's Punch cartoon 'A Pathetic Appeal' illustrates. (1878)

"Mamma, shall you let me go to the Wilkinson's Ball, if they give one, this Winter?" "No, Darling."

"You've been to a great many Balls, haven't you, Mamma?"

"Yes, Darling, and I've seen the *Folly* of them all."

"Mightn't I see the folly of *one*, Mamma?"

(A very long pause)

She must lure obliquely; maidenliness decreed that her charms, like her clothes, be subtle.

> The woman of true refinement, such as I dress, will not wear any toilette that draws attention to her, but will so mark herself that he may read "a charming woman" by her quiet attire and its exquisite simplicity of design. It is true that the materials are fine and the gown fits "a mervielle". But the effect is entirely unostentatious. (Worth, 1914)

Spinsterhood was considered a failure of girlhood. There was an 'excess' of unmarried women, partly due to an imbalance in the sex ratio, which increased steadily from 1871 to 1911. 'The problem ...affected middle-class women most. In 1892, Clare Collett, a social investigator, reported that in the richer suburbs unmarried women aged 35-45 outnumbered men by over three to one and only one third of these were domestic servants.' ((Lewis, 1984: 4) Female childhood sanctuary was undermined by uncertain future status and economic security. The unspoken issue threatened their comfort and credibility. It accounts for the feelings of Molesworth's child heroines, 'deep down' as Hoodie had, of unhappiness and anger.

To Be *and* Not To Be

The only way forward was to develop selflessness, rising above the constraints and doubts of girlhood and family life. Molesworth encourages watchfulness, creating a sense of self that was the greater from self-scrutiny and the lesser from self-abnegation. Connie exemplifies this duality. (*Sweet Content* (1891)

> You see, I had been selfish all my life. I had never even *thought* of its being wrong. Once I did begin to think of it I was perfectly startled and horrified to find how wide-spreading and deep-rooted my selfishness was.... It was not only selfishness I had to fight against. I was exceedingly, absurdly, really *vulgarly* self-conceited and stuck-up.

> And now and then nice things happened to make me feel I was getting on a little; some of these I will tell you about, though I also have to tell you of some rather dreadful things that showed how very naughty and horrid - oh, I get hot still when I think of these ! - I still was. (137)

Connie's enthusiastic, detailed, constant probing into her motives and feelings feeds her self-worth while she wears a hair shirt. Humility and self-effacement co-exist with self-esteem; self, an eternal presence, is continually reinforced and withdrawn. This was the Victorian answer to childhood will; checks, balances, seriousness, and dedication supported the self while ensuring that self was conquered by the very means of its support. Connie's absorption in her feelings combines the moral discipline of Victorian Puritanism with the earnestness of the self-improvement creed that had seeped into middle-class consciousness. If there was any hypocrisy in a simultaneous approach of proposal and cancellation, it was no different from the Victorian way of thinking, in which double standards were the understood means of dealing with the shortfall between aspiration and reality.

The key to improvement, Molesworth felt, was unselfishness. Selfishness had been Sheila's 'great enemy.' (193) 'Selfish people have *no* idea what happiness they miss'. *The Rectory Children.* (185) Selfishness had an insidious grip. 'There is a sort of selfishness inherent in the mere fact of youth and health and vigorous life' ('Coming Out' *Studies and Stories*). For Molesworth, however, girls were more at risk.

Good women were revered for their dependent, maternal image; bad women feared for their sexual power and independence. The dangerous slide from respectability to degradation dictated female upbringing. The problem was exacerbated by a girl's recognised proximity to her emotion. Ruskin described the difference between the sexes in 'Of Queen's Gardens': 'each has what the other has not: each completes the other.' (*Sesame and Lilies:* 115) Emotion and femininity were linked. Girls, unlike men, could express their feeling. But not too much. Since passion, a lack of self-control, led to depravity, girls' behavioural goals were norms of repression and conformity. More revered was saintly abnegation, like the retiring Margaret May in *The Daisy Chain*, or Christina Rossetti.

> Not to be first: how hard to learn
> That lifelong lesson of the past
> Line graven on line and stroke on stroke,
> But, thank God, learned at last.

('The Lowest Room', 1856)

By the late nineteenth century, the 'rebel girl' in literature demanded escape from conventional femininity. Molesworth's daughter-heroines conform painfully, at a time when conformity was changing. They debate self and selflessness, a contest as fundamental to Victorian thinking as the balance between duty, progress and tradition. Molesworth's exposition of the female cry tips the balance towards the daughter becoming, not yet first, but at last beginning to be heard.

Illustration 8: *Mary* (1893) illus. L. Leslie Brooke, p.10 London: Macmillan

Chapter 6

Refractile Relationships: Servants, Nurses and Children

My second Mother, my first Wife,
The angel of my infant life -
Robert Louis Stevenson, dedication to his nurse in *A Child's Garden of Verses* (1885)

'...feeling myself almost like one of the family, though in a humble way.'
Nurse Heatherdale's Story (1891: 52)

Beyond the paying of wages or the performance of duties the barrier between drawing room and the servants' hall is never passed.
Edward Salmon, 'Fortnightly Review' (1888)

Intransigence and Liberalism

The child-servant relationship followed a different course from that of a social equal. Like the deflection of the straight course of light, it bent to accommodate the class system. It included the tensions and limitations engendered by social boundaries, while simultaneously based on the closest possible early mental, moral and physical intimacy. It meant that a straightforward affinity between child and nurse or servant was almost impossible, and, by the mores of the time, judged undesirable.

Molesworth's books illustrate this refractile nature of child-servant relationships. They suggest, radically, that a servant might be wiser and more loving than her employers. However, she never allows the child/ servant relationship to exist beyond the nursery. The child straddles the gap between servant and employer, reflecting inferiority through immaturity, and superiority through class, until age and hierarchy widen it irrevocably. In exploring the tension between child, servant and status, Molesworth is uneasy with its discrepancies. Her incompatible ideologies introduce into her novels a grey area of uncertainty making a fruitful ground to assess the disparate attitudes that structured the nineteenth-century child.

Children and servants were linked by inferiority. Inferiority called for patronage, as one employer explained: 'Servants - as well as children -

require to be managed with *kindness* and *firmness*.' (Horn, 1986: 129.) Both their living spaces, as Davidoff points out, the children's night and day nurseries, and the servants' quarters, were separate from the main part of the house. (Davidoff, 1973: 87) Their food was based on similar principles. *The Book of the Home* (n.d.: 259) gives a recipe for 'Economy Jam - for nursery or kitchen use.' The ingredients are apple peel, cores and pips.

Child/nurse closeness was equally welcomed and disparaged. No middle-class mother was without a nurse for her children. Demand for nurses rose from one advertisement a day in *The Times* in 1822 to 12.2 a day in 1882. From 1850 on, 'a thorough nurse in a genteel tradesman's family' was a common advertisement, until 'by the end of the century you were barely considered middle-class if you didn't have at least a nursemaid for the children.' (Gathorne-Hardy, 1972: 66) However too much association with the lower classes was undesirable; the children might lose their sense of caste. *The Woman's Book* (1911: 485) recommended, to counteract this possibility, engaging 'a lady to be with the little ones for a few hours daily' for children between babyhood and governess age.

Early nineteenth-century evangelical literature's emphasis on wicked hearts discouraged class superiority. Mrs Sherwood's texts warn of the sin of temporal vanity. By the late nineteenth and early twentieth century, even the Fabian E. Nesbit shows how class had taken root. A housekeeper

> does not understand anything about writing books. She thinks Albert's Uncle copies things out of printed books when he is really writing new ones. Many servants are like this. (Nesbit, 1901: 69)

Molesworth, unusually, has servants playing heroic roles, reflecting the large part they played in real children's lives. She tests the boundaries surrounding the nurse/servant-child relationship. Herself a combination of boldness and intransigence, she inserts liberal thinking into inexorable rules. While upholding tradition she aimed to teach her middle-class audience a new sensitivity.

The mother-nurse

Molesworth's fictional children artlessly love their nurses. When adult they look back with gratitude and tenderness – and move on. The sadness this might have entailed is not an issue. Social rules have by this time become part of their psyche. But the debt owed to the good nurturing nurse *is* an issue, and Molesworth is unique in establishing it, as she examines the bond between nurse and child.

In *A Charge Fulfilled* (1886) the heroine, Avice, is a farmer's daughter, a lower-class girl. Widowed, fragile (fragility being the hallmark of a lady) Mrs Redmond asks Avice to look after her two daughters. One dies, the mother drowns, and Avice is left in sole charge of Juliet, who nearly dies too. Her recovery strengthens the bond between them. Meanwhile, Mr Withers, Juliet's cruel guardian, wants her fortune, dismisses Avice, says Juliet is epileptic, and sends her away, expecting her to die of neglect. Avice, now married to a farmer, Luke Warden, searches for Juliet, and finds her running away, dirty and very ill. The melodrama of their reunion underlines their love.

> As she covered the little face with kisses, and forgetting all risk - everything except that it was her own little Judy she held again in her arms - spoke to her in the tenderest tones: "Oh my darling; oh, my little Judy, my own little girl," the child, fainting, half-dead as she had been,...whispered low but clearly, "Adie, dear Adie, come for Judy."

Juliet is brought up by Avice and her husband, who, to hide her from Mr Withers, re-name her Dolly Warden. She is their 'dolly'; they are wardens. Her childhood is spent as a farmer's daughter. As she grows older, Avice drives a wedge between them, reminding her that she was born 'a lady', correcting her speech, ('I've never wanted you to speak like us') and has her educated beyond a farmer's daughter's expectations. Dolly is confused –'I want to be your own Dolly always,' and upset, at eighteen, when an eligible bachelor appears. 'I don't want him to patronise me as a little country girl.' She is torn between being simple Dolly and Miss Redmond.

For Molesworth there is only one possible ending. Juliet must be restored to her place in society. In emphasis, she is now a great heiress with duties and responsibilities and she marries the eligible bachelor, who is her cousin. Though she will always be Avice's child, she belongs elsewhere. Avice's rural, nurturing haven is suitable only for children. At eighteen, she must move on. All Molesworth's hallmarks are here; honesty, sensitivity, loyalty, and a rigid application of the rules.

Avice represents the middle-class ideal of the working-class nurse. She had originally worked, unpaid at home, as a dairymaid; her milk connection establishes her as an icon of nurture. With comfortably-off farmer parents she did not need to work outside the home, an important distinction. Molesworth writes to her publisher about a Newnham graduate.

> I am anxious to find a post for a girl of twenty-four...She is a lady belonging to a family of excellent position and she is not *obliged* to work, but has nothing to do at her own home in the country, and wishes to put her education to good use. (1908)

This was acceptable. A woman who did need to work was considered more rapacious. 'The angel who left the house was, on some metaphorical level, seen by the more conservative elements of Victorian culture as a streetwalker,' (Michie, 1987: 31), was a potential threat to the structure of society. Her wage-earning capacity showed masculine capability; she rebutted the whole 'angel' discourse. A lower-class female wage-earner was considered more unnerving. The *Morning Chronicle's* survey of the nation's poor (1849-51) made it clear that working women made bad mothers. Shaftsbury's reports (1862) found working-class women 'strangely bold in looks and manner.' They were seen as physically different. Their scant clothes revealed bodies that middle-class corsets and petticoats concealed. Nead, analysing George Elgar Hick's painting, 'The Sinews of Old England' (1857) points out that the woman's strong arms and tan 'provide the point of closure between the middle class and the class below it.' (1988: 43). The working-class woman was deemed ominously sensual.

Avice-types, however, not in need of work, were working-class women with a middle-class outlook. A nostalgic artistic and literary discourse presented rural women 'elevated as goddesses of harvest and fecundity,' (Sayer, 1995: 101), combining pastoral innocence with the cottage idyll and simple domestic bliss. They were the most prized servants, considered honest, happy, uncomplicated, thrifty, industrious and nurturing. Sayer (43) also point to an official discourse that 'worked to support the cultural hegemony of the ruling class through a mechanism which linked the rural poor to Englishness, the organic community and femininity, and made rural women the carriers of industry, thrift and domesticity.' They made ideal nurses.

They feature in many of Molesworth's books, creating a haven of security and comfort. In *The Story of a Spring Morning* (1890) Bertha, the nurse, disobeys her master when she considers her charge unjustly punished. In

Nurse Heatherdale's Story (1891), the nurse understands and encourages an unloved child and helps to promote better feeling. The story purports to be written by Nurse Heatherdale, so hers is the conclusive authorial voice. Few other contemporary writers similarly promote the nurse, an exception being Mrs Ewing's Nurse Bundle (*A Flat Iron for a Farthing*, 1871) Mrs Bundle's peasant-like, instinctive wisdom, however, differs from Molesworth's intelligent, analytical nurses.

Molesworth highlights the nurse's difficult position. She could provide love and understanding, but lacked power in family dynamics. Nurse Heatherdale can only help by working behind the scenes. Bertha, speaking frankly, gets dismissed from the room. The servant's stance of love without power shows both child and servant the class chasm.

Molesworth's next step - to consider the servant as sympathetically as the nurse - was more contentious. Though she played with the idea - fascinating, forbidden territory –she felt equality was impossible.

The Unbridgable Gap

Attitudes everywhere dictated that servants were different. Derogatory generalisations abounded.

> Firewood is used far too freely by servants, who are given to employing as much again as is necessary. (Davidson, n.d. vol 4: 258)

> Maids are apt to be very wasteful with fried bacon.
> Many employers fail to realise that servants often prefer a coarser style of food than appeals to a cultured palate. (Davidson, n.d., vol 3: 31)

> Servants talk about People. Gentlefolk talk about Things. (Horn, 1986: 68)

Servants were judged by employers for build, like judges at a cattle market. 'A parlour maid should be tall and elegant...and rather slight so that she can...be graceful in her movements.' (Jack, 1911: 52) *A Few Rules for the Manners of Servants in Good Families* (Jack, 1911) shows that behaviour required of servants was as exacting as that demanded of aspiring gentlefolk in etiquette books.

> Always stand still and keep your hands quiet when speaking to a
> lady or being spoken to; and look at the person speaking to you.
>
> Never begin to talk to ladies and gentlemen, unless it be to always
> speak of the children of the family as 'Master' – 'Miss.' (Horn,
> 1986: 126.)

Molesworth wonders what it felt like to be treated as a servant. She
explores the subject - but entirely from the viewpoint of a lady; her daring
leaps behind respectable parameters. In *Philippa* (1896), written for older
girls, headstrong Philippa altruistically pretends to be a lady's maid to her
dim sister Evelyn when Evelyn visits her husband's rich relations. She
wants Evelyn to make a good impression, to help her inherit a fortune.

Philippa gets prepared. She calls herself Phillis – 'a *perfect* name for a
maid,' (60) wears unobtrusive clothes, 'A lady's maid wears no uniform,
but ought to be quietly and neatly dressed when in attendance on her
mistress.' (Jack, 1911: 54) and changes her voice. 'It was slower and more
monotonous than its wont, with a slight suggestion of choosing her words,
as might be done by an intelligent girl of a lower class with enough
education to make her aspire to perfect correctness.' (66) Instantly there is
an insulting change in the indifferent way she is treated by strangers.

Horrified Evelyn laments: '*You*, my beautiful Phil, sitting at table with a
crew of *servants* - common servants.' Phillipa won't allow such sweeping
class-ridden judgements: 'They were not all common. Some...were very
*un*common,' (190) and makes friends with the housekeeper. But
Molesworth never totally disregards class.

> Though not in any conventional sense superior to her class, the
> good housekeeper was one whom no true woman of whatever
> position, need have hesitated to have called a friend. (87)

Real friendship is obliterated by the patronising adjective 'good.' Servants
are people too - but only up to a point.

A vindictive lady's maid recognises Philippa, now socially restored, and
nearly destroys her with unsavoury rumours casting doubt on Philippa's
status as a lady, which jeopardise a brilliant marriage proposal. Philippa
emerges triumphant – just, marrying a less worldly, more sensitive man.
Though her unorthodox behaviour reveals the better man, the book is not
a plea for the unconventional. The danger she risked is emphasised at

every turn. The gap between lady and servant is shown to be unbridgeable.

Molesworth's stories demonstrate the convoluted nature of class interaction. The nineteenth-century construct of the child combined inferiority of status with progress as the child moved from lower-class care to an adult middle-class world. If, as Molesworth's books illustrate, transition flowed inevitably, with question, but without rebellion, so did the precepts of the period infiltrate the character of the child. As the child realised that different classes required appropriate expressions of affection, how did it affect the child's character? How did he/she think?

The child's exit from the sheltered nursery to the uncertainties of the adult world required duty and self-discipline. These two watchwords of the century reflect a middle-class fear that otherwise the whole safe structure of society would be undermined. They imposed stability and tradition on a period of rapid change. Likewise, these were the attributes required from a young man leaving the safety of England for the Empire. Progress demanded discipline. The construct of the child and the century were founded on the same tenets. Consciously upheld, in literature, in schools, in the army, in every middle-class facet of life, they were unconsciously absorbed in the nursery. As Molesworth shows, teaching began early. Children love their motherly nurses, and go beyond their reach. Older girls understand servants' tribulations, and maintain the divisions. Stability with sensitivity was the background currency, while relationships, affections, and maturing fell into place around them.

The nurse, as child-guardian, was peculiarly in charge of the home's most valued content. Home's sacred nature pertained to the nurse. Her image - pure, inferior, with duties but without rights -contributed to the 'angel' ideal. Ncad defined the Victorian middle-class women as 'firmly secured in a subordinate position through notions of mission, duty and responsibility. She was economically, legally, socially, and ideologically dependant.' (1988: 14) Molesworth's books show how the good, nurturing nurse, lower-class, but with a middle-class outlook, is an exaggerated form of the way in which Victorian women were regarded.

This affected men and women differently. Though both understood the 'angel' image and the sanctity of home and family, while men drew from this respect for the purity of socially equal girls, they understood from their childhood that nurses and servants were subordinate, inferior and powerless. The rich anyway thought the poor another breed. The author of

My Secret Life noted a prostitute was 'not warmly enough [clad] perhaps for well-to-do people, but enough so for her class who don't feel cold as we do.' (Gathorne-Hardy, 1972: 103)

Nead shows how 'Eve as sign defined woman as weak and fallible, fallen from her Edenic purity and leading men into sin and chaos.' The message that lower-class women were different was learnt in the nursery. Molesworth's allure lies not just in her delineation of character and plot, but in the clues concealed in her texts to the orthodoxies that informed Victorian thinking. The rules that governed behaviour created a different mindset.

Illustration 9: *White Turrets* (1896) Illus. W. Rainey, p.215, London: Chambers

Chapter 7

Angels at Home

Why, having won her, do I woo?
Because her spirit's vestal grace
Provokes me always to pursue,
But, spirit-like, eludes embrace;
'Husband and Wife', 1854, Coventry Patmore

'On the whole, it might be better if you asked the headmaster to
explain all about the disgusting side of life.' And then half to
herself and half aloud, she added, 'Not that I myself have ever
*found it **exactly** that.'*
Mrs Lees-Milne to her son, James, c 1916, from his autobiography,
Another Self, 1970, Faber & Faber: 32.

Red-brick and ashlar, long and low,
With dormers and with oriels lit,
The windows all wide open thrown;
And some-one in the study play'd
The Wedding-March of Mendelssohn.
'The Cathedral Close,' 1854, Coventry Patmore.

The Real Girl

Molesworth's books ring with hitting, crying, kicking, and squeezed-out
tears falling down hot cheeks. There is wriggling, pouting, flouncing;
streaming, untidy hair, grimy faces, clothes flung pell-mell out of drawers,
dressing, undressing, breaking things, hugging, stroking, eating. She
creates a very physical sense of childhood.

Mary (1893) is a typical example. This book describes a little girl's
everyday life.

Nurse had lifted Mary out of her bath by this time, and was rubbing
her with a nice large 'soft-roughey' towel – 'soft-roughey' was one
of Mary and Artie's words – it meant the opposite of 'prick-
roughey.'[1] They did not like 'prick-roughey' things. She wrapped
Mary all round in the big towel for a minute; it was nice and warm,
for it had been hanging in front of the fire; then she gave Mary a
little hug. (11)

The repetition of the invented, intimate baby-language, the simplicity of the words, the images of roundness, softness, warmth and enclosure from the bath, the towel, the fire burning in the room and the hug, lead a young reader into literary awareness of physical experience. (Mary is four; the book is aimed at young children.) The passage underlines the safe boundaries of early childhood, in which enjoyable body-sensations from loving care play a large part.

Jasper (1906) was written for older children. Thoughtless Leila and Chrissie, aged ten and eleven, react badly when their parents lose all their money. On the first day without servants Leila reads in bed instead of getting up in time to dress properly, while Chrissie hurls pillows at her and throws their clothes on the floor. At breakfast

> Leila's dark locks were in an extraordinary state of confusion...And her face hardly looked as if she had washed it at all. She grew scarlet when she felt all eyes upon her

> "I can't tie up my hair myself," she said.

Emotion, leading to physical disarray, is unwomanly, threatening ultimately loss of respectability, caste and status; Leila's scarlet face is an echo of a scarlet woman.

The Victorian female middle-class sexual instinct was considered non-existent. The male was the instigator; the female the passive receiver of sexual drive. The *Westminster Review* (1850) confirmed

> If the passions of women were ready, strong and spontaneous, in a degree even approaching the form they assume in the coarser sex, there can be little doubt that sexual irregularities would reach such a height, of which, at present, we have happily no conception. (Greg, 1850, vol. 53: 456-7)

William Acton writes in 1865

> I should say that the majority of women (happily for them) are not very much troubled with sexual feeling of any kind. What men are habitually, women are exceptionally. (112)

Yet writers of Victorian novels, both male and female, use language that is, as Mitchie observes, 'rich with metaphoric allusions to the body,' which 'appears only as a series of tropes or rhetorical codes that distance it from the reader in the very act of its depiction.' (1986: 5) The middle-class nineteenth-century female body was not only obfuscated by crinoline or bustle, but was also hard to reach through whalebone corsets and underwear layers, fastened with tiny buttons and fiddly ribbons. Likewise, literary and artistic allusion to female form was indirect; in Pre-Raphaelite paintings, the erotic body is disguised and swathed, alluring and forbidden. Overt sexuality was the reverse of womanliness.

Respectability and purity were the hallmarks of the middle-class feminine ideal. Nead notes that the difference between 'respectable' and 'fallen' women was constantly being defined. The importance of the distinction was continually emphasised. The goal of female upbringing was respectable femininity, based on self-control quelling passionate instinct.

The borderline between child and adult shifted throughout the Victorian period. At the beginning of the century childhood for working-class children was brief. The age of consent for a girl, until 1875, was twelve, thirteen until 1885, when it was raised to sixteen by the Criminal Law Amendment Act. Mayhew, mid-century, observes street arabs without 'childish ways;' an eight-year old watercress seller has a wrinkled face 'where dimples ought to have been;' a boy has 'the face of a child with no trace of childish goodness.' Evangelical thinking together with the romantic interpretation of childhood was slowly beginning to apply to the poor, enforced by Acts of Parliament. Middle and upper-class children enjoyed a prolonged childhood. The longer girlhood lasted, the more assured was innocence. Girls' 'impure' instincts were quashed. A letter to *The Girl's Own Paper* from a twelve year-old girl asking whether 'a girl of twelve years old may have a lover,' received the answer, 'a rag doll is the best love for such a silly little girl as you seem to be.' (July 28th, 1894)

The Victorian mind split knowledge into two: private acknowledgment and public front. Revelations of female response belied the approved perception of womanhood. Queen Victoria's disgust at childbirth in 1870 – 'the animal side of our nature is to me – too dreadful...' (Longford, 1971: 377) – was a commonly understood point of view, placing women, 'Quick, tender, virginal, unprofained,' (Patmore, 'To the Body', 1854) on an immaculate pedestal. To keep her there, girls were left in ignorance, from Patmore's

> Pure as a bride's blush, when she says
> 'I will' unto she knows not what: (1854)

to Dr Marie Stopes,

> One highly educated lady intimately known to me told me that
> when she was about eighteen she suffered many months of
> agonising apprehension that she was about to have a baby because
> a man had snatched a kiss from her lips at a dance. (1918: 29)

The veil remained for generations; in a 1930's novel an unmarried heroine
is surprised by her sexual eagerness. 'I didn't know I was *like* that.'
(Kennedy,1930: 311)

Molesworth appreciated the problem. Her child heroines are energetic.
Leila and Chrissie, handsome and healthy with abundant hair, burst
noisily into rooms. They are destructive. They are clever. Victorians
considered clever girls suspect; over-stimulated brains tended to
precocious maturity. 'Be good sweet maid, and let who will be clever.'
Charles Kingsley's 1858 adage addressed society's hope for the Angel.
Their appetite for life is matched by their appetite for food. Showalter
describes the Victorian heroine who refuses to eat as, an 'incorporeal
angel...literally turning herself into a "little woman." (*The Female Malady*
1987: 129) Michie notes that 'the Victorian social novel rarely depicts
heroines in the act of eating or starving'. (12) If hunger is equated with
desires for sexuality and power, heroines in canonical literature show their
hunger secretly. Miss Jenkyns and Miss Matty suck their oranges behind
closed doors in *Cranford*; Jane Eyre creeps to Miss Temple's room for tea
and toast. Maggie Tulliver is set apart by her bigness and dark colouring;
more usually pallor and a tiny waist were the mark of the icon angel.

Conversely, Molesworth's heroines enjoy eating. Leila and Chrissie
complain of a poor lunch.

> "I hate cutlets done like this," said Chrissie. "They're so dry. I like
> them with that nice reddy sauce."

> "Tomatoes," said Leila. "So do I. And I don't see why we should
> have plain potatoes, instead of mashed or browned, just because
> Mummy's away."

> Then came the next course.

> "Apple pudding! I hate cooked apples!" exclaimed Christabel. "Is
> there no cream ?" (34)

Victorians linked a carnivorous diet with sexual forwardness. Doctors recommended a low-protein diet to delay puberty. But Molesworth uses hunger – and meat – as a symbol of health: good girls eat plenty; naughty girls are picky, while she also stresses the dangers of energy.

Jasper's message is self-discipline. Leila and Chrissie send their delicate brother into a fever-ridden house to retrieve a lost prayer book. They confess when he nearly dies.

> Christabel, the tears pouring again from her still swollen and aching eyes, flung herself on the floor beside her aunt...the miserable little face hid itself on her aunt's shoulder...

> ...It was, under the circumstances, a terrible confession to hear, though at the root of it all was nothing worse than childish carelessness and disobedience, followed, alas, by concealment and deceit.

> But when Leila, too, flung herself upon her, in less stormy but still agonised penitence, saying, "...I was older and I knew how wrong it was. Poor Chrissie, you were no naughtier than I was," a strange sort of calm, almost of joy, came over Aunt Margaret. (200)

All their flinging conforms to the conventional female norm; Leila and Chrissie's physicality is now expressed as a sorrowing, comforting heap. The sub-text points to vigour's dangerous link with downfall. A small girl is safe; four-year-old Mary, wrapped in her bath towel, sexless in Molesworth's pre-Freudian eyes, may innocently give herself up to pleasurable sensation. Ten-year-olds must beware of their natures. While Coventry Patmore's Angel is a child-like woman,

> She grows
> More infantine, auroral, mild,
> And still the more she lives and knows
> The lovelier she's expressed a child. (*Angel in the House*: 30)

Molesworth sees the woman in the child. Her books warn of the animal within. Self-vigilance and self-knowledge, a cross-roads of Victorian values and a Freudian-like reliance on analysis, armed a girl to battle for control.

Molesworth was suggesting obliquely in literature just what Dr Blackwell was daringly stating in public. Girls, she said in her *Counsel to Parents in* *the Moral Education of their Children (*1879) like boys, had 'a natural passion' damaging to their moral development, and should strive for purity. (Forster, 1984) Josephine Butler rebutted fiercely the double standard. She also thought both sexes equally capable of love and desire. The double standards that presented the prostitute as wicked, the man as only satisfying 'natural urges' was, they said, a sham; the division between the wicked prostitute and the 'good' girl utterly false.

Molesworth's stories show the death throes of the child-woman Angel. Dora Copperfield's childishness echoed the tininess and sweetness of the inexperienced Mayflower, the young Princess Victoria. Lewis Carroll's 1859 photograph of seductive, semi-clad little Alice Liddell dressed as a beggar was thought by Tennyson to be the most beautiful photograph he had ever seen. By the end of the century, Lewis Carroll stopped taking photographs; innocent eccentricity now seemed suspicious behaviour. If female sexuality was possible, then protection of innocence was even more important. Innocence, celebrated in the Romantic cult of the child, re-emerged strongly in children's literature, dividing the knowing adult from child purity. In contrast Molesworth suggests that what divided the girl from the gutter was not innocence but iron control.

'Keep a stiff upper lip.' 'Hold your tongue.' 'Children should be seen and not heard.' These period axioms of childhood, signals for silence, suggest a multitude of thoughts unsaid. Molesworth's rebellious heroines are evidence of the difficulty in absorbing the convention that divided behaviour from feeling. Her 'difficult girls' tales are many: *Hermy* (1881), *Hoodie* (1882), *Rosy* (1882) *The Rectory Children* (1889), *The Children of the Castle* (1890), *Sheila's Mystery* (1890), *Sweet Content* (1891), *My New Home* (1894), *The Ruby Ring* (1904), and *Jasper* (1906). Upbringing must, she suggests, subvert the beast within. Her spirited heroines are tamed. The next question – what does an intelligent, healthy girl *do* with her energy and fortitude? – equally occupied Molesworth. She showed it was possible for old restraints to find new expression if the home were reinterpreted as a source of enablement.

Power House

The middle-class Victorian home was a shrine to marriage, family, domesticity, and industry. The Great Exhibition in 1851, 'a temple to things,' as Queen Victoria, a frequent visitor, noted in her diary, reflected the feeling for home. Its displays of furniture, silver, china, glass, papier-mâché – all intricately ornamented in a way both complicated to create and to clean – new types of upholstery, new decorative techniques meant home was a place on which money was spent. Ruskin called it

> A sacred place, a vestal temple, a temple of the hearth watched over by household gods. Wherever a true wife comes, this home is always round her...shedding its quiet light for those who else were homeless. (1865: 117)

The middle-class Victorian woman as mistress of the house was the director of her servants and children. This limited extent of her sphere reinforced her Angel image, needing protection and worship. As Sir William Blackstone put it in 1765, 'the disabilities a woman lies under are, for the most part intended for her protection and benefit.' (*Commentary on the Laws of England*) Elizabeth Barrett Browning describes the effect

> She had lived
> A sort of cage bird life, born in a cage
> Accounting that leap from perch to perch
> Was act and joy enough for any bird.
> ...I, alas,
> A wild bird scarcely fledged, was brought to her cage,
> And she was there to meet me. Very kind.
> Bring the clean water, give out the fresh seed.
> (*Aurora Leigh* 1856)

Molesworth reinterprets this view of home, and shows how the intelligent middle-class girl, applying the power that accrues to the icon, can translate it into a source of self-knowledge and mental independence. The next step, a career *outside* the home, is hardly mentioned, despite contemporary Victorian feminist campaigners, such as Josephine Butler and Emily Davies. Revolutionary ideas were not a suitable subject for her girl readers; Molesworth kept liberal notions within safe perimeters. The homes in her books reiterate old values while proposing new ones. They show the Angel the door of the cage.

Freud considered houses and rooms, 'the space that encloses human beings' (1916) as symbols of the female. Molesworth's detailed, lingering descriptions of her heroines' houses are full of significance. House and home in her books are, far from a cage, a place of growth. *The Cuckoo Clock* (1877) that tells of lonely Griselda's adventures with the Cuckoo, begins with the house.

Once upon a time in an old town, there stood a very old house. Such a house as you could hardly find nowadays, however you searched, for it belonged to a gone-by time, a time now quite passed away.

The incantation of 'once upon a time,' linked with the house, places the house on the borderline between fantasy fulfilment and realism. The Cuckoo clock itself is a magic miniature house, the entry into a fantasy world, and the fount of the wisdom and imagination that finally connects with Griselda. The house symbolises time, imagination and self-empowerment.

Robin Redbreast (1892) describes in detail the house that bears the title's name. Jacinth and her siblings, children of Empire-building parents, live with a 'vinegar aunt.' Jacinth is befriended by Robin Redbreast's owner, fierce old Lady Myrtle Goodacre, who becomes as a mother to her. Jacinth, lacking her real mother, has become supercilious and unchildlike. Softened by her love of Lady Myrtle and Robin Redbreast, she learns to respect her parents. In her will, Lady Myrtle leaves her the house and money enough to maintain it in good style. Now Jacinth has learnt how to be a proper child, she is given the adult, empowering status of householder, and provides a home in it for her parents. The name of the house – redbreast – reflects the nurturing, educative, female nature of home, especially when linked with the old lady's name; the myrtle, an emblem of love.

The hall was wainscoted in oak half-way up, where the panels met a bluish-green Japanese paper. A really old oriental paper it was, so thickly covered with tracery of leaves and flowers and birds and butterflies that the underlying colour was more felt than seen. A short staircase of wide shallow steps ran up one side, disappearing apparently into the wall...There he (the butler) threw open a door, papered like the walls so cleverly as to be invisible...A glow of colour met her eyes, for (it) opened on to a gallery, three sides of which ran round an inner hall on the ground floor, while the fourth – that facing her – was all conservatory... of the most perfect kind...The girl started, half-dazzled by the unexpected radiance...The butler threw open a door leading in among the flowers. She lingered a moment to enjoy for half an instant the fragrance and beauty around her....Jacinth's usually cold, unimpulsive nature was strongly moved. (111)

Molesworth frequently describes a labyrinth of complicated architecture leading the heroine to ecstatic bursts of sensation. *Hermy* (1881) written for younger children, is about eight-year-old Hermione, whose parents are in India. Misunderstood at her aunt's home, she hides her feelings and appears inarticulate and witless. She runs away to a strange house where Miss Lavinia, an elderly invalid, lives. Miss Lavinia helps Hermy to understand herself and Hermy learns how to communicate. When her parents return, she is no longer a misfit.

> The servant crossed the neat little hall, opened a door dividing it from the back part of the house, and Hermy followed her. But for a moment she stood still in amazement. "When the door was opened," not only did it seem that "birds began to sing," but flowers to bloom, the sun to shine, trickling streams begin to flow. Hermy began to feel she had stepped into fairyland by mistake! After all, it was very simply explained. The short back passage ran into a beautiful little conservatory, gay with lovely bright flowers; in the centre a little fountain was playing, and several bird cages hung from the glass roof; and over all the sweet spring sunshine was brightly falling...Hermy looked all round the comfortable little sitting-room, half-library, half-boudoir – brightened by a small fire burning cheerfully in the grate, and by a glass door...letting in the sunshine and brilliance of the conservatory...

When Hermy meets Miss Lavinia here,

> suddenly something seemed to rush across her face, she gave a little cry, and, throwing her arms around the lady's neck, burst into tears: Hermy, dreamy Hermy, whom everyone set down as having no heart or affection!

Molesworth uses the house to represent the female self. The search for self-knowledge and fulfilment is like pioneering in mysterious terrain. In *Robin Redbreast* and *Hermy* the house of exploration belongs to someone else; Jacinth and Hermy examine new territory. In finding their individual self-worth and growth, they jettison the early bonds of childhood and close familial ties.

Molesworth uses Empire children, particularly girls, to illustrate the search for fulfilment. Jacinth and Hermy are homeless and parentless. While ideally, middle-class Victorian girls enjoyed a prolonged childhood, Empire children, deserted by their parents, were challenged to early independence, as Kipling shows in his autobiographical story of unhappy childhood, 'Baa Baa Black Sheep' (1888). In finding themselves, Jacinth and Hermy 'house' themselves. The prize at the end of the quest is self-knowledge, self-worth and empowerment, discovered in another home that represents the inner self, after an escape from the familial home,

Molesworth presents the house as a fount of creativity, discovery and development. The images in these texts of flowers, birds, water, scent, and sunshine portray an explosion of inspiration from interiority. The realisation of beauty in domestic settings, she infers, releases hidden potential. An exploration of the house's secrets corresponds with a journey to self-enlightenment and closure of happiness. While Ruskin's vestal temple was a panegyric to a limited vision of womanhood, Molesworth finds in the home a source of female energy and enablement. Her home is a nurturing place, a stronghold teaching strength, self-command, and with it, command.

Harvest Home

Home held no security without money. Without it single women were particularly vulnerable. 'A single woman with a narrow income must be a ridiculous old maid, the proper sport of girls and boys, but a single woman of fortune is always respectable.' (Austen, 1816). The 1851 and 1861 censuses estimated there were seven hundred and fifty thousand 'surplus' single women. Showalter points out that these women were regarded as peculiarly liable to mental disorder (1987: 61) though the novelist Mrs Craik thought lack of meaningful work led to depression or breakdown. Most Victorians, however, were wary of women making money outside the home, as this jeopardised class and femininity. By the late nineteenth century, the growing 'surplus' of single women meant that female status was as dependent upon inherited – or, rarely, earned – wealth as on class.

Married women were also insecure. Before the Married Women's Property Act (1870), a wife's money, as in the adage, 'my husband and I are one and I am he,' belonged to her husband. Patmore spells out his Angel's dependence, on her first honeymoon spending-spree.

> I, while the shop-girl fitted on
> The sand-shoes, look'd where, down the bay,
> The sea glo'd with a shrouded sun.
> 'I'm ready, Felix; Will you pay?'

The Married Women's Property Act in 1870 was a sort of trial measure, debated amid uproar and fear from both Houses of Parliament of consequent 'corruption of morals.' Not until 1882 was it amended to give a woman almost the same independence as her husband. Her income was now her own property. A separated woman had hitherto been at risk, as Molesworth, herself separated and dependent upon her earnings, must have appreciated.

In her fiction as in her own life, Molesworth's home is a means of female wealth and independence. In *Robin Redbreast* Jacinth inherits the house that helped her to be nicer, a fairy-tale reward for endeavour. Money, as Samuel Smiles's *Self-Help* (1866) demonstrates with every anecdote, lauded the rising man, the reward for Smiles's favourite virtues of industry, application, thrift, perseverance and determination. These were Molesworth's favourite virtues too, though she subjected money to classification; excess signalled *nouveau-riche* extravaganza or aristocratic libertinism. Jacinth is left just enough 'for real comfort without extravagance or display.' (290)

In *My New Home* (1894) orphan Helena is raised by her upper-class, impoverished grandmother. Grandmother had considered becoming a 'grand sort of housekeeper, which even quite ladies are sometimes,' [3] or a shop-assistant, but she doesn't want to part from Helena. Instead she makes a happy, cheap, rural home for Helena, eking out income by sewing and teaching. When Helena falls ill, Grandmother realises the cottage idyll isn't working. Now she earns by becoming a housekeeper to a cousin in London and a nurse to his invalid wife, thus able to keep Helena with her. Helena understands that Grandmother's first thought has always been to create a home for her.

In *The Story of a Year* (1910), when ten-year-old Fulvia Derwent's father goes abroad to retrieve his fortune, she and her mother leave home to live with Miss Leinster, a rich cruel miser aunt. After some dismal months, Fulvia falls ill and Mrs Derwent finds a happy new home with new friends, two old ladies, skilled embroiderers who sell their work. Mrs Derwent, hitherto a drawing-room embroiderer, is able to pay her way while Fulvia helps in the shop.

In both texts the home is a haven of love and security, presided over, like Ruskin's vestal temple of the hearth, by the mother. Molesworth goes further. Her mother-figure is not merely the presider, but creator and breadwinner. In both texts a child's illness is the catalyst of change, releasing the mothers' fierce, protective energy. The true meaning of home is, in Molesworth's view, not limiting but an instrument of female empowerment, embracing maternity, leading to enablement and financial capability.

While Acts of Parliament led to significant changes in a woman's position, education was opening its doors to women; London University began to admit women in 1878, Somerville and Lady Margaret Hall were founded in 1879; Cambridge degrees were open to women in 1881. Novels were reflecting a sense of movement. Jane Eyre and Margaret Hale, for instance, made rich by inheritance, are superior to their male counterparts. Margaret Hale, by the end of *North and South*, owns John Thornton's factories, and when they fail, he lacks the means to pay her rent. Jane Eyre's Madeira legacy puts her on a level with Mr Rochester's status. Both heroines' quests for self-fulfilment have ended in their enrichment and consequent independence. They contradict the submissive Angel image.

Molesworth's heiresses chart the changing Angel renegotiating the male/female relationship. In *That Girl in Black* (1887) Despard meets a girl in a misleadingly plain black dress. He thinks her name is Maisie Ford, that she is poor, intended to be a governess. In fact she is Lady Margaret Fforde, an heiress. Despard falls in love, but Maisie rejects him believing he only proposed when he knew who she was. Despard leaves England. Two years later, weakened, chastened, his career ruined, they meet again. Maisie realises her mistake, and proposes herself. She provides him with a job. 'All manner of things for poor people that I want to manage, and don't know how – and all our own – I won't say "my" any more – tenants to look after...'

Maisie had used the image of the Angel as a mask; she chose not to reveal her position to the easily-persuaded Despard. The Angel concept was a fiction made real by usage and acceptance. At the same time there were new examples of female capabilities, blazed by women such as Florence Nightingale and Elizabeth Blackwell in medicine, Emily Davies in education, and Josephine Butler on the double standards of morality. However conventional one's outlook, it was impossible to disregard contemporary trailblazers. Molesworth, a 'safe' writer for girls, never overtly discusses Woman's Rights but by making heiresses of her heroines, she highlights rising female status. She shows that the Angel image has become a myth – still perhaps exploitable, but untrue, paving the way to more level relationship between the sexes.

As a novelist Molesworth was an example of a woman working at home, like her friends, Mrs Craik and Mrs Humphrey Ward, and contemporaries, Mrs Oliphant and Mrs Trollope. Lady novelists were common; as Frances Power Cobbe commented 'it is now a real profession to women as to men to be writers.' (*Fraser Magazine*, 1862: 609) Poovey notes: 'if the feminisation of authorship derived its authority from an idealised representation of woman and the domestic sphere, then for a woman to depart from that idealisation by engaging in the commercial business of writing was to collapse the boundary between the spheres of male and female ideologies.' (1989: 125) Molesworth's letters to Mr Craik, her publisher at Macmillans (and the husband of novelist Dinah Mulock Craik) combine charm and commercialism as she negotiates her payments. (British Library, Folio 1 54930) She turned home – physically as her workplace and metaphorically as the scene of her domestic novels – into a fertile source of income.

Home was the birth-place of Victorian feminism. There were drawing-room meetings and lectures for Barbara Leigh Smith's Langham Place Group committee. Teas, soirees, at homes all led to the formulation of new female philosophies and action. Female networking and friendships as of Emily Davies, educationalist, and Elizabeth Garrett, doctor, crossed sections of the movement, making it more widely based. Josephine Butler's unassailable home-orientated status as a wife and mother made her an indomitable opponent of the 1869 Contagious Diseases Act. The ideology of the home was used to suggest female superior morality transposed from the domestic to the public sphere.

Girlhood, Molesworth said, was in 'a state of transition...especially as regards its upper strata.' ('English Girlhood', *English Illustrated Magazine*, 1889) By the end of the century figures show that prejudices were diminishing. By 1891 there were 53,057 nurses, the great majority of whom were trained; there were 146,375 female teachers, an increase of 66,358 since the 1861 census. (Strachey, 1978: 226)

Molesworth discusses the duties owed to independence and tradition in *White Turrets* (1895). Difficult, mannish Winifred, the heiress and artist Celia, sisters in their twenties, live in a stately home. Winifred longs to escape and gets a job in London. Wrong, says Molesworth. Her real duty is managing her estate; a wealthy girl in paid employment deprives a needy girl of a job. Winifred is disciplined by the family ghost, an ancestress who willed the house to the female line, promising doom if disregarded. The ghost, the crux of the plot, represents woe, power, stealth and home, the mixed symbols of Victorian womanhood. Forced to do her duty, Winifred's character softens, becoming more feminine with success.

Celia escapes to study art. There was a duty, Molesworth considered, to develop talent, though she limits possible outside-home careers to 'womanly' talents like art. Women artists however struggled to be taken seriously, as Helen Allingham discovered. Unlike male artists, she had to serve a double apprenticeship since the Royal Academy refused to recognise qualifications issued by the Royal Female School of Art. Celia marries; radically, Molesworth suggests that work after marriage is possible. Her friend, Mrs Adrian Hope, exemplified a similar success. She was a professional artist from an aristocratic family, painted the Royal children, and illustrated one of Molesworth's books. Celia represents the restraints and advancements of the Victorian female work ethic.

To Molesworth, however, the most important duty of all, in fact, the whole point of home – was being a mother. The matriarchal icon, like Queen Victoria, strong in her home, with widespread influence, is a frequently used image in her texts.

Queening the Pawn: The Angel and the Endgame

Queen Victoria represented a domestic creed of middle-class culture; as Lord Salisbury said: 'I have always felt that when I knew what the Queen thought, I knew pretty well what views her subjects would take, and especially the middle class of her subjects.' Her activities in public life and government (St Aubin)[4], her Diamond and Golden Jubilees in 1887 and 1897 brought national admiration; girls wanted to emulate her. A Diamond Jubilee song proclaimed

> Let ev'ry English maiden make this her frequent prayer
> That she the same high purpose with her sovereign share.

Though the Queen herself was opposed to what she called 'this mad, wicked folly of "Women's Rights"'(Longford, 1981: 9) her status and character made her a role-model of female supremacy, while Bagehot's definition of sovereignty, 'to be consulted, to encourage and to warn' turned her into the nation's mother. By the end of the century, female potential and fulfilment were encapsulated by the Queen's example.

Lewis Carroll parodies queens in his *Alice* books. 'Their pompous formality and arbitrary laws of etiquette can be seen as a grotesque version of the very proper and formal court of Queen Victoria...The King of Hearts, like Prince Albert, takes second place to his consort.' (Lurie, 1990: 22) Nevertheless, their power indicates an area of female domination that extends beyond domesticity. Molesworth's Queen Victoria-like, rich, stubborn, awe-inspiring widowed matriarchs, like Carroll's queens, reign with arbitrary rule over family and events.

Molesworth admired the Queen and the Royal Family. She often sent her children's books to the Princesses through friends of hers who were courtiers; they were apparently read with pleasure. Molesworth's letters to her friend, Mrs Du Cane, in 1893, ask anxiously for instruction in correct protocol in addressing Royalty when she sent her books. Family stories were thus written with an underlying awareness of *the* Family.

Children's fantasy literature frequently posited a goddess/queen-matriarch as an emblem of power and morality, for instance Frances Browne's *Granny's Wonderful Chair* (1856), Charles Kingsley's *The Water Babies* (1863), and George Macdonald's *At The Back of the North Wind* (1871) and the *Princess and Curdie* books (1872 & 1877). Molesworth's fantasy tales follow this tradition. Their publication dates coincide with the approach and aftermath of the Golden Jubilee in 1887, reflecting the impact of the icon-power-Queen; *Four Winds Farm* (1887), *The Children of the Castle* (1890), *The Magic Nuts* (1898), *The Ruby Ring* (1904).

Molesworth's version of maternal influence echoes that of the Queen to her people, embracing quasi-religious connotations. Mothers in Victorian children's literature are frequently holy figures: 'the God to whom little boys say their prayers has a face very like their mother's.' (*The Little White Bird,* Barrie) While patriarchal, fictional fathers were God-like, the mother was frequently Jesus-like: a symbol of goodness, doomed to untimely, sacrificial death, and worshipped thereafter, like Mrs May in *The Daisy Chain* (1856). Molesworth, in contrast, knew mothers had faults, but thought a child's trust in the mother a preparation both for the trust asked by religion and a bulwark for life's vicissitudes. Children's

> lovely belief in 'mother' is the very breath and sunshine of their lives – and the greatest possible incentive to mother herself to be worthy of this exquisite trust.

> Nor is this faith a false one. It is God-given, as a shelter and support to the infant character till the day comes when the man or woman must stand alone and see things with full-grown vision. (*Atalanta* ('On the Art of Writing Fiction for Children', May 1893: 583-6)

Her emphasis anticipates Freud's assertion that the child's trust in its mother, when fulfilled, teaches love and empathy. (1905: 145)

The good mother, Molesworth says, is synonymous with home. 'What matters most to children is not *where* their home is, but *what* it is.'(*The Carved Lions,* 1895) Here Geraldine leaves her happy home for an unsympathetic boarding school when her parents go abroad to recoup their fortune. Geraldine runs back home, even though home is 'let'. In her desperate, futile search 'never, I think, was a child's heart more nearly breaking.' (146) Home for Geraldine *is* mother. Geraldine, following Molesworth's usual pattern, finds happiness in a new, un-familial home. The trust originally learnt from home-and-mother has empowered her.

Was Molesworth's creed different from the Angel fiction? The old Angel's power was limited by home. Molesworth's own life told her a wife could be stronger and more financially reliable than a husband. Her heroines find in home self-knowledge and achievement; she shows how the Angel had spread her wings. With new legal rights, new ambitions, financial force, a public voice, she was a new phenomenon. Molesworth shows the forceful child's growth into the real woman repressed but unstoppable.

Notes

1. 'Prick' was a euphemism for the penis from the seventeenth century, still commonly used in the nineteenth century. (*Dictionary of Obscenity, Taboo and Euphemism, 1988*) Stephen Marcus (*The Other Victorians* 1964) notes the Victorians, forced by convention to omit explicit sexual references, used less direct methods to convey meaning. In saying 'prick-roughey' is disagreeable, it is impossible to guess whether or not Mrs Molesworth knew the sexual meaning, or whether she was unconsciously warning her readers.

2. Victorian women were often described sexually in terms of tea-time food: 'tart,' 'biscuit,' 'cake,' 'crumpet.' (*Dictionary of Obscenity, Taboo and Euphemism,* 1988) A woman at the tea-table, presiding over the vestal flame of the teapot (silver teapots sat on stands with a burner underneath) exemplified Ruskin's goddess of the hearth. Her tea-gown made her even more alluring...

> The woman who knows not how to appreciate the poetry of the tea-gown is either "emancipated," and therefore not worth troubling over, or has yet to live and learn, in order to taste the joys of

feminine success. [Those} who dwell on the defects of the tea-gown affirm that it must bring in its train (that very delightful *frou frou-ing* train) all sorts of immoralities; but beauty-lovers are right when they declare that it is a joy for ever. In a cotton dress a pretty woman may look charming, in tailor-made clothes delightful, in evening dress regal; but in a tea-gown she will appear just "adorable" – and what more can a woman want to be? (*The Lady's Realm,* Vol 1, Nov 1896-April 1897: 90)

3. Queen Victoria was responsible for the Public Worship Regulation Act (1874), the Vivisection Act (1874), the Royal Titles Act (1876), and the law allowing the verdict 'Guilty but Insane' (1883).

4. As, for instance, *Silverthorns* (1886), *The Third Miss St. Quentin* (1888), *Robin Redbreast* (1892), and *The Three Witches* (1900)

Chapter 8

The World of Manners

Don't use a knife when eating minced meats or curry.
Don't wear a large number of rings; it looks vulgar.
Don't use the word "dress" when you are speaking of a gown; say
"gown" or "frock."
Etiquette for Women by One of the Aristocracy (1902)

Books of etiquette, indeed ! It is only on the social stage that you
can practise. There only can you learn the "je ne sais quoi." My
dear...to the seeing eye, the manner in which you offer a cup of tea,
or accept it, is conclusive as is the formation of a flower's petal for
its classification to the botanist.
The Lady's Realm, Vol 1, Nov 1896-April, 1897: 216

Molly married the Marquis,
What a thing to do...
Now Molly went out to dine one night,
Resolved that she would be most polite,
But some of her ways were not quite right
Which rendered her husband gloomy.
When asked if she took champagne or not,
Some Benedictine or chartreuse hot,
She answered, "Oh, thanks, I'll take the lot;
A cupful of each will do me."
'Molly the Marchioness,' Music Hall song, based on the actress,
Rosie Boot.

Structure and stricture

'The English, more than any other people, not only act but feel according
to rule.' (Mill, 1869) To appreciate the rules of society that affected every
nuance of daily life is to understand middle-class Victorian thinking.
Their significance was evidence of the allegiance to duty and upward
mobility, itself an obligation. 'To push on, to climb vigorously on the
slippery slopes of the social ladder, to raise ourselves...out of the rank of
life in which we were born, is now converted into a duty.' (Froude, 1888)
'Those who ignored the system, or even worse, took a stand against it,
were seen as potentially hostile...The sanctions which could be invoked by
Society in terms of ostracism, ridicule and exclusion from sources of
power were extremely powerful.' (Davidoff, 1973: 39) The working-class

remained, as Disraeli described it mid-century, another nation; bitter, rebellious, and removed from the upper and middle-classes' acute preoccupation with social codes.

The rules stopped outrageous leaps by bounders; newly-risen families followed a blue-print code.

> It is a good thing for everyone that there are rules by which Society is held together and enabled to work smoothly...it changes very fast and you must keep up with it or you will stand out and no woman wants to attract comment, or she is not a gentlewoman. (*The Lady,* February, 1893)

Bagehot's maxim: 'The first duty of society is to protect society' (St George: xviii), applied also to its conduct disciplines. Old families had to maintain standards; new ones had to follow tradition, camouflaged in the discipline of manners. 'Manners are social control self-imposed, and etiquette is class-control exercised'. (St George: xiv) Manners were a tacit social constitution that ensured stability.

The need for stability came not only from a new fluidity in the class system, but also from uncertainties engendered by the speed of change, in which new thoughts raged against established ideas, from Darwin's revolutionary, blasphemous thesis of evolution in his *Origin of Species*, to railways and industry, Poor Laws, Reform Bills and the Working Men's College. Parents wanted for their sons 'an education which shall enable him to ring with confidence the visitor's bell at double-belled doors; in a word, which shall lead to advancement in life.' (Ruskin, 1864, 'Of King's Treasures': 5) Knowledge of behaviour gave confidence to the doorbell-ringer, establishing his status for the double-belled door-keeper. It also gave birth to the minutiae of etiquette.

> Etiquette is not a mere code of formal, foolish rules; it comprises the whole range of good manners, and consequently good breeding. (*Etiquette for Women,* 1902: 12)

Etiquette created pitfalls. Everyone knew evidence of breeding was betrayed in accent, expression, dress, gesture, reaction, even instinct. The nineteenth-century's preoccupation with class spilled into novels. As Avery notes, 'Observation of the interplay of various sections of society inspired some of the greatest English novels; the material that class structure provided is possibly one of the reasons for the pre-eminence of the nineteenth-century English novel.'(Avery, 1965, 189)

'Many of [Molesworth's] girl novels turn on small points of propriety and etiquette magnified into such importance that they can now only be read as curiosities.' Lancelyn-Green's observation (1969: 59) shows how Molesworth's novels are contemporary evidence of the way things worked. Letters to her publishers in her role as publisher's reader reveal her instinctive classic realism.

> It is really a *caricature* of a vulgar parvenue family, and yet it describes these people (people one *never* meets) as more or less "in Society"...They are supposed to be immensely rich; there is talk of a mansion in *Earl's Court*...There are other mistakes - *riding* in her carriage. (Letter to Mr Macmillan, May 15th, 1896, British Library).

The mistakes were obvious to Molesworth. No parvenue family could enter Society; Earl's Court was then an unfashionable suburb; 'you don't "ride" in a carriage – you drive.' (*Etiquette for Women* 1902, 118) Similarly

> A mistress so refined as Miss Clifford wd. certainly not have had so vulgar and illiterate a servant. No proper parlour-maid would be so common. (Letter to Mr Craik, November 6th, British Library)

Molesworth's own books comment critically on rigid class conventionality.

I am his Highness's dog at Kew. Pray tell me, sir, whose dog are you? (Pope)

Blanche (1893) shows how the rules were upheld with some desperation to confront the uncertainty caused by the crossing of barriers. The wounds of class warfare are as cruel and minutely painful as lacerations inflicted by Lilliputian swords.

In *Blanche*, well-born Mrs Derwent and her daughters move to Blissmore, her childhood village. Everyone she once knew is dead. Feudal Blissmore has changed into a town, with villas, breweries, schools and a new middle-class population. Knowing nobody, the Derwents' can't get introduced to their own – the upper – class. A grandee says 'no-one else is calling on them, and I really don't see why we need to.' They refuse to consort with the middle-class, despite their loneliness. Stasy, aged sixteen, who explodes, 'I would rather leave off being at all grand, and get some fun,' is corrected by her sister, Blanche. 'It is one's duty to live in one's own class, unless it is clearly shown it is necessary to leave it.'

Charity rescues them. They run millinery classes for the local guild girls which lets them meet their own class without any loss of face. When Rosy Milward of Crossburn wants to go to a meeting at their house, her grandmother, who has forbidden her to know the Derwents, explains, 'That sort of thing is quite different. You can go anywhere for a fair or a charity entertainment.' (183) Charity can have a dual meaning; Lady Bountiful establishes herself, as well as genuinely wishing to help. Mrs Derwent is 'delighted to be the means of giving pleasure to others. Nor was she sorry to assert her position.' She finds her twofold view logical, just as Rosy's grandmother does. The complications of nineteenth-century class were tacitly understood.

The Derwents lose their house and money, forcing them to set up in town as milliners. Their hats are wonderful; because they are ladies, their taste is considered exquisite. Suddenly they have novelty value. Smart invitations pour in. But Molesworth shows that their right to the smart circle is due as much to their breeding as their courage and self-help, when an old, titled friend finally turns up and adopts them as his heirs. Now the Derwents find the most disagreeable grandee 'not bad, after all.' Class demanded loyalty within its divisions. As milliners, though, their distinction shone like gold through disguise, like Hans Andersen's *The Princess and the Pea* (1835), described by Molesworth as 'a clever little story with a very delicate and true undermeaning.' (*Time*, June, 1888) Hodgson Burnett's *Sara Crewe* (1888) and *A Little Princess* (1902) reiterated Molesworth's theme that honourable codes of behaviour, the true meaning of 'good breeding,' must apply in adverse circumstances.

Molesworth is radical in transforming 'ladies' into workers with no loss of status. Working women were viewed with mistrust. They lost caste. Their rapacious image refuted the image of the dependent Angel and questioned the sanctity of the home. As a letter to the *Englishwoman's Journal* (1866) said: 'If a woman is obliged to work, at once (although she may be a Christian and well-bred) she loses that particular position which the word "lady" conventionally designates.' *Blanche* shows old standards applying to new situations.

Where class was in question, behaviour loomed ever more important. How did trying to behave like a lady affect a girl? What did it mean to be a 'lady'? The answers constitute the nub of Victorian female middle-class upbringing.

Tell me, is she a *lady*? (Molesworth, *Lover and Husband*, 1870, vol 3, 14)

While the aristocracy and the working-class were *outré* enough to impose their own rules, middle-class children had to behave like ladies and gentlemen. Literature reiterated these rules in text and sub-text. There is a gender-split, however. In nineteenth-century novels descriptions of men as 'gentlemen' are more overt than of women as 'ladies.' The qualities of a gentleman was a valid, popular discussion, deliberated by authors such as Thackeray, (*Book of Snobs*), Dickens, (*Great Expectations*), Mrs Craik, (*John Halifax, Gentleman*), and Frances Hodgson Burnet, (*T. Tembaron*). Smiles' *Self-Help* comprises biographies of the rising man, a phenomenon requiring definition and debate.

The rising woman, however, was hardly recognised. A Victorian woman took her class from her natal family and her husband; she seldom independently achieved a rise in status. In novels her social definition, unlike her male counterpart, seldom forms their crux. While Pip in *Great Expectations,* for instance, finally achieves new status, Jane Eyre, is restored to her rank by marriage, after wobbling on the edge of her class as a governess. Attributes of lady-like behaviour, such as the control of passion, dividing respectable from fallen women occur not in the text, but the sub-text.

Children's literature follows the same pattern. Learning to be a gentleman was the middle-class creed; as Squire Brown says when Tom goes to Rugby: 'If he'll only turn out a brave, helpful, truth-telling Englishman, and a gentleman, and a Christian, that's all I want.' (*Tom Brown's Schooldays*: 72) Susan Coolidge's definition of a gentleman in *What Katy Did at School* is typical of boys' teaching – in content, and in its overt expression.

> It's being gentle and nice to everybody, and just as polite to poor people as to rich ones...and never being selfish or noisy, or pushing people out of their place. A gentleman is a gentleman inside – all through! (1873: 152)

Girls' literature seldom openly states this basis of upbringing. Molesworth, however, stands out in underlining, in dialogue, description, text and sub-text, precisely how girls should behave, look and define themselves socially. Her fictional children's 'precocious sense of class superiority' (Avery, 1965: 169) has earned her a snobbish reputation. Her exposition of class deserves investigation as it forms the framework of her books and explains the construct of nineteenth-century middle-class girlhood.

Class structure was deeply ingrained in nineteenth-century, middle-class childhood psyche. Raverat, as a child, ridiculed her governesses. 'Some of them had Family Circumstances; and some of them had Religion as well...if you were rude or disobedient to Miss X, a governess you rightly despised, you felt rather pleased with yourself afterwards.' (Raverat, 1952: 215) Leila and Chrissie similarly insult their governess, meek Miss Greenall. (*Jasper,* 1906) They make her cry, telling her she is not a lady. Miss Greenall sobs to their mother:

> "I never have pretended to be one. Father was only a shopkeeper, and mother is a farmer's daughter. Leila said I couldn't understand what it was to have no maid – 'of course *you*,' she said, 'have been used to huddling on your clothes anyhow, - and," Miss Greenall continued, "I *know* I am not untidy, though I dress plainly. Mother brought us up to be very neat." (153)

Pretension lay at the heart of class warfare, emphasising the gap between the rising man and the status quo. Smiles links pretension with dishonesty: 'always endeavour to be really what you would wish to appear.' (236) Miss Greenall's lack of pretension is more lady-like than Leila and Chrissie's rudeness. Their mother is 'unspeakably ashamed.'

Smiles's rising man succeeds with the middle-class, Protestant work-ethic of 'sense, industry, good principles and a good heart.' (1866: 235)

> His qualities depend not upon fashion or manners, but upon moral worth. The poor man ...may be honest, truthful, upright, polite, temperate, courageous, self-respecting, and self-helping, that is, be a true gentleman.' (Smiles, 1866: 243)

Equally in Molesworth's eyes a lower-class girl could become a lady, provided she embraces middle-class behaviour and morality. In *The Rectory Children,* Celestina, the newsagent's daughter, helps Biddy, the clergyman's daughter, to be good. Celestina is quiet, gentle, thoughtful, self-controlled, the innate qualities of a lady; while Biddy, a lady by birth, is rude, lazy and heedless. The authorial voice notes the class differences: Biddy eats in the dining-room and sits in the drawing-room; Celestina has a parlour. Celestina prepares tea in the kitchen; Biddy has servants. Celestina says 'Miss Biddy.' Biddy's mother is appalled at their friendship; Celestina's father tells her not to 'be getting any nonsense in your head of setting up to be the same as ladies' children.' (11) But their friendship proves lifelong, 'a *real* friendship...friends whose love and trust in each other even death cannot destroy.' (212) As adults, Celestina becomes a French teacher at a girls' school, while Biddy helps in the parish at home. Molesworth makes a radical move in mapping their equally-based adult friendship and Celestina's rise in the world.

Similarly in *The Carved Lions* (1895), Geraldine, daughter of impoverished gentry parents who go abroad, runs away from school, finding refuge in Mr Cranston's shop. Here lies happiness and a new home with Myra Raby, the shopkeeper's granddaughter. Myra's mother, the shopkeeper's daughter, had married a clergyman, information causing Geraldine's brother to exclaim

> 'A clergyman, and he married a shopkeeper's daughter.'
>
> 'There are very different kinds of shopkeepers,' said mamma. 'Mr Cranston is very rich, and his daughter was very well educated and very nice. Still, no doubt Mr Raby was in a higher social position than she, and both Mr Cranston and his wife are very right-minded people, and never pretend to be more than they are.' (30)

Molesworth charts the merging of class boundaries. Myra and Geraldine share a home, governess, and friendship. Myra finally marries Geraldine's brother. A passage that reads snobbishly today then united trade with gentry, a revival of a more fluid eighteenth-century stance. Vickery notes in *A Gentleman's Daughter* (1998) how the vagaries of marriage, inheritance, and fortune reversal in Georgian England shifted people between trade, profession and landed gentry, blurring the Victorian precision of class division.

Wealth played no part in defining a lady. Leila, scoffing Miss Greenall's lack of maids, has missed the point. Wealth was suspect anyway. Davidoff shows how by the 1880s, agricultural depression began to undermine the landed aristocracy's economic base. Affluence and display became pointers to trade and the *arriviste*. The expensive clothes of Nurse Heatherdale's previous children, for instance, are too much: 'when you come to look *into* them...embroidery and tucks and real Walansian!' (*Nurse Heatherdale's Story,* 1891: 9), Hodgson Burnet's poor, well bred Emily Fox-Seton in last year's shabby gown, captures Lord Walderhurst's heart, despite competition from a designing American heiress flaunting her picture hat. (*The Making of a Marchioness,* 1901) Simplicity proves the lady whose essence lay not in her trappings but within.

Molesworth lists a lady's attributes for young children in *The Ruby Ring.* (1904) Sybil is transformed by magic into Matty, a gypsy. Sybil dislikes the coarse food and misses nursery meals laid with silver and a white cloth. Molesworth dismisses this as faddiness; after all, the food she is offered is wholesome. Molesworth notes critically her helplessness combing her long hair, and her lack of physical confidence, running wild with the gypsy children. But, commendably, Sybil insists on a morning wash, refuses to beg with Johnny, her gypsy 'brother' and disdains a money reward when they find a child's watch. 'I'd *so* much rather not.' She puzzles the child's mother: 'She seems to have the feelings of a lady.' (168)

The Sealskin Purse (*Studies and Stories* 1891) is a burlesque-like short story for older girls with a serious message. Upstart Nora mistakes well-bred Cecil Wode (pronounced Wood) for a nobody, and accuses her of the theft of her purse. On learning at a hunt ball how grand Cecil really is, Nora faints with shock and shame. Cecil's ladylike magnanimity keeps Nora in the place she deserves, a fall from grace, collapsed on the floor: 'Don't try to prop her up. Lay her quite flat. I will see to her.' Nora's outsider position is constantly confirmed; she doesn't know Wood means Wode; her bearing is 'a loud, rather boisterous gaiety'; her clothes are 'resplendent...prosperous-looking,' ominous adjectives redolent of opulence; her tone of voice is 'not of the *very* purest quality.' She calls her husband's cousin, Sir Edric, whom she has just met, 'Teddy.' 'Don't speak of persons by their Christian names directly you get to know them.' (*Etiquette for Women* 1902) Despite her respectable background (a solicitor's daughter) and an upwardly mobile marriage, her manner and behaviour, barometers of class, lower her. Molesworth plays a period game of class warfare, much enjoyed by its upper-class team, of unmasking the interloper.

The precariousness of class was a subject uncomfortably close to Molesworth's heart. The daughter of a businessman whose prosperity had bought his family into rural Cheshire society, Molesworth suffered from her aristocratic husband's sneers when dining with her father, 'especially if the faintest odour of Manchester shd unfortunately cling to [guests'] garments,' (Cooper, 2002: 114) she told Lord de Tabley, a close friend. Molesworth's father once sent Lord de Tabley, to his disgust, a brace of rare wild duck. Molesworth rushed to defend her father of de Tabley's accusation of toadying. 'It wd be very new to him to be suspected of anything so low & in his independent position so *absurd.*' (Cooper, 2002: 118) Harsh judgements were readily drawn. The duty of the poor was to rise; the duty of the well-born to stay put, their sport to mock gatecrashers. Meanwhile the rising class risked minefields.

How was an ambitious girl to survive the snapping jaws of upper-class piranhas? The answer, Molesworth felt, was refinement. Refinement meant self-control in sexual and social behaviour. It safeguarded a girl's modesty and purity; it meant submission to the feminine mores upheld by the conventional middle-class; it meant acceptance by the arbiters of class; it invited the possibility of betterment. Molesworth saw refinement as the salvation of women on the edge of poverty, loneliness, and respectability, and did what she could to help. She asked Mr Craik for assistance

> in the Reading Room for women students to be started in Bloomsbury...It is to be a sort of club where students, *many of them almost ladies*, can meet...Many of them lead most pitifully isolated lives and almost fall out of touch with refinement, becoming complete Bohemians. (April 17th, 1891)

'The lives of struggling women were so hard. Sometimes such nice ones went under because temptation was so great.' (*The Making of a Marchioness,* 1901) It was all too easy to fall into the slippery abyss of the seedy pit. To prevent the descent to Bohemia and the *demi-monde,* upbringing demanded instinctive reaction, so that girls behaved like ladies and were aware of the gap between themselves and the lower classes. Thus class distinctions in Molesworth's books abound, reflecting and influencing her readers. They infiltrate judgements about pronunciation. 'You mustn't get into the way of dropping your "h's," whatever you do. That matters more than baby talking; it's *vulgar,*' says an elder sister. (*Robin Redbreast,* 1892). They invade attitudes to toys and dress. In *A Christmas Posy* (1888) sisters address a disappointing new doll: 'We'll make her some new clothes, and then perhaps she won't look so vulgar.' (73) Little girls breathed in early the pointers of class.

In Molesworth's texts class and morals are equally important. 'Why should you learn to be self-helpful? Because it would be good for your own characters,' naughty Chrissie and Leila are informed. (*Jasper,* 1906, 31) Children's struggle to be good finds expression in religion. 'Saying our prayers is like opening the gate into being good,' says Beata in *Rosy* (68) 'If we do our best – what we *think* the best, that is the best; and even if we do wrong, thinking it right, it's like as if it wasn't wrong. I mean God **counts** it so,' concludes Hermy. (*Hermy,* 158) Class, morality, and religion were inextricably linked, different expressions of the same edifice of late-Victorian thinking.

Together they formed the background to the daily round of middle-class life. Representative of her class, sex and age, Molesworth presents trying to be very good as the only sure way to be happy. Thus was a girl's conscience clear, her position in society assured; her role as a woman unsullied. Molesworth shows in the strictures of upbringing, the hope that an awareness of class-obligations, a striving for high moral endeavour and an iron self-control, might help a girl to achieve, to take her place in the world, and to be safe.

****

It is hard to get under the skin of another era. The way late-Victorian girls dressed, for instance, tight-laced into corsets, weighed down behind by bustles, constrained by length of gown, gave their every movement a particular sensation. Their custom of speech, freely among themselves, and with restraint in front of the servants; the way their meals were cooked, served, eaten; their means of keeping clean and healthy, all speak of another sort of behaviour, and another frame of mind. It is only with a leap of imagination that we can make the nineteenth-century world our own.

It never can be. The past vanishes for ever, as memories die, and evidence is open to interpretation by later ages with other expectations and experiences. It is impossible to know if, in the far-off air it breathed, the nineteenth century thought with the same instincts, or reacted as we do to life, death, joy and disappointment. It is all familiar; it is all strange. If the past is unrealisable and unknowable, it is also, finally, unjudgeable. What is left? It is books like Molesworth's, with their overall and detailed picture of the precepts of upbringing, that help one to begin to understand people who were the same as ourselves, and yet profoundly different.

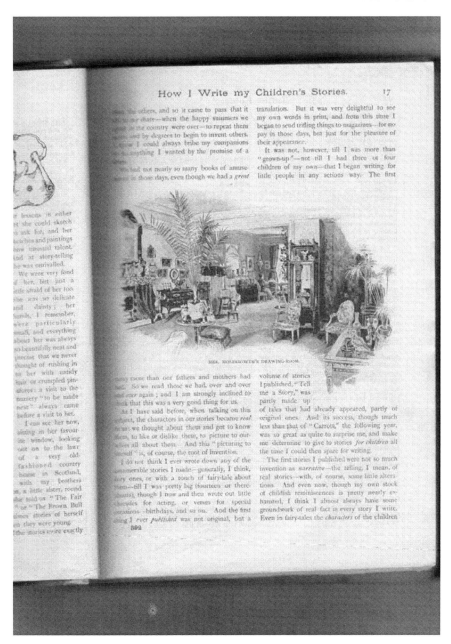

Illustration 10: Mrs Moleworth's drawing room

Bibliography

Works By Mrs Molesworth

Carrots: Just a Little Boy (1876), London: Macmillan

The Cuckoo Clock (1877), London: Macmillan

Hermy: The Story of a Little Girl (1881), London: Routledge

Hoodie (1882), London: Routledge

Rosy (1882), London: Macmillan

A Charge Fulfilled (1886), London: S.P.C.K.

The Rectory Children (1889), London: Macmillan

The Story of a Spring Morning, and Other Stories (1890), London: Longmans

Sweet Content (1891), London: Griffith Farran

Robin Redbreast (1892), London: Chambers

Studies and Stories (1893), London: A.D. Innes

Mary: A Nursery Story for very little Children (1893), London: Macmillan

Blanche: A Story for Girls (1893), London: Chambers

My New Home (1894), London: Macmillan

The Carved Lions (1895), London: Macmillan

White Turrets (1896), London: Chambers

Philippa (1897), London: Chambers

English Illustrated Magazine (1889), 'English Girlhood', October London

The Three Witches (1900), London: Chambers

The Ruby Ring (1904), London: Macmillan

The Wrong Envelope, and Other Stories (1906), London: Macmillan

Jasper: A Story for Children (1906), London: Macmillan

The Story of a Year (1910), London: Macmillan

Letters from Mrs Molesworth to Macmillan. (1875-1917), British Library. Folio 1. 54930.

Other Sources Cited

Acton, William (1865) *The Functions and Disorders of the Reproductive Organs*, London

Austen, J. (1816) *Emma*

Avery, G. (1965) *Nineteenth Century Children* London: Hodder & Stoughton

Avery, G & Briggs, J. (eds.) (1989*) Children & Their Books* Oxford: Clarendon Press

Barrett Browning, E. (1886*) Poetical Works* London: Smith, Elder & Co

Barrie, J. (1902) *The Little White Bird* London: Hodder & Stoughton

Bronte, C (1847) *Jane Eyre* London: Smith, Elder & Co

Carey, R. (1889) *Not Like Other Girls* London: Richard Bentley & Sons

Carroll, L. (1865) *Alice in Wonderland* London: Macmillan

Carroll, L. (1871) *Alice Through the Looking-Glass* London: Macmillan

Castle-Smith, Mrs. ('Brenda') (1875) *Froggy's Little Brother* London: John F. Shaw

Coolidge, S. (1873) *What Katy Did At School* London: Warne

Cooper, Jane (2002) Mrs Molesworth, East Suessex: Pratt's Folly Press

Cunningham, H. (1995) *Children & Childhood in Western Society since 1500* London: Longman

Davidoff, L. (1973) *The Best Circles* London: Croom Helm

Davidson (ed.) (n.d.) *The Book of the Home; A Practical Guide to Household Management* London: H.C. Gresham

Eliot, G. (1876) *Daniel Deronda* London: Blackwood

Ewing, J (1871) *A Flat Iron for a Farthing* London: Bell & Sons

Forster, M. (1984) *Significant Sisters. The Grassroots of Active Feminism 1839-1939* London: Martin Secker & Warburg

Foster, S., & Simons, J. (1995) *What Katy Read* London: Macmillan

Fraser's Magazine, (1862) 6th November, 609

Freud, S. (1916): *Introductory Lectures on Psychoanalysis* reprinted 1991London: Penguin

Freud, S (1905) *Three Essays on the Theory of Sexuality*, Penguin, London, 1991

Froude, J. (1888) *Short Studies on Great Subjects* London

Gaskell, E. (1852) *Cranford* Household Words.

Gaskell, E. (1855) *North and South* Household Words.

Gaskell, E. (1864) *Wives and Daughters* Cornhill Magazine.

Gathorne-Hardy, J. (1972) *The Rise and Fall of the British Nanny* London: Hodder & Stoughton

Gosse, E. (1907) *Father And Son* Reprinted 1983, London: Penguin,

Hodgson Burnet, F. (1913) *T. Tembaron* London: Hodder & Stoughton

Horn, P. (1986) *The Rise and Fall of the Victorian Servant* Gloucestershire: Alan Sutton

Houghton, W. (1957) *The Victorian Frame of Mind, 1830-1870* U.S.A: Yale University Press

Jack, F. (1911) *The Woman's Book : Contains Everything a Woman Ought to Know* London: T.C. & E.C. Jack

Jones, K. (1991) *Learning Not to be First; The Life of Christina Rosetti* Gloucestershire: Windrush Press

Kennedy, M. (1930) *The Fool of the Family* London: Heinemann

Kipling, R. (1888) *Wee Willie Winkie & Other Stories* London: Macmillan

The Ladies Realm Vol. 1. November 1896-April 1897, Hutchinson & Co, London

Lancelyn-Green, R. (1961) *Mrs Molesworth* London: The Bodley Head

Lesser, M. (1984) *Clarkey; A Portrait in Letters of Mary Clark Mohl* Oxford: O.U.P.

Lees-Milne, J. (1970) *Another Self* London: Faber & Faber

Lewis, J. (1984) *Women in England 1870-1950: Sexual Divisions and Social Change* Sussex: Wheatsheaf

Longford, E. (1971) *Victoria R. I.* London: Weidenfeld & Nicolson,

Lurie, A. (1990) *Not in Front of the Grown-Ups* London: Bloomsbury

McDonald, J. (1988) *A Dictionary of Obscenity, Taboo and Euphemism* London: Warner

Mitchell, S. (1995) *The New Girl* New York: Columbia University Press

Mitchie, H. (1986) *The Flesh Made Word* Oxford.O.U.P.

Nead, L. (1988) *Myths of Sexuality* Oxford: Blackwell,

Nesbit, E. (1901) *The Wouldbegoods* London: T. Fisher Unwin

One of the Aristocracy (1903) *Etiquette for Women* London: C. Arthur Pearson, Ltd

Patmore, C. (1909) *Poems* London: George Bell & Sons

Poovey, M. (1989) *Uneven Developments: the Ideological Work of Gender in Mid-Victorian England* London: Virago

Raverat, G. (1952) *Period Piece* London: Faber and Faber

Reynolds, K. *Girls Only* (1990) . Harvester Wheatsheaf, London.

Reynolds, K. & Humble, N. (1993) *Victorian Heroines* London: Harvester Wheatsheaf

Rosetti, C. (1904) *The Poetical Works of Christina Georgina Rosetti* London: Macmillan

Ruskin, J. (1864) *Sesame and Lilies* London: Milner & Co.

Salway, L. (ed) (1976) *A Peculiar Gift: Nineteenth Century Writings on Books for Children* London: Kestrel Books

Sayer, K. (1995) *Women of the Fields* Manchester: Manchester University Press

Sherwood, M. (Part 1,1818, Part 2, 1842, Part 3, 1847) *The Fairchild Family* London: John Hatchard,

Showalter, E. (1987) *The Female Malady; Women, Madness and English Culture, 1830-1980* London: Virago

Smiles, S. (1866) Reprinted1996, *Self-Help* London: IEA Health and Welfare Unit

St. Aubin, G. (1991) *Queen Victoria, A Portrait* London: Sinclair-Stevenson

St George, A.(1993) *The Descent of Manners : Etiquette, Rules & the Victorians* London: Chatto & Windus

Stone, L.(1990) *The Family, Sex and Marriage in England 1500-1800* London: Penguin

Stopes, M. (1918) *Married Love* London: Putnam

Strachey, R. (1978) *The Cause* London: Virago

Thomas, D. (1996) *Lewis Carroll. A Portrait with Background* London: John Murray

Vickery, A. (1998) *The Gentleman's Daughter: Women's Lives in Georgian England.* New Haven & London: Yale University Press

Westminster Review (1850), London.

Winterburn, F. (1914) *Principles of Correct Dress* New York: Harper & Brothers

Yonge, C. (1856) *The Daisy Chain* London: Macmillan

Woolf, V (ed.1995) *Killing the Angel in the House* London: Penguin

Mary Sebag-Montefiore

The Woman Known as Brenda

Liz Thiel

BRENDA (Georgina Castle Smith) 1845-1933

On January 3, 1934 *The Times* newspaper carried an obituary of Georgina Castle Smith, 'known to most of us as "Brenda." ' It was an effusive eulogy for the author who was remembered primarily for her second children's book, *Froggy's Little Brother* (1875) – and the *Times* correspondent waxed lyrical in his praise of Brenda: 'So real, so lifelike did [London's poorest children] appear to us that it seems as though [Brenda] must now be –greeted in Paradise by Froggy and his little brother,' he wrote. 'Not even Florence Montgomery's "Misunderstood" or Hesba Stretton's and Mrs O. F. Walton's stories can rend our heartstrings or move us to tears as "Froggy's Little Brother" has done.' The obituary detailed several of Brenda's street arab tales, reminded readers that the actress Ellen Terry was among those who had loved *Froggy's Little Brother* and extolled Brenda's 'deep insight and reverence for all those who serve in the Kingdom of God on earth for the very poor…for doctors, for lay-missioners and for the clergy.' Yet, despite its significant length of some eight column inches, the *Times* obituary presented what was essentially a one-dimensional portrait of the woman known as Brenda. Nowhere was there mention of Georgina Castle Smith the individual; the public face of Brenda was that of a worthy Victorian woman whose command of 'exquisite pathos' and 'gift for…sympathy' had earned her immortality.

But to characterise Georgina Castle Smith solely as a worthy creature devoted to the exposure of poverty and suffering is clearly inaccurate. She was also a Victorian woman whose writing extended beyond the street arab genre to encompass middle-class life and the social issues of class and temperance, and who chose to confront the scandal of female alcoholism in her adult novel, *The Secret Terror* (1909). Her writing career spanned some 59 years and the last of her 23 books, *Opened Doors: The Story of Sonny Baba* (1932), was published just a year before her death at the age of 88. Moreover, despite her ability to 'rend heartstrings,' her subject matter was often less than harrowing. She also wrote of Victorian middle-class childhood and did so successfully; in a rare critical analysis of Brenda, J.S. Bratton observes that 'Mrs. Castle Smith writes well when she takes the nursery child as her subject…She describes beautiful, well-cared-for children with animation and humour' (Bratton, 1981: 100).

Lamentably, Brenda's tales of middle-class life are rarely referred to in critical studies or encyclopaedias of Victorian writers. Today, best remembered almost entirely for her second children's text – as she was at her death – Brenda is consistently gauged against other street arab authors, particularly Hesba Stretton. But while Stretton is invariably praised for her genuine dedication to child welfare reform, Brenda is deemed altogether less commendable; Bratton, for example, counts Brenda among '[the] lesser writers in [the street arab] genre' and accuses her of 'falsification, sentimentality and condescension' (101). Gillian Avery, referring to street arab writers other than Stretton, speaks of those who 'one suspects, wrote up their accounts of starving crossing sweepers, waifs…and cruelly used children…from the abundant journalism of the 70s and 80s, because it was so profitable' (Avery, 1975: 117). Brenda is not necessarily implicated in her words; in fact, Avery wrote the introduction to a 1968 reissue of *Froggy's Little Brother* in which she asserts that Brenda, like Stretton and Silas Hocking, was 'genuinely moved by the desperate plight of the poor at that time' (Avery, 1968: 7). Nevertheless, this frequent comparison with Stretton implicitly diminishes Brenda's reputation and has consequently served to impede curiosity about her other writings.

First Impressions

Somewhat perversely, however, it was this distinct lack of curiosity about Brenda and her other writings that captured my interest and ultimately initiated my research. I had enjoyed *Froggy's Little Brother*, and wanted to know more about Brenda, but little information was readily available; there were only scant references to Brenda in mainstream directories. At first, I assumed that both Brenda and her other work had been subsumed beneath the success of *Froggy's Little Brother*, but later deduced that this was only a partial truth. While the emphasis on *Froggy's Little Brother* had undoubtedly impeded interest in Brenda and her remaining texts, it had also been her salvation. Without *Froggy's Little Brother*, Brenda might have been entirely forgotten.

Yet this deduction was less than reassuring. *Froggy's Little Brother* had last been reissued, but in abridged form, in 1968, and as my frequent book searches had shown, the original illustrated text was largely unavailable, other than in private collections or the British Library. The remainder of Brenda's books proved equally elusive. Despite the fact that Brenda had once been a popular children's author, she was patently fading into obscurity. My research sought to re-establish her reputation within

Victorian children's literature, and create a record of a writer whose identity and place in literary history were under threat.

A Worthwhile Subject

It was a fascinating project, and Brenda – or Georgina as she will be referred to hereafter – proved an engaging subject. While a number of her books can be categorised as street arab tales, they possess an intrinsic value that identifies them as more than Stretton imitations. Their worth, particularly that of *Froggy's Little Brother*, appears to have been recognised and celebrated by at least two prominent social reformers of Georgina's time – Lord Shaftesbury and Lord Arran. But Georgina was not only a writer of street arab tales, and as Bratton has suggested, Georgina's stories of Victorian middle-class childhood are among her more memorable texts. *Lotty's Visit to Grandmama: A Story for the Little Ones* (1877), *Little Cousins or Georgie's Visit to Lotty* (1880) and the lengthier *The Pilot's House or The Five Little Partridges* (1885) are written fluently and with obvious enthusiasm, and while they may sometimes incline towards whimsy, each demonstrates an acute understanding of the child's world. Yet they are more than simply enjoyable texts. These domestic narratives are essentially historical documents that offer valuable, first-hand insight into Victorian middle-class life. Georgina was an author whose writing supported a widowed mother and, later, supplemented her family's 'reduced circumstances', but she was also a wife and mother-of-five who drew inspiration from her own middle-class world.

Little had been published about Georgina prior to my work, other than Charlotte Lennox-Boyd's article in *Signal* (Lennox-Boyd, 1990) and I am grateful to Lennox-Boyd, whose work guided me to Georgina's great granddaughter, and so enabled me to begin my dissertation research in earnest. Since then, others have proved themselves invaluable; Georgina's grandsons, Peter and Roger Castle-Smith and Dudley Rouse, enthusiastically combed family albums and memories on my behalf. They too were fascinated by the lady who, according to Dudley, appeared stern but had something of 'a twinkle' about her (Thiel, 2001) wrote prolifically, and stored the manuscript of *Nothing to Nobody* in the small writing desk known by her descendants as 'Brenda's Box.'

Today, the desk is owned by Georgina's great granddaughter, Brenda, who is named in memory of her Victorian ancestor. It still contains Georgina's possessions, although now they are the souvenirs of her life. Some items

Illustration 11: A rare published photograph of Georgina accompanying a review of *Mary Pillinger: Supreme Factor.* Publication unknown

may have been stored there by Georgina herself, others, perhaps, by her daughter Eva, who was patently devoted to her mother, but each discloses something about Georgina's existence – from the carefully pasted book reviews to the letters of condolence sent to her husband, Castle Smith, following the death of his wife.[1] Beautifully inlaid with shell, the small, walnut roll-top desk proved to be a veritable doorway into Georgina's world, although many of its contents initially perplexed me and generated rather more questions than answers. However, despite its mysteries, some of which remain unsolved, it was a valuable resource and an excellent introduction to my subject. It was, essentially, with 'Brenda's Box' and the memorabilia of her life that my research truly began.

Notes

1. Although Georgina was known as Mrs. G. Castle Smith, her husband's first name was Castle and, consequently, was never hyphenated with Smith. Her children also used the surname Castle Smith and it was with only the third generation, Georgina's grandchildren, that the name became hyphenated.

Chapter 9

A Doorway to the Past

The family home that now houses 'Brenda's Box' might be perceived as a treasure trove of Brenda memorabilia. Framed original illustrations for *Froggy's Little Brother* are displayed just inside the front door; they were drawn by Georgina's husband Castle Smith, a solicitor and artist, who also provided the illustrations for Brenda's third children's book, *Especially Those: A Story on the Prayer 'For All Conditions of Men'* (1875). Another Castle Smith original hangs in the study – a portrait of Benny, Georgina's nurse, who gave her name to Froggy's sibling and whose likeness is dated 1876 and signed 'Cas,' Castle Smith's pseudonym.

There are books by Brenda on the shelves, mostly inscribed by the author to her children – among them an edition of *Especially Those*, presented 'To My Dearest Eva from "Brenda" ' in 1910. There are gifts too from Georgina to her husband; a copy of her non-fiction history book *Old England's Story in Little Words for Little Children* (1884) is dedicated 'To Castle Smith with Love from his Wife, "Brenda" ' and an edition of her *Victoria-Bess: The Ups and Downs of a Doll's Life* (1879) carries the inscription 'To Cas With fondest love from "Dora." ' Undoubtedly an overt reference to Dickens' *David Copperfield*, Georgina's words – the inscription is clearly in her handwriting — suggest that Georgina, like David's wife, may have delighted in her role as helpmeet to her husband, and that Georgina perhaps perceived Castle as the more creative force. It may be that Georgina tended her husband's pens and pencils as he drew, or copied out papers for him, as Dora did for David; Georgina's daughter Eva recalled that her mother's first 'scribblings' as an embryonic writer 'took the form of copying out long chapters of any author she admired'. Whatever the implications of the inscription, the notion of Georgina's creativity as secondary to that of her husband is questionable and, indeed, a large volume by the bookcase testifies to her creative and commercial success as a writer. The presentation edition of Milton's *Paradise Lost*, produced by Cassell, Petter and Galpin, with full-page illustrations by Gustave Doré, was given to Georgina as a wedding gift by John F. Shaw and Co, who published 15 of Georgina's books, including her first novel, *Nothing to Nobody* (1873), and *Froggy's Little Brother*. Shaw's gift is lavishly bound and the embossed inscription inside its front cover reads: 'To Miss Meyrick on her Marriage with the Best Wishes of her Publishers, John F. Shaw and Co.' Although records for John F. Shaw have long been lost, Shaw's generous gift to Georgina implies that the author and her works were of substantial value to the publishing house.

Pride in Achievement

Within 'Brenda's Box' lies further evidence of Georgina's success as an author. There are newspaper reviews of *Nothing to Nobody*, carefully cut out, pasted on cloth and labelled, in Georgina's hand, with the name of the relevant publication. These dozen or so reviews of her first published work are from a variety of regional newspapers and journals and each was, no doubt, avidly perused by the young writer whose identity proved of interest to more than one publication. 'Although this volume is published under the *nom de plume* of "Brenda," we believe we are not violating any confidence in stating that the talented authoress is Miss G. Meyrick, daughter of W. Meyrick Esq., of London,' revealed a newspaper identified only as 'Pembroke paper.' The *Hampshire Chronicle* of January 17, 1874 found Georgina's pseudonym altogether more intriguing, describing *Nothing to Nobody* as 'an interesting little story by a lady who conceals her name under the *nom de plume* of "Brenda." ' All the reviews are complimentary and Georgina, as a newly-published author, would have been pleased and encouraged by the comments, particularly those of the *English Churchman and Clerical Journal* of February 5, 1874, whose reviewer wrote,

> This little tale ...is admirably told, and is replete with real pathos. We have no key to the discovery of the author. 'Brenda' is probably the *nom de plume* of some young lady; but whoever she may be, this first effort of her pen should not be her last, as she evidently has (a great gift and power in a writer of tales) the art of appealing with great power, in natural and unaffected language, to the best sympathies and kindliest emotions of the human heart.

There are other reviews in 'Brenda's Box,' although and paradoxically, none relating to *Froggy's Little Brother* or to Georgina's tales of middle-class life. Her ninth publication, *Without a Reference: A Christmas Story*, published by Hatchards in 1882, was précised by *The Pall Mall Gazette* in April of that year as a tale of 'a brave woman's struggle with the world and, with what is harder than the world, a helpless husband with a turn for the bottle.' It was, declared the *Gazette*, written 'in excellent taste and with some literary skill.' *The Literary World* of December 1881 thought *Without a Reference* 'a touching and pleasant Christmas story' and *The Saturday Review* of the same month praised Brenda's writing: 'Brenda always knows how to be pathetic without being either sentimental or moralizing (sic) and consequently her stories are invaluably pleasing and wholesome,' they commented. The review of *A Little Brown Tea Pot* (1902), printed in *The Standard* and forwarded to Georgina by press cutting and information agency Romeike and Curtis, was similarly enthusiastic; *The Standard* thought it 'a very pretty story.'

While Georgina obviously treasured her reviews – many are carefully mounted to ensure their longevity – her pride in her work is most clearly demonstrated in her treatment of the numerous newspaper notices of *The Secret Terror*, her adult novel about female alcoholism, published by Stanley Paul in 1909 when the author was 64 years old. The reviews are generally no more complimentary than those relating to other texts, but Georgina's decision to mount them in a special notebook that isolates them from other reviews, suggests that *The Secret Terror* was a particular favourite. It may be that *The Secret Terror* represented a departure from Georgina's long-established style of work, or that she perceived herself as something of a literary maverick; the theme of temperance had featured in some of her earlier stories, but drunkenness had invariably focused on the working class, and this new book took as its protagonist a well-born woman who was also an alcoholic. It is impossible to guess at Georgina's own response to her work, but it is feasible to assume that her adult novel, praised by *The Scotsman* of June 10, 1909 as 'necessarily sombre…[but] wrought out impressively without sensationalism,' provided her with a sense of achievement, and that this is evidenced by the 'little black book' of cuttings that today is stowed inside her memorabilia box.

Public Acclaim

If Georgina's 'little black book' of newspaper cuttings is an expression of pride in her work, she was, without doubt, equally proud of the letters of commendation written by her readers, who appear to have ranged from Sunday School pupils to members of the aristocracy. A number of letters from eminent individuals have been stored in 'Brenda's Box'; there is a note of thanks from Victoria of Hesse, granddaughter of Queen Victoria and the grandmother of the current Duke of Edinburgh, and a series of letters from the 6th Earl of Arran with whom Georgina appears to have enjoyed a lengthy friendship. Perhaps of particular historical interest is a letter written by the nineteenth-century social reformer Lord Shaftesbury, who was largely responsible for the 1842 act forbidding the employment of women and young children underground in mines, and who campaigned for the establishment of ragged schools to provide free education for the poor.

Shaftesbury's letter, written to a Miss Eyre on January 30, 1875, but presumably forwarded to Georgina, is difficult to read; the handwriting is, at times, little more than a scrawl, and the frequent blotting of Shaftesbury's pen serves to further confound translation. But, the letter, believed by Georgina's descendants to allude to *Froggy's Little Brother*, is an altogether impressive tribute to the power of Georgina's writing. While I have attempted to decipher those words that are virtually illegible, I freely acknowledge that they may be inaccurate and so have placed them in parentheses:

> Dear Miss Eyre. The second time I have to thank you for a book. The second one will (I doubt not) – I shall read it at my first leisure – be equal to the first but that is saying a great deal.
>
> If writings such as these, produced the effect that their genius and her (persuasion) ought to command, we should see much misery and degradation erased from our land. Truly yours, Shaftesbury.

If this letter does indeed refer to *Froggy's Little Brother*, it would seem likely that Shaftesbury had also received Georgina's *Nothing to Nobody* and that this is the text he refers to as 'the first.' In Shaftesbury's campaign to improve the lives of working children, writers such as Georgina were invaluable; Shaftesbury had already praised Stretton's *Jessica's First Prayer* (Bratton: 1981: 85). Three years later, The Ragged Schools Union publicly gave their approval to Georgina's work. *The Ragged Schools Union Quarterly Record* of July 1878 featured *Nothing to Nobody* in its 'Books and What is Thought of Them' column, and the reviewer commended it as 'a touching and interesting tale' that would 'well repay a perusal.'

But Georgina's books were of interest to a wider readership and while they were useful tools of social reform, they were also deemed enjoyable by members of the aristocracy. Unlike Shaftesbury, Victoria of Hesse wrote directly to the author from Schloss Darmstadt – her family home in the small German duchy of Hesse – to thank Georgina for sending one of her books.[1] Victoria's letter reads:

> Dear Madam,
> I thank you for sending me that nice copy of your book. It will be greatly appreciated by my sister who always likes the stories you write very much.
> Yours truly, Victoria of Hesse

It was commonplace for authors to send copies of their books to the Royal household, and it may be that a text was sent to Queen Victoria and passed to her grandchildren, although Victoria of Hesse's letter suggests that Georgina sent the book directly to Germany. Lamentably, Victoria's words give no indication of which book she received and the letter is dated only May 9, but although it is apparently merely of superficial interest, Victoria's comment about her younger sister extends the profile of Georgina's readership. Victoria's sister Alix later became Alexandra Feodorovna, wife of Tsar Nicholas II of Russia, and was assassinated with her family during the Russian Revolution. It is admittedly a speculative suggestion, but it may be that the girl, who was clearly fond of Georgina's work, took her books with her to Russia, and that the last Russian Royal family was familiar with Georgina's tales.

Friendship With 'A Complete Stranger'

There was also enthusiasm for Georgina's work from within the English aristocracy. Arthur Jocelyn Charles Gore, the 6th Earl of Arran, who in 1903 became Hon. Treasurer for the Children's Country Holiday Fund,[2] apparently enjoyed a friendship with Georgina towards the latter part of her life. Having re-read *Froggy's Little Brother* after some forty years, he wrote to offer his congratulations on what he perceived as 'the most touching story in the English language' (Gore: Letter 1). Apologetic for the fact that he was 'a complete stranger' who had ventured to write to Georgina, Arran was generous in his praise of *Froggy's Little Brother*, asserting that it 'must have proved to be the most powerful agent in existence for procuring assistance to many charities for children.' In his work with the Children's Country Holiday Fund he had 'never heard anything quite so sad,' he told the author. Moreover, having been 'so struck by [the] beautiful story', he 'venture[d] to ask whether it [was] a true one' and estimated Froggy's age at 55 years.

Arran's relatively humble letter to an author he patently admired – he closed his communication with the words 'your most faithful servant' – marked the beginning of what was seemingly a lengthy correspondence. Only six of his letters to Georgina remain in 'Brenda's Box,' although their contents suggest that there were many more, and while most are dated solely by the day and month, they appear to span the years from after the First World War to 1929.[3] Arran, some twenty years younger than Georgina, clearly cherished his friendship with the writer who had, by now, entered her sixties, while she, as an elderly lady, must assuredly have been pleased by his obvious admiration. Sadly, Georgina's replies to

Arran have vanished; despite an extensive search among the current Lord Arran's memorabilia, much of which contains personal letters from the 6th Earl, no trace of Georgina has been found. But the personal nature of Arran's letters, with their detail of his own life and experiences, provide fascinating historical reading and Arran's willingness to confide in Georgina at what was possibly a most tempestuous time of his life, suggests that she provided comforting words, albeit largely, perhaps, by letter.

He wrote to her about 'the last horrible outrage of the Germans' (Letter 2) and of the burning of his ancestral home in Southern Ireland during the country's political unrest following the Easter Risings. He had voted against the Treaty of 1921 which sought to allow the establishment of an Irish Free State and told Georgina that 'he had no wish to live under a Government [that had] won its way to power through the murder of [his] brother officers and friends' (Letter 3). His news was traumatic and his correspondent was no doubt appalled by the events. Yet, within the space of a paragraph, Arran had refocused his reader on more palatable issues, commenting on the film that had been made of *Froggy's Little Brother*[4] and inviting Georgina to visit him in London for 'luncheon or dinner.'

Arran obviously perceived the older Georgina as a wise friend with whom he could share his thoughts, and a letter written in 1920, six months after their last meeting and in the wake of both the continuing Irish troubles and the First World War, would undoubtedly have been of vicarious comfort to him and might also have offered a panacea to Georgina. 'We live in anxious times,' wrote Arran. 'You and I have seen the world as it was and as it never will be again. You have the tremendous consolation of knowing that through your books you made the world better for many children than it was before, and that the result of your work will always remain – whatever upheaval may come' (Letter 4).

Closeness and Loss

There were further letters; an apology for being unaware of Georgina's visit to London and genuine dismay at having 'missed the great pleasure' of seeing her (Letter 5), and vociferous thanks for a signed copy of one of Georgina's books, although Arran fails to specify which text this was (Letter 6). This last note, written from London's Alexandra Hotel, was indicative of the close nature of their friendship; Arran spoke proudly of a woman who would appear to be his second wife, Lilian. Having suggested that he might visit Lyme Regis 'during the spring or summer', he asked for

Georgina's permission to bring his wife to see her, so that Georgina might know 'how gentle, unselfish and sweet tempered a creature' could come from St. Mawes. Arran married his second wife in 1929 following the death, two years earlier, of his first wife Maud (Tompsett, 2001). But there is no further documentation to show whether or not such a meeting ever took place. The last of Arran's letters, written in January 1934, was one of condolence and mourning that was sent to Castle following Georgina's death (Letter 7).

Arran had responded swiftly to the obituary notice in that morning's *Times* and his letter once again demonstrated his attachment to Georgina. He wrote,

> Dear Mr Castle Smith,
> I venture to write to you to try and express my sympathy at the terrible news which I read this morning in the Times. Your loss will be shared by all the thousands and thousands of readers of "Froggy" and be the cause of heartfelt mourning to those who like myself were honoured by Mrs Castle Smith's friendship. Nobody could have written "Froggy's Little Brother" who did not possess the heart of an angel of the Almighty – and I do not think that anything in English literature – even that written by Dickens – can equal the pathos of "Benny's" life and death. The description by today's correspondent of how it was impossible to read aloud "Froggy" is one which was experienced by myself when I tried to read it to my son fifteen or sixteen years ago – I could not do so without breaking down. I pray for your comfort, Yours very sincerely, Arran.

As a devoted reader of Georgina's work, Arran was not alone in suffering a sense of loss. A second letter of condolence in 'Brenda's Box' was written, possibly also in response to the *Times* obituary, by Beatrice Rochdale, wife of Colonel George Kemp, Baron of Rochdale, from her home in Lingholm, Keswick. Dated January 5, 1934, the letter is clearly a spontaneous gesture from 'a total stranger,' anxious to offer her sympathy. It reads,

> Dear Sir,
> Having seen the obituary notice in the paper of "Brenda", a name connected in my childhood with happy memories of beloved stories – I felt you would forgive and might appreciate a total stranger writing to express sympathy. I have my mother's copy of Froggie's little brother (sic) which must be over 50 years old – a book beloved by countless people. Please forgive my writing as it is an

expression of thanks which I would so gladly have given to your wife, and it was being attracted by the name of the book which made me read further. Lyme Regis I know, as I nearly always spend a short holiday each year at Axmouth.
Believe me, Yours truly Beatrice Rochdale.

There were undoubtedly other such letters, although only those from Arran and Beatrice Rochdale have survived. But someone – possibly Eva or her father – chose to retain them along with newspaper and journal cuttings that recorded Georgina's death, and stored the mementos in 'Brenda's Box.' The local newspaper notice[5] of Georgina's burial in the cemetery at Lyme Regis briefly mentioned that the deceased was 'an authoress' who wrote under the name of 'Brenda,' but devoted a greater space to the funeral service and to listing the names of the mourners – a small group, comprising Castle and his children. Another cutting, taken from what would seem to be a parish magazine, was a more lavish tribute and, in the manner of the *Times* obituary, praised Georgina's 'outstanding gift' as a writer, a gift that enabled her 'to enter deep into the heart of the very poor, and so to clothe the appeal from the lonely and the unwanted as to stir the feelings of numbers who otherwise would not have cared.' She was, said the article, a woman whose life was 'characterized by a very real Christian piety.' But as the contents of 'Brenda's Box' show, she was also a wife, mother and friend who took pride in her work and whose stories attracted a broad readership that included some of the eminent names of her day.

Unsolved Clues

While many of the items in 'Brenda's Box' are reasonably self-explanatory and clearly serve to illuminate Georgina's character and existence, others have proved more obscure, although each could ultimately provide details that would enhance an understanding of Georgina's life. Among them is a newspaper cutting from *The Standard* of September 13, 1877 referring to the death of Dr. Meyrick, a surgeon, who travelled out to the Russo-Turkish frontlines with the National Aid Society, and who died from disease in Constantinople. Information from the British Red Cross Society – which evolved from the National Aid Society – identified the young man as Francis Gethley Meyrick. Sent out to the 1877-1878 conflict, he treated the wounded near Yeni Saghra and later at Karaboundar, working night and day as one of only two doctors for an army of some 40,000 men. Buried in the British cemetery at Scutari, Meyrick, some ten years younger than Georgina, may possibly have been a cousin; the inclusion of the cutting in 'Brenda's Box' would certainly suggest a close family tie.

An equally intriguing item is the sheet of song lyrics, signed by what appear to be the initials R.K. and dated 1865. The lyrics are those of 'My Queen,' a Victorian ballad written by Jacob Blumenthal, pianist to Queen Victoria, and are part romantic fantasy, part tribute to Her Majesty. The song begins,

> When and how shall I earliest meet her,
> What are the words that the first will say,
> By what name shall I learn to greet her,
> I know not now but t'will come some day,
> With the selfsame sunlight shining upon her,
> Streaming down on her ringlets sheen,
> She is standing somewhere, she I would honour,
> She that I wait for, My Queen, My Queen.

It may be that Georgina simply acquired the song sheet, but the embossed address on the paper and the fact that it was stored in 'Brenda's Box' are undoubtedly significant. The address is that of Aynhoe Park in Banbury, a stately home and former residence of the Cartwright family. R.K. was perhaps a guest at the house as, indeed, Georgina may have been. The house is no longer home to the Cartwrights, but records show that they were absent during 1865 and had rented the house to David Fullerton, second son of MP George Downing. It may be that Georgina was invited to the mansion by Mr Fullerton and, during her stay, the unknown R.K. presented her with the hand-written lyrics of a favourite song[6].

There are other 'unsolved clues' in 'Brenda's Box' – a photograph of a late Victorian/Edwardian man; an invitation for Castle to attend a dinner 'on behalf of the Dockland Settlements' at the Mansion House in London where he would meet the Princess Helena Victoria, daughter of Queen Victoria; a sketch for a memorial stone to 'Brenda', drawn perhaps by Castle, that was never constructed but that features two small children. Also in the box is a part-review of Georgina's twentieth book, *Mary Pillenger: Supreme Factor* (1912), a patriotic story of maternal influence and the Boy Scout Movement. While the final page of the review is missing, the document may have been cherished for its illustration. The photograph of Georgina that appears on the page (see 152) is a rare published portrait of the author and it is consequently no surprise that whoever chose to place it in 'Brenda's Box' perceived it as a notable memento.

The contents of 'Brenda's Box' are sometimes extraordinary and frequently illuminating; the newspaper reviews, letters, obituaries and tidbits of

Georgina's life substantially enhance her known biographical details and give breadth to an understanding of her world. Yet Georgina's life-story, the memories of her daughter, Eva, and the reminiscences of Georgina's remaining descendants are similarly fascinating and, in conjunction with the items that lie in 'Brenda's Box,' provide a comprehensive portrait of a woman who, at first glance, appears to have led something of a quiet life. As a writer of 'worthy' tales, a supportive wife and a mother-of-five who adored her children, Georgina seems, in many ways, to have epitomised the Victorian ideal of womanhood. But to perceive her simply as a stereotypical 'angel of the house' is to disregard her individuality. Georgina Castle Smith, neé Meyrick, was born and raised in a middle-class London home and grew up in the midst of society. And, as her daughter's memoir also reveals, she was an engaging Victorian woman with a vitality and enthusiasm for life.

Notes

1. Victoria's letter is not addressed directly to Georgina, but because it is in the writing desk and refers to a female author, the recipient was undoubtedly Georgina. The letter is written on black-edged notepaper; Victoria may have been in mourning for her mother, who died when she and her sister Alix were aged 15 and six.

2. The Society was founded in 1884 and was originally named The Country Holidays Fund to Provide Fresh Air for Ailing London Children.

3. This reckoning is based on historical content and I have numbered the letters accordingly.

4. A silent film of *Froggy's Little Brother* was made by Oswald Stoll in 1921. However, Georgina was upset that the story was 'cut about,' according to Eva's notes. Apparently, Benny did not die in the film version and Arran too was unhappy at this change. 'It will reduce the awful pathos of the true story,' he wrote to Georgina (Letter 3).

5. My assumption that this cutting was from a local newspaper is based on its phraseology; the small article begins, 'The internment took place at the Cemetery on Saturday.'

6. Georgina later featured the song in *The Secret Terror*. It is performed as an after-dinner entertainment by protagonist Reine Claveryng (40).

Chapter 10

An Engaging Victorian Woman

Georgina was born on May 9, 1845, coming 'into the world,' as Eva's memoir states[1], at the family home in Cambridge Terrace, London. The Meyrick house, located in the All Saints district of Paddington, lay some three hundred metres north of Hyde Park and Kensington Gardens, and although Georgina's parents were to move home again during her childhood, they would remain for many years within the same, solidly middle-class, district.[2] The fourth of eight children, Georgina spent her teenage and young adult life at 5, Talbot Square, All Saints, in the company of her siblings, two housemaids, a manservant, a nurse and a cook.[3] While little is known of Georgina's parents, her father, William Meyrick, a London solicitor, seems to have been sufficiently prosperous to provide a comfortable home for his offspring and for his wife, Eliza, daughter of 'solicitor and agent' James James of Temple Square, Aylesbury,[4] whom he married at St. Mary's Church, Aylesbury on July 18, 1837.[5]

Family life for the Meyricks was, apparently, largely unremarkable – although, according to Eva, Georgina displayed signs of inherent 'worthiness,' even at a young age. There were trips to nearby Hyde Park with nurse Mary Bennett, or 'Benny' as she was known by the children where, says Eva,

> [Georgina's] old nurse…would often tell what difficulty she had in getting 'Miss Georgie' past a poor dirty baby in a pram – more than once she escaped Benny's vigilant eye and was found embracing – a poor…babe as if indeed it was the most beautiful thing in the world. Tears the little girl often shed at the sight of those ragged little families in Hyde Park so often in charge of the eldest brother whose care and tenderness for the baby was and still is a touching sight for the observant.[6]

Eva's memories – presumably drawn from conversations with her mother – are patently romanticised, but nevertheless provide a highly visual portrait of both the young Georgina and her local environment. Yet the image of Georgina as a child, rushing to embrace urchins in the park, contrasts with Eva's description of her mother's seemingly withdrawn early childhood. 'Never strong as a child,' Georgina was 'much hindered in her education up to six years of age by being unable to talk.' In fact, as the memoir continues, although Georgina eventually spoke, she did so with a stammer until 'a kind old friend of her mother's fresh from India took a great fancy to little Georgie Meyrick and…[spent] much time in patiently helping the child conquer her stammering tongue.' According to Eva, the lady 'never allowed her pupil to stammer over a word but made her go back over and over again till the tiresome obstacle was safely overcome.' Eventually, and perhaps fortuitously for the young Georgina, 'speech was improved and nervousness…less marked.'[7]

It may have been Georgina's 'affliction' that drew her towards the written word; Eva suggests that 'the apparent drawback' of poor speech served to develop Georgina's imagination, and that because she was 'thrown back on her own resources and amusement, she found an outlet through the medium of her pen.' An admirer of good handwriting, Georgina took to "'scribbling' with pencil and paper…shyly concealed," although her mother was clearly aware of her daughter's interest – Eva reports that '[Eliza] used to declare that she never remembered the time when Georgie was not scribbling.' At first, the 'scribblings' took the form of copying out chapters of admired authors that included Charlotte Bronte; Georgina copied sections of *Villette*. It was, says Eva, 'a form of self-education and self-preparation for the place Georgina was to take in England's literature for children.'

Torturous days

Despite overcoming her stutter – and surviving the ministrations of the 'kind' family friend – Georgina's childhood remained a difficult one. She fell prey to hay fever as she approached her teenage years, was misdiagnosed by 'the old family doctor' as suffering from a cold and was taken out into the strong summer sun and into the garden of the Meyrick's London home. As Eva states: 'The [summer], instead of being a joy, became a time of dread' and Georgina would spend long sunny days in darkened rooms, becoming 'exhausted by the constant sneezing added to a form of asthma'. Not surprisingly perhaps, the adult Georgina depicted London summers as unendurable; *The Pilot's House or The Five Little Partridges* opens with a description of a parched and airless landscape that may well be based on memory:

> The month of August had come. The London season was quite over, and the grass in the parks and Kensington Gardens was dried up and scorched to the colour of hay under the fierce sun-rays that had beaten upon it all the hot summer through. Everything looked burnt up and withered; every little blossom was hanging its head as

if thirsty…Everybody slept with their windows wide open and were thankful for the lightest breath of sultry air that came in and stirred the curtains. (10)

But there was escape from London, the hay fever and asthma, and Georgina and her nurse, Benny, were sent to Brighton, where they spent 'many happy hours' on the beach. Eva believes that 'the scenes of happiness stamped themselves indelibly on the child's…memory and…imagination' and, indeed, a certain nostalgia for the seaside permeates several of Georgina's texts. In *Lotty's Visit to Grandmama*, Lotty is entranced by her first vision of Seabeach: she wakes up in the morning to see 'the garden and the sunny beach and the blue sea coming in over the sands and a fisherman having his breakfast under the shade of an old boat' and responds by crying out, ' "Oh, how beautiful!" '(48). In *A Saturday's Bairn* (1877), the fictional town of Crabhaven is portrayed as highly desirable:

[It is] a very amusing gay place. The beach is crowded with little boats and pleasure-yachts perpetually going out and coming in. The parade is cheerful with loungers, carriages and flys; bands are playing, nigger troupes are performing…and there are all the other sights and sounds which make a seaside balcony in our childhood seem such a very delightful place…Then the drive back to Warburton along the coast-road in the evening, with the moon rising on the waters, and the lights twinkling out at sea, is so very delightful! (294)

Froggy too abandons London for the sea; in *More About Froggy: A Sequel to Froggy's Little Brother* (1914), he is lured by the call of the ocean – 'The sea was calling, calling to him persistently, day and night' (147) – and becomes an enthusiastic and well-travelled sailor. If hot city streets were an anathema to Georgina and were associated with illness and misery, then the seaside appears to have represented health and happiness.[8]

However, as Georgina grew into young adulthood, childhood ailments seem to have vanished; Eva makes no further mention of her mother's ill-health – in fact she depicts Georgina as a robust and lively young girl. A keen horsewoman, Georgina rode in Rotten Row, Hyde Park, a sandy track that was a favoured spot for Victorian society, and may also have used the women-only Ladies Mile.[9] Eva reports that Georgina's riding master was the 'well-known' William Allen and that Georgina used to love riding in the Row, commenting that 'those days everyone [was] so well turned out, a good seat and figure being…shown off by the paces of a good mount and the side saddle seat.' Eva was clearly unimpressed by more modern riding trends. She speaks disparagingly of riding astride – 'Stride legs never suits a woman [as well as] the other' – and compares her mother's 'erect' posture with 'the ornaments of present day society' who she describes as 'curved like a banana.' For Eva, 'the appalling sights to be seen between 12 and 1 in the season at Hyde Park Corner beggar[ed] description.' In contrast, Georgina was a graceful woman possessed of 'a beautiful figure' who could nevertheless have fun – albeit elegantly, according to her daughter: 'Women were wonderfully athletic despite long skirts. Georgie was a very fleet runner and used to catch up her long dress and fly lightly over the ground with very little effort, even beating her own husband.'

It may be that Georgina honed her running skills in the Talbot Square schoolroom, pitting her speed against that of her brothers or sisters, rather than those of schoolmates. She would certainly seem to have been educated at home; there is no mention of school in Eva's memoir although Georgina's brothers undoubtedly received their education away from the Meyrick household. Indeed, William Stephenson, two years younger than Georgina, attended Westminster School for two years. At 15, William gave evidence to the Public Schools' Commission and complained of the 'excessive bagging' in college of the junior boys. Lennox-Boyd notes that William Meyrick Senior also gave evidence and 'poured out' to the Commission that he had not himself been to a public school, that he had held high hopes of his son's getting a scholarship from Westminster to Oxford and becoming a barrister, and that these hopes had been abandoned when the boy was taken away from the school.[10] William appears to have gained a scholarship to Westminster which was of 'considerable importance' to his father who described himself to the Commission as 'not at all a rich man.'[11] It seems unlikely that William became a barrister; he left Westminster for Kings College, London and although little more is known of him, Westminster School records indicate that he died in South America in 1880.[12]

First Success

It was about the time of William's removal from Westminster School that Georgina herself entered society. Eva states that Georgina had to wait her 'full time' in the schoolroom before she 'came out,' implying that her mother was 17 or 18 when she began to take part in the social season. Nevertheless, despite the wait and the frustration of living with three older sisters who were already 'out,' Georgina – described by Eva as hazel-eyed, of medium height and fair – appears to have enjoyed her freedom when it eventually arrived. Georgina made her debut into society as 'quite an interesting personality, very bright and gay, fond of dancing and music' and balls 'were a delight to her.'[13] She apparently had something of 'a soft spot' for the army; Eva says that her mother would have been a soldier had she been a man. In addition, Georgina and her sister Augusta were engaged in charitable work, an occupation that undoubtedly informed Georgina's street arab tales. The sisters were, apparently, 'a much sought after couple to perform at…penny readings' for East End audiences.[14] Georgina played the piano while Augusta's 'fine contralto' used to 'easily bring tears to the eyes of those poor folk who loved the sweet old ballads and rather sentimental stor[ies] that …flowed from them.'[15] But while Eva's description of her mother's social life and charity work is both illuminating and entertaining, her memories of Georgina's literary career are less clearly defined.

Eva states that Georgina published her first story, *Nothing to Nobody*, at the age of 16 but this is undoubtedly incorrect; the book was produced by John F. Shaw in 1873 when Georgina was 28 years old. Furthermore, Eva claims that the writing desk containing the manuscript of *Nothing to Nobody* – the desk now known as 'Brenda's Box' – was lost in the move between Cambridge Terrace and Talbot Square, although this would suggest that Georgina had written her first novel at 13. However, although Eva's recollection of the dates of the move and of Georgina's literary debut may be awry, her details remain fascinating and the tale of the missing writing desk not only emphasises its importance to the emergent author, but also confirms the provenance of 'Brenda's Box'. Eva writes,

> [T]he little Chippendale desk,[16] now much treasured by her sons and daughters, containing the ms of *Nothing to Nobody* was for a time lost, or anyway, Georgie thought it was. She was loath to part with it, her great treasure, so now there was a great to do…Mr Sanderson was the kind friend who interested himself on the girl's behalf, found the desk and with her consent read the story through.

In fact, the 'kind' Mr Sanderson would seem to have been instrumental in launching Georgina's career as an author. Having read the text, he was, says Eva, delighted with the 'fresh simplicity' of it, drew Eliza's attention to it and arranged for its publication. As a result, says Eva,

> [Georgina] sprang into importance in her family circle at once and a good cheque was the result; the publishers Shaw of Paternoster

Row [were] very pleased at the good sale of the book and made it known to the authoress that they would be glad to take anything further from her pen.

According to Eva, Georgina's 'nom de plume' of 'Brenda' was chosen by Eliza and Georgina declared that it brought her luck. Whatever the case, the success of her first novel, the publication of *Froggy's Little Brother* some two years later, and her marriage to Castle Smith on October 7, 1875, ensured that by the age of 30, Georgina's life had completely changed.

A Family of her own

Georgina and Castle Smith were married at Trinity Church in Marylebone in Castle's home parish. The marriage certificate indicates that both fathers – William Meyrick and William Castle Smith – were present and that the marriage was witnessed by a William Meyrick who may have been Georgina's brother, and by Castle's 17-year-old sister, Sophia. Eva says that the marriage 'caused quite a sensation in Georgina's circle and beyond' and that her mother often told of 'that sparkling morning…when, after the service, she and her husband came down the church steps to find a very large crowd struggling to catch a glimpse of the young author, a radiant bride.' The couple honeymooned in Venice; Georgina had travelled only a little and 'it was a great pleasure to her husband to see her delight in the beauties of that water city.'

Castle, born on May 17, 1849 at New Broad Street in the City of London, and a solicitor like his father and father-in-law, was also an accomplished artist; he provided the illustrations for *Froggy's Little Brother*, and Eva notes that 'Father did the wood cuts' for Georgina's most famous tale. It is unlikely that Georgina was living in Talbot Square when the couple married. As Lennox-Boyd points out, the Meyrick family had moved out of the London directories by 1872 (116) and their later whereabouts are as yet unknown, but it may have been during the period following her marriage that Georgina's father died and her writing became more than a pleasurable pastime. Eva writes that although Eliza was 'left badly off as a widow,' Georgina was 'a devoted daughter'; 'her pen was often the means of adding to her aged mother's comfort up to the time [Eliza] died'.

Georgina and Castle began their married life in Avenue Road, Hampstead, and Eva remembers the period in the 'little bright house' as a most happy time. Georgina's children were raised in an atmosphere that was obviously enjoyable if fairly strict; Georgina apparently became 'a pastmaster at the

169

arranging of children's parties…A Xmas tree, sometimes, or a conjuror from Whiteleys, or great delight [and] surprise a real Punch [and] Judy show erected in the drawing room,' recalls Eva. And despite the fact that Georgina could often be found 'sitting in the big arm chair surrounded by MSS, cuttings, notes, etc [and] a huge ink-pot [and] quill pen,' she found time to educate her daughters in both needlework and selflessness. Eva notes,

> Her dolls dressed by her own clever fingers as court ladies were covetted (sic) by all the little girls. Her own two small daughters were often taught unselfishness on these occasions. They were never allowed one of these dolls, but were taught to present them to their girl friends with a good grace…We were disciplined in those days.

Eva's portrait of her mother suggests a busy but rewarding life that allowed Georgina to enjoy motherhood and simultaneously fulfil her artistic desires. Castle appears to have been a supportive husband; Eva tells how Georgina sewed 'continuously' for her young family while Castle often cut out the 'little outdoor coats.' As an artist himself, Castle was undoubtedly sympathetic to his wife's literary ambitions; although he practised as a solicitor, the many works of art that have survived indicate that his true love lay not in the law, but in artistic creativity. As well as illustrating *Froggy's Little Brother* and *Especially Those: A Story on the Prayer 'For All Conditions of Men,'* he painted a portrait of his wife, shortly after their marriage,[17] and, probably during his later years, painted watercolours and carved paper knives – which remain within the family.

Later years

In 1905, the family moved from Avenue Road, to Netherhall Gardens, Hampstead; the house in Avenue Road was demolished in 1906 to make way for a block of flats. By this time, the three boys had completed their schooling at Upgrants, Westminster and Georgina had published some 18 children's books. There are few details from this period in the Castle-Smith family archives, but the small collection includes holiday 'snaps.' Georgina, Castle and their children had initially favoured Deal in Kent[18] as their summer holiday resort, but later spent their vacations at Seaview on the Isle of Wight. The island had become a fashionable holiday spot for the late Victorians; Queen Victoria bought Osborne House in 1845 and she and her family were often in residence during the summer months, while her youngest daughter Beatrice continued the royal patronage by regularly visiting Carisbrooke Castle in the early 1900s.

It was during one of these seaside holidays that Georgina's daughter Lucy met the young man she was to marry. Lucy's son Dudley Rouse recalled that his father's family used to holiday in Bembridge, just south of Seaview, and that one of his father's brothers told Athol of '...two beautiful girls' at Seaview.[19] The girls, it transpired, were the Castle Smith daughters, Lucy and Eva, and although, according to Dudley, Eva was perceived as the more beautiful, Athol chose, and later married, Lucy at St. John's in Hampstead.

Illustration 12: Georgina at the Rouse family home, 1931. Picture: courtesy Dudley Rouse

More difficult days

Although Georgina and Castle had no doubt enjoyed their holidays on the Isle of Wight with their children, their final visit to the resort was possibly less joyful. Their finances had suffered a blow and while this period of their history is obscure, Dudley, the eldest of Georgina's surviving grandsons, believed that Georgina and Castle lived in rooms at Craigmore, Fairy Road, Seaview, prior to finally moving to Lyme Regis; he remembered staying with them on the island in 1918 when he was a small boy. There had clearly been a crisis of some sort, but whatever the cause, Georgina and her husband became financially dependent on their sons although Georgina was still writing; six of her books were published during the period 1901 to 1932, including *The Secret Terror*. Nevertheless, according to Peter Castle-Smith, Castle was supported by his sons for the remainder of his life, principally by Hugh, the eldest.

It was through the auspices of the three boys that the Castle Smiths became resident in Lyme Regis sometime around 1920, living first in Bradford House and then moving into The Corner Cottage in West Hill Road, a house that had been built for them and paid for by their sons.[20] Their unmarried daughter Eva accompanied them and lived with her parents until their deaths, continuing to live at Lyme Regis, although not in The Corner Cottage, for her remaining years. There is very little information about the Castle Smiths' retirement; despite extensive research in the Lyme Regis area, no further details have been forthcoming. The couple seem to have lived quietly, no doubt attending St. Michael's Parish Church where Georgina's funeral was held, but otherwise blending unobtrusively into the local community.

Georgina's last book, *Opened Doors: The Story of Sonny Baba*, a religious tale with roots in Britain's colonial past, was published the year before her death at The Corner Cottage. The story is largely unremarkable, but for Georgina to have written such a novel at the age of 87 was, in itself, surely an accomplishment. A published author for some 59 years, she had, during her long life, combined her literary skills with the duties of daughter, wife and mother-of-five, had suffered 'reduced circumstances' and, finally, had retired to a quiet seaside community worlds away from the London of her girlhood. Her final resting place in the cemetery at Lyme Regis is as unobtrusive as Georgina appears to have been in later life, but gives no clue to her versatility – as either an author or a woman. The inscription on her tombstone simply reads:

In Memory of Georgina Castle Smith
"Brenda"
Author of "Froggy's Little Brother"
Died December 27 1933
Their Works Do Follow Them

Linked in perpetuity to *Froggy*, despite her many other texts, Georgina will thus always be remembered for her work about the children of the slums.

Notes

1. Eva's hand-written memoir is undated, but its inaccuracies suggest it was never read by Georgina and so may have been written after her death. It ends abruptly and there is little mention of Georgina's later life.

2. The assumption that All Saints was a respectable middle-class area is based on Booth's 1839 Descriptive Map of London Poverty. Cambridge Terrace no longer exists; it is now known as Sussex Gardens.

3. Lennox-Boyd's information about Georgina's household is taken from the London census of 1861.

4. *Surname Index to Robson's 1839 Directory of Buckinghamshire Names.* http://www.met.open.ac.uk/genuki/big/eng/BKM/Directories/bucksdirg.html. Accessed 15.10.01

5. Marriage details of William Meyrick and Eliza James from *Family Search*. www.familysearch.com. Accessed 12.10.01.

6. Eva comments that, in later years, 'Brenda' used to hold that boys made the best and kindest mothers. Froggy, of *Froggy's Little Brother*, would seem to exemplify that notion.

7. The corrections to Eva's memoir suggest that dogged persistence, rather than gentle persuasion, was employed to correct Georgina's speech. The teacher was originally described as a 'kind' friend of Georgina's mother, but the word 'kind' was deleted.

8. For a further exploration of Georgina's seaside writings, see Chapter 12.

9. Information about Rotten Row from D. Pool (1993) *What Jane Austen Ate and Charles Dickens Knew*. New York: Touchstone (51).

10. Lennox-Boyd, 14.

11. Lennox-Boyd, 14.

12. My thanks to Charles Kidd of Debrett's for this information.

13. It is unlikely that Georgina was presented at court. Charles Kidd confirms that only the daughters of gentry were officially allowed this privilege, although impoverished aristocrats sometimes arranged presentations of middle-class girls for a fee.

14. Eva does not specify the dates of performances, but it is probable that they were prior to her marriage.

15. Georgina may also have written songs. The British Library catalogue lists a Georgina Meyrick as the author of a ballad entitled 'In this bark, sweet Mary,' published 1865.

16. See introductory chapter.

17. Eva mentions this portrait in her memoir and describes her mother's face as 'full of life, humour and observance.' Unfortunately, none of Georgina's descendants know its whereabouts.

18. Georgina's *The Pilot's House or The Five Little Partridges* clearly draws on memories of family holidays at Deal. For more information, see Chapter 12.

19. L. Thiel. Interview with Dudley Rouse.

20. L. Thiel. Interview with Dudley Rouse.

Chapter 11

The Children of the Slums

Georgina may well be remembered as a writer of street arab stories, but, in reality, only three of her texts, *Nothing to Nobody*, *Froggy's Little Brother* and the later *Wonderful Mates* (1900), conform in any substantial way to the formula established by earlier writers of the genre. Her other stories of childhood poverty – *A Saturday's Bairn* (1877) and *Uncle Steve's Locker* (1888) – incorporate elements of the street arab style to varying degrees, but, overall, Georgina's classification as a typical street arab novelist is debatable. Her tales are replete with Christian emphases but sometimes seem to lack the religious certitude characteristic of the genre; her protagonists' release from wretchedness is more dependent on the auspices of a human being, or on chance, than on spiritual succour. Moreover, although Georgina apparently strives to portray Christian death as a 'beautiful' event in *Nothing to Nobody* and *Froggy's Little Brother*, she is ultimately unconvincing – although this may, on occasion, be deliberate. Although Georgina was a Christian, she was also a social commentator, and evidently perceived human intervention as the solution to the miseries of slum life, rather than blissful demise.

The 'fashion for the slum background' (Avery, 1975: 117) in children's literature, of which Georgina was clearly a follower, arose in the mid-1800s in response to prevailing social concerns. By the 1840s, social reformers had exposed the horrors of child labour and had begun to focus on the plight of the inner city poor. Henry Mayhew's *London Labour and The London Poor*, a series of articles published in volume form in 1851/52 and 1861/2, is the most famous social study to emerge from this period, but journalist John Hollingshead, commissioned by the *Morning Post* to investigate the impact of the harsh winter of 1860/1861 on the labouring poor, produced a series of articles that ultimately formed the basis of his *Ragged London in 1861* – a book that was less intentionally shocking than Mayhew's, but was, perhaps, more insightful. Hollingshead resisted Mayhew's impulse to sensationalise; instead he offered a detached, factual tone that lent his words a stark reality, and his description of the inhabitants of the Shoreditch area, where Georgina's Froggy was to be located some 14 years later, was highly disturbing. However, and despite its horrors, Hollingshead's report on Shoreditch captured a sense of the generosity that could be found amidst the squalor – a generosity that Georgina frequently acknowledged in her tales of London poverty. Hollingshead wrote,

> Within a few doors of [an illegal sporting theatre] is a family who were found …without food, without fire, or any other necessary, in a room nearly bare, their furniture having been seized for rent. There were a father, mother, and several children standing shivering within the bare walls, the children having nothing on them but sacks tied round their bare waists…In Old Nichols Street, a turning in this district leading off from Shoreditch, we have a specimen of an east-end thieves street…its houses are black and repulsive…Even here [however]…there is something to admire. A woman…has picked an orphan boy from the streets, and given him a place among her own children. The boy was tossed about for many days…until he found a home with people who were nearly as poor as himself. (41)

It is possible that Georgina visited the slums of Shoreditch; she performed penny readings for East End audiences and her comments in *A Saturday's Bairn* suggest that she visited the homes of the poor (see 212). But it is also likely that Georgina, as an educated middle-class woman, was a reader of Dickens' social commentary novels and that she was familiar with the work of Mayhew and Hollingshead by 1873 when *Nothing to Nobody* was published. Whatever her sources, her portrayal of slum housing in *Nothing to Nobody* is seemingly informed by fact: Mary's home is 'a very old [house], in bad repair…on each floor [there are] one or two families, so beneath this roof there [sleeps] at least forty persons, every night' (18). Furthermore, the book's implicit compassion for the inhabitants of the slums, coupled with its ambivalence towards premature death, suggests that Georgina was more concerned with life on earth than with the consolation of heavenly reward.

A Waif and Stray

Nothing to Nobody opens with a description of the weather and locality in which the story is to unfold:

> It was a Sunday afternoon in London; a cold, dark, miserable afternoon late in November. At three o'clock in the city, near the river-side, there was hardly a person to be seen in the streets. The fog was getting so thick and yellow that everybody whose business obliged him to be out was hurrying along as fast as possible. (1)

No one should be outdoors on such an afternoon, but Barbara Russel, Sunday school teacher and daughter of a clergyman, hurrying to her teaching duties, encounters 'a ragged child, with only half a bonnet on and no shawl' cowering in the doorway of a shop, 'the chin of her pale wretched face almost touching her knees, as if she were trying to keep warm' (3). The 13-year-old waif Mary Sulivan, nicknamed 'Daddy Long-legs' because of her lengthy limbs, is an honest creature; she alerts Barbara to her presence by telling her that she has dropped 'her handkercher' (3). Barbara, possessed of a 'kind warm heart' and a 'divine charity' that forbids her from leaving the 'poor waif and stray on the door-step,' invites Mary to Sunday school, and, although Mary declines – ' "I should *hate* school," ' she says – Barbara promises to see her again (7). There are several Dickensian-style sub-plots before the story concludes, but ultimately, Barbara introduces Mary to Sunday school, Jesus, the seaside and her own household where Mary is finally engaged as a servant by 'kind, dear, old' Mrs. Bush (133), the faithful housekeeper, and becomes 'something to somebody' at last (142).

Mary's escape from poverty and wretchedness is clearly the result of human intervention, but the narrator insists, in the final pages, that her happy condition has derived from learning 'to love Jesus' (176). It is a comment that sits awkwardly within the text and it is ultimately as unconvincing as Georgina's portrayal of a supposedly 'beautiful' Christian death. Jem Russel, Barbara's young sailor brother, mortally wounded as he swims to save another man, gasps, ' "It's very hard – dying" ' (126) to his assembled crewmates, although the text stresses that it 'was no fear of death that made him clutch the captain's hand so tightly; it was only that life was still so strong within him, his spirit had to struggle to get free' (125). The captain of Jem's ship presses Jem's hand and utters, "He that believeth in Me shall never die!" (126), but his desperate attempt at consolation fails to diffuse the horror of the moment. It may be that Georgina, like the captain, sought solace in religion but lacked conviction; the sometimes unconvincing nature of her religious emphases suggests a striving for belief, rather than a reiteration of unshakeable views.

An Indictment of Society

Although Georgina's religious emphases may have sometimes appeared unconvincing in her debut tale, she had obviously consolidated her thoughts prior to writing her second book. Like *Nothing to Nobody, Froggy's Little Brother* is ambiguous in its attitude towards death – but *this* ambiguity is altogether more purposeful. Despite being positively awash with Christian dogma, the death scenes in *Froggy's Little Brother* remain distressing to the reader; Benny's 'beautiful' dying moments are particularly harrowing:

> "Froggy darlin', I dreamt I was dead and gone from here. I think I
> was in heaven, cos there was angels and all the little children's
> faces was bright and there was no tears. Nobody seemed hungry
> and nobody seemed thinkin' about their rent"...At last Benny's sobs
> grew gradually less, and Froggy felt that by degrees Benny's little
> arms were loosening about his neck, as if he would shortly fall
> away from him..."Yes, Froggy, I can hear the angels singing'
> again!" said Benny faintly, and a peculiar light shone over his face.
> (204-5)

Had she been writing some fifty years earlier, Georgina might have
concluded her tale by affirming that a 'beautiful' death was highly
desirable for both the deceased and his mourners. But, unlike the authors
of comfort tales for children, she offers no celebration of Benny's passing.
Instead, the comment that follows Benny's last sigh is a clear indictment
of an uncaring society: 'There was nothing else to tell that in London's
sorrowful army of starving, struggling people, another little sufferer had
fallen out of the ranks, because there seemed no room for it here' (206).
Delivered in the same gentle voice as Benny's last moments, it is a
criticism that is all the more effective for its muted tones; the content of
the statement is in stark contrast to its delivery. And the fact that Benny
has gone 'to be consoled and comforted for ever more in the bosom of
[his] Saviour' (206), is a similarly ambiguous remark. Georgina, as author,
might well have believed in everlasting life, but her use of such a
placatory statement at this juncture may be a deliberate attempt to expose
the inherent hypocrisy of a society beset with religious platitudes.
Although the prospect of eternity in Jesus' bosom was unquestionably
desirable to her readers, even glory itself seems inadequate compensation
for Benny's harsh, needlessly short, life.

A Sprinkling of Guilt

There are other, more explicit, asides to the reader within *Froggy's Little
Brother*. While *Nothing to Nobody* had offered only tentative and largely
implicit authorial comments, Georgina appeared to find her voice in her
second novel which may, in part, explain its potency and enduring
success. Moreover, she had earmarked the audience for whom she was
writing – an audience that was potentially influential and capable of
orchestrating social change. In the first page of *Froggy's Little Brother*,
she identifies her reader profile: 'Every morning [Froggy and his family]
used to sally forth from their home in Shoreditch to go to wealthier
neighbourhoods, where people could afford the luxury of *Punch*' (8). Her
reader is not only familiar with Punch, he is also an individual who

disdains rags; 'even *rags*, my little readers, are precious things in some homes!' she says (10). In addition, he may be a child – or adult – who laments the 'dullness' of Sundays. The narrator asks, 'Do we ever think enough of its preciousness to weary workers when sometimes Sundays are called *dull* days in luxurious homes by people who are idle, or only idly busy, all the week?' (11). Thus having identified the reader, addressed him and sprinkled him with guilt, Georgina allows the story to unfold.

Throughout the tale, the narrative voice intervenes to emphasise the plight of the poor and to give it relevance to the middle-class reader's life. When Froggy's father dies and the boys become orphans, their friendless state is emphasised and linked to the reader's everyday reality:

> What a sad reflection – motherless, fatherless, and friendless! But so it was; and this is the condition of hundreds of our poor little brothers and sisters in great London. Let us think of this next Sunday when the petition comes in our beautiful Litany, "That it may please Thee to defend and provide for the fatherless children and widows, and all that are desolate and oppressed!" (37)

And this same voice intrudes into the narrative to contrast the children of the slums with traditional visions of childhood:

> Froggy was but eleven, and he should not have been feeling like an old tired man…London has nothing more sorrowful to show us…than its old children…[on whose faces] hard Care is stamped, instead of the glad expectancy and joyous carelessness which we generally associate with childhood. (99)

Finally, in the closing pages of the book, comes a direct appeal to 'parents and little children', especially those 'who are rich' (222). It is unashamedly manipulative, reminding readers of Judgement Day as it requests financial help for 'schools, and Homes and Kindergartens', and is self-consciously biblical in tone; there is talk of hoping 'to partake of the same citizenship in the one Everlasting City', and of being content to wait for reward 'till that Day when the truth of the saying, "Cast thy bread upon the waters and thou shalt find it after many days", shall be manifested to us' (223).

The closure of *Froggy's Little Brother* is immensely persuasive and no doubt procured additional funding for the various children's charities of

Illustration 13: Froggy dreams of happier days. Illustration by Castle Smith from *Froggy's Little Brother* (n.p.)

the day. Georgina had identified and directly addressed a specific readership and, having found her voice and target audience, proceeded to write further tales of social deprivation. She seemingly made little attempt to identify with a working-class readership, although her books were frequently presented as Sunday school prizes; indeed as author of *Froggy's Little Brother*, she has been criticised by Bratton for assuming that 'the reader is well-off, comfortable [and] completely insulated from the story' (100). But it is, perhaps, an assumption that Georgina, as a middle-class woman, was entirely qualified to make. And although, as Bratton suggests, a ragged school child might have found *Froggy* a 'sham' or an 'insult' (100), Georgina's plainly sentimental but powerful tale was a success with the affluent classes for whom she continued to write.

Striking Contrast

Georgina chose to focus – at least initially – on the children of those affluent families for her third story of childhood poverty. *A Saturday's Bairn*, published two years after *Froggy's Little Brother*, is, like *Nothing to Nobody*, a rags-to-relative-riches tale, in which 13-year-old Jean Hart, her widowed mother and family, are deprived of their legacy by an unscrupulous relative, rescued from the grime of 'Baxter's Court,' reunited with their lost funds and transported to 'a pretty little house' at Crabhaven (367) through the auspices of philanthropic Lily Duberly. Jean and her mother are Christian souls; despite her poverty, Mary 'keeps the eye of faith fixed steadfastly on the Saviour' (28), and she and her daughter cherish the religious scroll hung in their hovel by 'loving fair-haired' visitor, Lily (29). Moreover, Jean preaches at the water pump about 'the well that *never* fails' (57) and contends with abuse from less worthy 'locals' as she does so.

Although the emphasis of the tale is very much on poverty, its effectiveness derives primarily from the structure of its opening chapters; the story begins in the luxurious nursery of six-year-old Musgrave Warburton of Grosvenor Square and his older sister, Meta, and then subsequently focuses on the poverty of Jean. Introduced as 'a rebellious little couple' (2), Musgrave and Meta are as mischievous as Jean is good, and Musgrave is entirely ungrateful for the food that would nourish Jean and her family; in fact, he throws a bag containing his dinner of Yorkshire pudding and potato out of the nursery window (15) where it is found by Jean as she gathers logs in Hyde Park. As the story progresses, rich and poor lives are brought into ever-closer play: 'Long before Meta and Musgrave were out of their little dainty muslin-hung beds, or had even opened their eyes, Jean had washed [clothes]...scrubbed the floor, washed the baby and little brother Jack (46). Eventually the Grosvenor Square children and Jean and her family make contact, although not directly; their cousin Lily, the Hart's visitor, tells Musgrave and Meta about the Harts, and, having overcome his prejudices about the poor and their propensity for crime, Musgrave offers to send chocolate creams and his 'new little steam engine that goes by clockwork' to Jean's little brother Jack (224).

Georgina is patently critical of affluent society in this tale, but her criticism is aimed specifically at ingratitude or ignorance. Despite their naughtiness, Musgrave and Meta escape any real reprobation; Georgina had given birth to her eldest son Hugh the previous year, and she had evidently become enamoured of motherhood. Talking of Sunday morning in Grosvenor Square, she describes Musgrave and Meta's preparations for the day, commenting; 'A *fresh* little couple they look this morning when they are finished. I think Aurora must pass by sometimes and give little children a kiss before breakfast, or they would never look as suggestive of cream and roses as they do' (204). However, while her fictional children escape severe criticism, they provide the author with the opportunity to remind the reader of his own fortunate state – and be grateful. Having described Jean's poverty, the narrator states, 'Oh think of this, little children, the next time you are tempted to grumble because there is only Yorkshire or rice pudding for dinner' (44).

More substantial criticism is reserved for the adult reader and *A Saturday's Bairn* is notable for its authorial condemnation of those who seek to do good works, but behave thoughtlessly. In what is essentially a three-page lecture on visits to the poor, the author advises,

> [The] nerves [of the poor] are often strung at a painful tension from a hundred worries and anxieties that we know nothing about, and makes them keenly sensitive to all outward influences. Without intention, it is easy to ruffle them; but then, also with consideration, it is easy to soothe them; and *soothing*, not ruffling, should be one of our first cares towards our poorer brothers and sisters, whose lives very often are one vast struggle from cradle to grave...I have seen people [really kind-hearted people sometimes] go into the homes of the poor and pick their way about, with silk dresses caught up...as if they were treading on hot bricks all the while...and then I have heard them wonder...why the poor are always such a grumpy, unget-at-able set. (251)

Fascinating in content, the episode is also indicative of Georgina's own involvement in home visiting, and demonstrates her desire to influence a readership whose culture she shared. As author, she may have striven to raise awareness of childhood poverty, but it would seem that she also felt moved to improve the social skills of the rich.

A More Traditional Format

With *Uncle Steve's Locker*, published 11 years later in 1888, Georgina returned to the slums of London and to her more traditional format. The tale tells of young Dorothy, whose loving aunt is forced into the workhouse and sends her niece away from the city to live with her uncle in his 'boat-hovel' by the sea. While she is at Kale, Dorothy, assisted by the children of the local gentry, uncovers truths that clear her father's name and reclaims a bag of rubies that is her birthright, thus ensuring both her own future and that of her aunt. The religious emphases of Georgina's earlier work remain – Dorothy's middle-class London relatives are less than Christian towards their impoverished niece while her aunt Betty, dressed 'in a [tattered] purple gown to celebrate the Eve of the Nativity of Christ' (16), is comforted in her poverty by her belief in angels and by the notion that 'in the evening time there shall be light' (35).

Georgina's agenda as author of *Uncle Steve's Locker* is similar to that of her other tales of childhood poverty; she draws the reader's attention to the appalling conditions in which Dorothy and her aunt live and implicitly pleads for compassion. However, in this text she also focuses on the duty of parents and those who instruct children. Four years before the publication of *Uncle Steve's Locker*, Hesba Stretton had helped found the London Branch of the National Society for the Prevention of Cruelty to Children and Georgina, as narrator, identifies the 'root' of the problem as a lack of early education. Dorothy's kindly Uncle Steve is abused by local boys because he is 'old and poor and defenceless' (209), and, having described their attacks, the narrator proceeds to broaden the subject.

She asks,

> Is there anything on earth more pitiless and cruel than a cruel boy?...In many instances, in most, I am inclined to think, this cruelty arises from want of thought and early teaching. How often we see mothers and guardians...not confined by any means to the lower strata of society, allowing to pass unnoticed the reckless stamp of the small foot on the worm in its path...[societies such as the NSPCC] are good, and do a noble work; but if we want to pluck

> the evil they fight against out by the root, we must aim at the *young*
> of the land, inculcate early in the well-to-do nurseries…that it is a
> base…thing to hurt, to harass, to hunt, to render unhappy anything
> that has *life* in it, of whatever degree. (209)

Although escape from poverty remains central to her text, Georgina's comment, addressed directly to her reader, would have given her tale a contemporary significance. Social comment had long been a feature of her stories, although she had dwelt primarily on the sufferings of the poor. *Wonderful Mates*, published in 1900, continued both traditions.

Like Dozens of Other Little Boys

The central protagonist of *Wonderful Mates* is Sposh, whose nickname derives from his occasional job as a newspaper vendor at Waterloo Station; his cry of 'special edition' becomes muddled, emerging instead as ' "Sposh dishun!" '(35). Discarded by his step-family, Sposh is described as being 'like dozens of other little, half-fed, growing London boys' (27). He is evicted from home and becomes resident in a condemned house which he shares with a black cat, a former tenant, whose 'love for its old tent [was] so strong upon it that miles of distance could not keep it away' (14) and befriends Sarah of Slum Passage, a cheery child, who educates him and whom he eventually marries.

While the story, in typical Georgina fashion, is one of rescue from the slums and achievement of a better life through chance and moral rectitude, it is also a criticism of thoughtless bureaucracy and of the evils of drink – although the two are tackled quite separately. The visit from the 'responsible-looking gentlemen in black coats and tall hats' (9) that introduces the story, is an indictment of government without compassion or forethought; the tenants of the buildings they subsequently condemn are ordered out without delay. Not surprisingly, 'the inhabitants [feel] as much put about as if they had been told to prepare for an earthquake' (10); the condemned buildings are their homes. But the authorities are portrayed as unsympathetic. In boarding up the houses, 'they meant…that no home-sick persons should creep back – "sentimental rubbish" they would have called the ache that could have brought anyone back to such a place' (13).

Criticism of such a system was undoubtedly relevant at the time; towards the end of the century, London was engaged in a controversial slum clearance programme that frequently led to more overcrowding and squalor. However, although the narrator is clearly unhappy with the brutal demolition of the slums, she reserves her true vitriol for the evils of drink. Sposh and his sister are sent to collect a jug of beer from 'The Goat and Compasses,' a public house whose name, Sposh later learns, has evolved from the expression 'the Holy Ghost encompasses us' (26) – and the narrator is spurred into violent criticism by the notion of children entering such premises. She states: 'Oh! The wickedness of ever sending little children into [the gin palace]. Many a father and mother could trace the downfall of some bright dearly-loved boy or girl in after years to their having put a jug once into the hand of a little child!' (26). Indeed, drink is the cause of Sposh's mother's downfall, although she, too, is a victim. Unequal to arguing any more with 'her big, rough, drinking husband' (23), and shut up in London, away from the 'salt breezes and fresh thoughts' of her previous home in Portsmouth, she begins 'falling away' and starts 'taking a drop like other women' (34). Although Georgina's other texts largely refrain from such vehement criticism, this preoccupation with temperance and the evils of alcohol is common to a number of her tales and culminated in her adult novel *The Secret Terror*, published nine years after *Wonderful Mates*. Perhaps temperance was Georgina's new 'cause'; by 1900 there had been a multitude of social reforms and it is unlikely that the Froggys and Bennys of turn-of-the-century London would have suffered the fate of their 1875 equivalents. Whatever the explanation, although poor children had previously featured in Georgina's work and would continue occasionally to do so, *Wonderful Mates* was the last of her texts to dwell, at length, on the plight of the children of the slums.

Georgina's tales of inner-city deprivation, wretched children and despairing adults were very much of their time, and her five books that take childhood poverty as their theme sought both to inform her affluent readers and solicit practical aid. In common with the street arab genre, they invariably displayed a Christian emphasis, although, in Georgina's work, it was rarely religious faith alone that saved the day. More inclined to champion the value of human assistance in times of need, she strove to engender compassion in her readers and even today, her depiction of Victorian slum life can provoke a sympathetic response. While her books resist classification as typical street arab tales, her contribution to the genre was nevertheless significant; *Nothing to Nobody* was adapted as a Service of Song[1] – along with Stretton's *Jessica's First Prayer* and Mrs. Walton's *Christie's Old Organ* – and *Froggy's Little Brother*, praised by Georgina's eminent contemporaries, has long remained a classic. Yet, as Georgina's extensive career suggests, her literary achievements ranged beyond those books that focused on poverty. Middle-class childhood was also a source of inspiration, and took her away from the decrepit streets of

London into what was a more cheerful, frequently humorous, world. And it was from that other, very different, but familiar environment, that some of Georgina's most delightful children's stories emerged.

Notes

1. In *Chapel: The Joyous Days and Prayerful Nights of the Nonconformists, 1850-1950*, Kenneth Young explains that 'the Service of Song consisted of the reading of "an edifying though not necessarily religious" story, with breaks for the singing of hymns, solo or anthems [that] was often held on a Sunday afternoon' (cited in Cutt:205). According to *The Ragged Schools Union Quarterly Record* of 1878, the 'abridgement' of *Nothing to Nobody* was carried out by Mr. Alfred Wells, who 'interspersed [the tale] with fifteen well-known and well-adapted songs' (43). It would, said the *Record*, 'enliven a winter's evening by means of a touching tale and well-selected music.'

Chapter 12

From a Personal Perspective

Georgina's tales of 'beautiful, well-cared-for children' (Bratton: 100) clearly addressed the same class of reader as her street arab novels but, and in contrast, avoided the slum landscapes of London's East End. They focused instead on territories more familiar to the affluent child – leafy London squares, shopping bazaars, seaside resorts – and, in general, depicted a secure, comfortable and caring world replete with kindly servants and benevolent relatives. Written specifically for younger children, indeed, perhaps her own[1], these tales of middle-class life are in many ways as didactic as Georgina's stories of slum dwellers, although her lessons are often subtly and unobtrusively woven into the text. Nevertheless, her books aim to teach, albeit implicitly, and might, to varying degrees, be perceived as manuals of good behaviour.

As a Victorian mother-of-five, Georgina's role was undoubtedly one of educator, and she appears to have taken her duties seriously. Her history book, *Old England's Story in Little Words for Little Children*, is an enchantingly naïve romp through the past, and was probably used as a teaching aid in the Castle Smith household. Dedicated to Castle Smith, 'With Love from his Wife "Brenda," ' an early edition owned by Georgina's great granddaughter is marked, in different places, with pencilled notes of Georgina's children's names and dates, apparently in Georgina's hand. It may be that she used her own text to educate her children in history; perhaps Mus had learned one particular fact on April 5th and another with Lucy and Maurice on June 25th. The pencilled legends 'Mus April 5th' and 'M, L and M June 25th' certainly suggest that this was the case. Moreover, while such a scenario might conjure notions of hard graft and endless repetition, lessons from Georgina's history book were unlikely to have been an arduous task. Chapter 1 begins:

> Once upon a time, a long long while ago, this pretty island we live in, called Great Britain, was not pretty at all...The English people *then* were not like the English people now, not at all. They were very wild and savage, and in summer when it was warm, they wore no clothes...Why did they paint their bodies blue? They did it to frighten their enemies, and I should think that what with their long hair, their shaggy beast skins, and their blue paint, and their savage shouts, they must have frightened their enemies very much – don't you? (1-2)

And just in case a child reader should envy this lifestyle, the text swiftly interjects, 'Do you think they were idle and did nothing but play all day? Oh no! the little children in those days were not allowed to be idle; they were set to work very early' (3).

Georgina's history of England might find a place on school bookshelves today – but strictly as a Victorian artefact. The narrator's assumptions are frequently questionable, although it might well have been the case that Julius Caesar disliked Britain because it was 'too dull and foggy after his own beautiful country' (9), and Queen Elizabeth I, although brave, may have been 'a very foolish woman in some ways...fond of dress and...vain of her good looks' (159). Only the narrator's comments on Queen Victoria can be perceived as potentially valid, but, even then, should be treated with caution; they are clearly more Royalist propaganda than objective fact. The final pages of the book counteract the anti-monarchy criticism that was obviously prevalent at the time, and remind the reader of his fortunate state:

> [R]emember what a great and good Queen it has pleased God to place over us! I am sorry to say, in these days, you may often hear people wishing that there was no queen, and that England could be governed by the people only. But the people who wish this surely forget that England has been a happier, richer, more powerful and more Christian nation under our beloved Queen, than at any other time in England's history. Victoria is, indeed, a Christian Queen and *this*, more than all her great talents, has been the secret of England's present prosperity and greatness. Let us, then, unite in saying from our hearts – God save the Queen! (227)

If lesson time concluded with such a lively exhortation, it was probably an enjoyable experience.

With Children in Mind

As an author of books for young children, Georgina evidently perceived reader enjoyment as a priority. Her books of middle-class life are written with enthusiasm, are pleasurable to read, particularly aloud, are frequently interspersed with humour and are obviously in striking contrast to her earlier work. Her motivation for what was essentially a change of literary direction is undocumented, but may have been initiated by her new role as mother; *Lotty's Visit to Grandmama* was published in the year following the birth of Georgina's first son, Hugh. And although neither *Little Cousins or Georgie's Visit to Lotty* nor *The Pilot's House or The Five*

Little Partridges appears to have been published to commemorate the arrival of other Castle Smith offspring, Georgina's growing family would no doubt have identified with, and relished, the exploits of characters who were essentially like themselves. For Georgina's children – and her other affluent young readers – the world of Lotty, Georgie and the Five Little Partridges would have been a most familiar place.

In fact, *Lotty's Visit to Grandmama* opens with the assumption that the reader is personally acquainted with the world of the main protagonist: 'Do you know little Lotty Frere?' asks the narrator (11). Although the answer is 'perhaps not,' as the narrator suggests, she assumes that the reader will at least *recognise* Lotty. She continues: 'no doubt you have often seen her in the Kensington Gardens, playing under the trees with her doll…she generally wears a white hat with a blue feather in it' (11). Within the first five pages of the book, the reader has been thoroughly introduced to Lotty and fully informed about her relatives, her home and daily life, all of which would probably have been reminiscent of his, or her, own. The narrator pre-empts the questions that a small child would be likely to ask; when the doll is described, she wonders, 'Who gave this great doll to Lotty?' (13) and subsequently provides the answer, while details of Lotty's home and her lessons are relayed in similar style. In addition, there are numerous details within these early pages to engage a child. The description of the doll and of its clothes, for example, would undoubtedly have interested a young girl:

> Lotty's doll is a very beautiful one, with eyes that can open and shut, and long eyelashes, and two little white teeth just showing between her pretty red lips. It has lovely wax arms and legs, and it wears white cotton socks and blue kid shoes, just like the shoes Lotty wears when she goes out to a party, and Nurse dresses her in her best…Lotty went to a toy-shop and bought it a hat, and Nurse trimmed it with a piece of blue ribbon and a pretty white goose's feather which Cook gave her. She also bought it some shoes and some socks, and some blue ribbon to make it a sash, and many other things besides. (12-14)

Throughout the book, there are frequent opportunities for dialogue between reader and text, and for engagement with the young protagonists' experiences. As Lotty prepares to leave her London house for her grandmother's seaside home, the narrator comments, 'How nice it is to see the cab drive up to the door, and the boxes put on the top, when you are going on a long journey, is it not?' (33), and when a mischievous child demolishes Lotty and her cousin Georgie's 'sand-heap' on the beach at

Seabeach, the reader is invited to predict his actions: 'and while their backs [were] turned, what do you think a naughty little boy did to their beautiful sand-heap?' asks the narrator (56). Furthermore, the book's many humorous moments – most of which derive from the interaction between 'Uncle William' and his nieces – would have delighted a young reader and, indeed, remain entertaining. Lotty, Georgie and Uncle William stage a cat race – Lotty's and Georgie's new kittens are pitted against Uncle William's cat – and grandmother promises a scent-bottle as first prize. Georgie wins, but is sorry that Lotty can't have a similar bottle:

> "And are you not sorry for poor me too?" inquired Uncle William, looking very sad.
>
> "No, not a bit," answered Georgie at once, "because you are a grown-up man with a moustache, and you can't want a scent-bottle – men never do have scent-bottles." (85)

While Lotty is consoled by grandmother's gift of 'a beautiful carved needle-book', Uncle William continues to lament his lack of reward:

> "And where is *my* present?" asked Uncle William. "Poor me! No one gives *me* a present. Now don't you pity me, Lotty?"
>
> "I don't pity you much, because you are a tall, grown-up man," said Lotty, "and you can buy what you like in a shop."
>
> "You are very unkind," said Uncle William, "and I shall go out into the garden, and have a good cry!" But the children knew he was only in fun, and that he went into the garden to smoke his cigar. (87)

More Serious Matters

Despite the jovial and sometimes 'exciting' nature of *Lotty's Visit to Grandmama* – there is a birthday party, a swim in the sea from a bathing-machine and a visit to a local home where the daughter of the house displays a walking wax doll – there are also serious lessons to be learned. But Georgina generally refrains from overt didacticism, and relies instead on the responses of the children and the comments of adult characters for emphasis. When Lotty and Georgie, along with maid Nancy, are dispatched to take provisions to 'a poor woman who lay ill in a cottage' (61), Georgie's disobedience ends in disaster; she frightens her cousin, falls and cuts herself, and drops and breaks the contents of the basket. Scolded by grandmother and Uncle William, she is sent to bed although 'when Georgie told [Grandmama] how sorry she was, and how she never meant to be so naughty again, Grandmama kissed her and forgave her' (81). The narrator comments,' How pleasant it is to feel forgiven!' (81) but ultimately allows the incident and the characters to emphasise the thoughtlessness of Georgie's actions. Similarly, when over-exuberant visitor Freddy Drake chases Grandmama's pet sheep and accidentally drives it into the drawing room, Freddy's contrition and apologetic behaviour are exemplary; he immediately claims responsibility for the incident and replaces a vase that was broken. There are instances of less implicit didacticism, and indeed the final chapter of the book is dominated, to its detriment, by a veritable blast of philanthropy that culminates in Lotty taking bags of shells to the children of Great Ormond Street Hospital (161). But, overall, Georgina as author forbears to preach, and prefers her characters, and their actions, to deliver her sentiments. Moreover, her realistic, and often highly visual, portrayal of childish behaviour imbues her characters with credibility, authenticates their actions – and suggests that Georgina was keenly observant. Lotty's interest in food, her barrage of questions prior to leaving London, and her fear of being bitten by strange animals, are all typically childish characteristics, and Georgina's image of Lotty and her cousin, forbidden to talk, but aching to chat, succinctly captures the moment: 'Then Lotty was undressed, and they never said another word, though they looked at each other all the while, as if they would have liked to go on talking very much' (44).

A Similar Tale

Georgina's sequel to *Lotty's Visit to Grandmama*, published three years later, is similar in many ways. Like its predecessor, *Little Cousins or Georgie's Visit to Lotty* invites the reader into the text – 'You remember, children, I told you about Lotty's visit to Grandmama; well, now I am going to tell you about Georgie's visit to London' (10) – and, in common with its companion book, depicts characters who are convincingly childish. Georgie raises her voice to her new French maid, not in anger, but because she cannot make her understand (14), is adamant that she will not rest during the train journey, but nevertheless falls asleep (36), and hopes that Cook has put 'lots of citron' into the cake she is taking to London (28). The text's portrayal of Georgie 'playing mother' with Lotty's baby sister Tottie – and mimicking her elders – is a particularly skilful and entertaining portrait of child behaviour:

> They played at 'visiting'…and Georgie was to show off Tottie as her baby.

"You must ask all about her food, and her teeth, and sleeping, you know, Lotty," said Georgie, "just as ladies do when they come to see babies."

"What food does your baby have?" inquired Lotty, sitting very upright with the nursery table-cloth pinned round her for a shawl.

"Ridge's Food," answered Georgie, dancing Tottie to and fro.

"Oh now, that's *quite* wrong," said Lotty…"you should give it nothing but rusks and milk, my dear Mrs. Frere; it would thrive much better. How many teeth has your baby?"

"Two," said Georgie, "the two back double ones."

"Oh you mustn't say that," cried Lotty, "babies never have their double teeth first…does she sleep well?"

"Yes, very good; she only wakes up for her bottle eight or nine times," replied Georgie.

"That's a great many times!" said the other little lady wisely, "that's because she isn't satisfied – it's because Ridge's Food doesn't suit her." (63)

There are further entertaining incidents in *Little Cousins*; Uncle William is staying in London, frequently engages in banter with the girls, and takes them to Madame Tussauds and to dinner. They are invited out to tea, visit Westminster Abbey and, on Lotty's birthday, are taken to the Zoological Gardens. Georgina, ever mindful that her middle-class readers would probably also visit the zoo, is swift to offer advice. The narrator warns: '[S]o quick are the monkeys in the Zoological Gardens that they have been known sometimes to seize the spectacles from off people's faces. That is why the board is put up to request persons wearing glasses not to approach too near the cages' (144). Unhappily, Laura Drake, a friend of the girls, fails to fully heed the advice of governess Miss Drake and loses her 'pretty and stylish' hat (148) to a mischievous monkey, who puts it on his head, snaps the elastic in his face and consequently, in anger, 'crumple [s] [the hat] into a complete ball' (148).

Children are rarely punished for minor accidents in *Little Cousins*, but Lotty's disobedience, which results in the injury of her little sister, is viewed with severity. Her spontaneous misbehaviour, reminiscent of Georgie' sudden outburst of naughtiness in *Lotty's Visit to Grandmama*, receives a similar punishment; she is sent to bed and this time it is Georgie who pleads on her behalf. Like Georgie in the earlier book, Lotty is as much concerned with the loss of her tea as with repentance – ' "try to make them pity me," ' she tells Georgie. ' "Tell them how lonely I am and what a poor tea I've made, and perhaps they may say I may have a little supper" ' (123) – and she and Lotty are anxious to remind each other, and the reader, of Georgie's own misdemeanour. However, ultimately all is well, Lotty is forgiven and receives 'a nice little supper of sponge cake and milk' (125).

Throughout *Little Cousins* the reader is encouraged to condone good behaviour, but rarely through the narrative voice. The girls' generous treatment of each other and the gentlemanly manners of Freddy Drake and of the reformed Dicky Fox, provide role models for the edification and education of the young reader, and Lotty and Georgie's kindness is further emphasised by their visit to Great Ormonde (sic) Street Hospital with Lotty's mother. Their purpose is to distribute 'pretty things amongst the little invalids' (173), and although a contemporary reader might balk at Georgie's whispered comment to her cousin – ' "They're common toys...but how [the children] like them," ' she says (175) – the girls' efforts are clearly deemed laudable. As a result of their visit, Lotty and Georgie plan to save money for Christmas boxes for the hospital, and the book closes with their correspondence, in which each reports on the success of her money-making scheme.

Georgina's portrayal of childhood in the two Lotty books is highly successful; she observes childish behaviour with skill and, despite her didacticism, rarely sacrifices the continuity of her tale to moral instruction. Her aptitude for portraying the world of the affluent, middle-class child with sensitivity and humour is evident, and the enthusiasm that permeates these texts is, in many ways, more memorable than the purposeful resolution that characterises her stories of slum life. Yet, and lamentably, despite the fact that she patently enjoyed her task as author of books for young children, Georgina produced only one other such text, although this final volume was undoubtedly enjoyable to write and a pleasure to research. *The Pilot's House or The Five Little Partridges*, published in 1885 when Georgina's family was complete, drew not only on familiar places and middle-class children, but was inspired by and featured her own daughters and sons.

Establishing the Facts

While Castle-Smith family legend had long held that the child characters of *The Pilot's House* represent Georgina's children, it was only recently that this was definitively verified. Georgina's great granddaughter, leafing through the pages of an elderly copy of the book, discovered notes,

Illustration 14: Dinner in the train en route to the seaside. Illustration by M. Irwin from *The Pilot's House* or *The Five Little Partridges*, p.41.

probably written by her grandmother Maude, that not only individually identified each of the young protagonists as Hugh, Eva, Lucy, Maurice and Mus Castle Smith, but also married fictional locations and events to the real-life experiences of Georgina, her husband and children. Always a delightful tale, *The Pilot's House* is now, in addition, a valuable resource, offering unparalleled information about the lives of the Castle Smiths as a family and, by implication, those of their late-Victorian counterparts.

The tale begins in London at the home of the Partridge family, where preparations are under way for the August evacuation to the seaside. Although '[e]verybody had packed up...and gone out of town' (11), one house remains open,

> [A] house of medium size standing in one of those rather dull, exactly-alike Squares with which that part of Bayswater near Westbourne Grove abounds. The house had nothing at all distinctive about it...[it] was just like fifty and one others in the neighbourhood, and the Square garden was just like all the other Square gardens in Bayswater; iron railings all round, a stiff gravel path running from end to end...a patch of burnt-up trodden grass in the middle, a black-trunked tree or two, and underneath a rustic seat or wooden bench, and at the gates a shabby notice board stuck up to say 'No dogs admitted,' (and some said the dogs did not miss much!). (11)

While the house boasts 'as quiet an appearance as all the others', the inside of the building is 'nothing but bustle and hurry and running to and fro' (12). Mr. and Mrs. Partridge have left for the coast to find lodgings, and the family is preparing to follow.

The overwhelming sense of frenetic activity and excitement that the author imparts to her early pages leaves no doubt that Georgina herself experienced such chaos; the absence of Mr. and Mrs. Partridge may just have been wishful thinking. But whatever the case, her description of the children's exuberance and the frustrations of the staff as they attempt to organise their young charges is highly entertaining and artfully depicted. The paragraph in which the author details the scene is replete with a host of different activities, and is delivered in a breathless rush:

> It had been rather a trying day for the children whose exuberance of spirits, whenever they thought of the little railway omnibus coming to fetch them away tomorrow, led them into outbursts of jumping about and rushing up and down stairs and general liveliness which

> was anything but helpful to the authorities, who were overcome with the heat, and perfectly distracted with the noise of the parish steam-roller, which had begun snorting and puffing as early as five o'clock that morning, and had been scrunching and pounding the road in front of No.7 ever since. (13)

However, the children, of course, adore the steam roller, '[wish] they were the men with the black faces to drive it' (14) and, in this way, are introduced to the reader. Dicky, aged eight and the oldest, is 'brimful of spirits' (15) and is, in reality, a fictional representation of Georgina's son Hugh, who was nine when *The Pilot's House* was published. The notes reveal that Hugh, like his fictional counterpart, was interested in machinery, particularly railway engines and steam-rollers, was fond of sticks and putty and delighted in history (15). Dicky also has a boat – he tells the Nurse that it is packed (18) – and this was probably also one of Hugh's possessions. In later life, Hugh and his brothers were keen makers of model boats; Hugh's Maltese water boat is currently in the Science Museum in London as are Maurice's models of a Deal galley and a Lerrit fishing boat. Mus, also a talented craftsman, built a model dinghy which is now in Queen Mary's Doll's House at Windsor Castle.

Further Introductions

The portrait of Dicky (or Hugh) is swiftly followed by descriptions of the remainder of the family, beginning with sisters Bel and Peggy, otherwise Georgina's daughters Eva and Lucy, who were aged approximately seven and five when *The Pilot's House* was published. Bel is depicted as 'a sweet specimen of a fair little English girl' who is 'very neat with her fingers' (16), while Peggy has 'violet eyes and dark lashes, and curly bronze-coloured hair' and is 'very quick and bustling in her movements' (16). The narrator comments on the girls' fondness for dolls: 'they liked getting into a corner together and pretending they were nurses, bathing and dressing their dolls', she says (16). Although it was clearly not her daughters who inspired Georgina's memorable portrayal of Lotty and Georgie 'playing at visiting' – Eva was only two years old and Lucy was a baby when *Little Cousins* was written – Georgina patently enjoyed observing Eva and Lucy's activity. Moreover, she was sensitive to the desires of her offspring. Four-year-old Fry, the fictional equivalent of Maurice and a 'roley poley…dear little fellow', adores his older brother; 'His ambition in life seemed to be to be like his elder brother Dicky,' says the narrator. Pocket crammed with items that resemble Dicky's possessions, he often '[stands] with his hands clasped behind his fat little back' because he has seen Dicky in similar stance (17). Finally, there is the baby boy known as 'the Partridge baby' (17), who the narrator apparently adores. Georgina had given birth to her youngest child, Mus, in the year that *The Pilot's House* was published, and her pride in this latest achievement was evidently undiminished:

> [I]f he could have understood all that was said to him, [he] would have been a very conceited baby; for he was told a dozen times every day…that he was the 'darlingest, sweetest, and dearest baby in all Bayswater.' The Patridge baby *was* very sweet, and Bayswater could not have produced a prettier – there could not be two opinions about it. (17)

There are other notable comparisons in *The Pilot's House* between the fictional lives of the Partridges and the true experiences of the Castle Smiths; the recently-found notes explain that the seaside town of Pebbledean to which the Partridges are travelling is Deal in Kent, the resort favoured by Georgina, Castle and their family when the children were small. The portable bath that the Patridges take with them and that is 'closely packed [and] bulging' with items (19) is also based on fact; the Castle Smith bath was, apparently, always packed with boots and shoes when the family vacated their London home for the sea. Drumadum Barracks, where the children's uncle, Captain Robert Maude, is based, is a representation of Marine Barracks, Deal, while references to the children's grandfather and rides in the park in his 'C-springed barouche' (52) are believed to have been based on Grandfather Castle Smith, who lived in Cumberland Terrace, Regents Park.

A Delightful Story

However, even without this 'inside information,' *The Pilot's House* is a most delightful tale. The exploits of the children and their experiences at Seabeach, ranging from bathing, to visiting Drumadum Barracks, are depicted with fondness and credibility, and although some events are more believable than others, the escape of a tiger from Boff's Menagerie is particularly suspect, the highly enjoyable nature of the text counteracts the occasional narrative extravagance. Georgina's portraits of childish behaviour are finely drawn throughout; Fry's assumption that the crowd on Seabeach station have come to greet the Partridges is typically child-like (51), and the children's pleasure, and anxiety, when playing in the prison cells at Drumadum Barracks is amusingly predictable:

> [A]fter that [they went] to see the solitary cells where soldiers were locked up if they behaved badly. Dicky and Bel and Peggy would

not be satisfied till Uncle Bob had put them into one of these solitary cells, to see 'what it was like' – but when the heavy door was shut, they very soon wanted to come out again. It was quite black darkness inside, and so still they could hear nothing. 'I should think the soldiers soon get good,' remarked little Peggy, 'when they are put into that nasty dark cupboard all alone by themselves.' (107)

Furthermore, *The Pilot's House* offers a detailed depiction of Victorian seaside resorts, from their bathing machines and bonneted children to the exasperation of their adult visitors, obliged to accompany their children on yet another donkey ride. In a heartfelt parental confession, the narrator, who is possibly Georgina, admits,

I always admire the British parents and guardians whom I see devoting themselves in this way; it is such utter self-sacrifice on their part...yet, I look upon it, they endure as genuine a martyrdom for the time being as any that have won martyr's crown or laurel wreath....Who, that has ever gone through it...does not remember the throes of that hour on the hot parade, keeping up at the side of the donkey, laden with every imaginable thing the riders don't want....And they must run...must gallop....And all the while the riders are in uproarious mirth and spirits...and with a pleasing conviction all the time, seeing the devoted soul running – because they can't help it – alongside so briskly, that *they* are thoroughly enjoying themselves too! (121)

As a mother of five children, Georgina clearly knew about donkey rides. Not surprisingly perhaps, in *The Pilot's House*, it is Mrs. Partridge and governess Miss Gay who accompany the excited Partridge troupe.

Model Behaviour

There are few authorial comments of this nature in *The Pilot's House*, although the narrator intervenes to comment on the children's hymn singing – 'There is not a purer and more beautiful sound on earth...than that of little children singing hymns' (104) – and to endorse Mrs. Partridge's seemingly unsympathetic attitude when Fry cries for tartlets that are delivered by mistake. 'Mrs. Partridge thought it well – and rightly – that [children] should learn early to be able to bear cheerfully little disappointments,' she says (82). As in Georgina's other books for young children, lessons are dispatched more frequently by example than with a sermon. The bad behaviour of the Prettyjohn children contrasts with that of the Partridges, the enthusiasm of the protagonists for the company of lodger Rev. Crosbie is emphasised, and the children are, at all times, polite to both family and acquaintances. They are also shown to be sympathetic to others less fortunate than themselves; having seen 'poorly clad, white faced little children' looking 'wistfully' after them as they set out for the seaside, they enthusiastically accept collecting cards to raise funds for out-of-town trips for the poor. Like Georgina's other books for younger children, *The Pilot's House* is essentially, if implicitly, a handbook on how to behave.

The Pilot's House was, perhaps, Georgina's crowning achievement as a writer for young children, although it might in fact be perceived as superior to *any* of her other children's books. Highly amusing, carefully crafted and replete with well-observed studies of children's behaviour, it also undoubtedly gave pleasure to the adult reader; its depiction of family life would have been familiar to those who shared Georgina's middle-class world. Inspired by her own experiences and by what was clearly a great fondness for her family, Georgina created a book that was an enthusiastic portrait of late-Victorian life. Like *Lotty's Visit to Grandmama* and *Little Cousins*, it offered an insightful vision of the child and did so with respect; while childish behaviour is often viewed with humour, Georgina forbears to patronise or in any way mock the actions of her young protagonists. Today, Georgina's stories for young readers remain of immense value as records of the past, but they have largely been forgotten. Superceded in the public and academic eye by other writers of the period, Georgina and her work for young children are rarely even considered in comparative discussions of late-Victorian, family-orientated tales.

Notes

1. *Lotty's Visit to Grandmama* is subtitled 'A Story for the Little Ones' and *Little Cousins or Georgie's Visit to Lotty* is similarly written for a younger audience. *The Pilot's House or The Five Little Partridges* features young protagonists and so is implicitly for younger children, but its portrait of family life might also have appealed to older readers.

Chapter 13

Beyond Preconceptions

Georgina Castle Smith, the woman known as 'Brenda,' is clearly an underestimated writer. Perceived today as little more than a yardstick against which other street arab authors, particularly Stretton, can be gauged, her true identity as a popular writer of children's books has been all but lost. In a career spanning some 59 years, she wrote prolifically on a variety of subjects and enjoyed a successful and productive working life. But while Georgina is at least referenced in contemporary critical analyses of street arab tales, her other books for children have been virtually forgotten. Like Georgina's identity as an individual, they appear to have been deemed of little value to literary history. Categorised within her own time as a stereotypical angel, the woman behind the cipher has remained largely unknown.

However, to characterise her solely as a writer of worthy tales is misleading. Georgina was also a popular author whose work encapsulated the diversity of the world in which she lived. She portrayed the slum-life of inner-city London and the affluent dwellings and families of the middle-classes with enthusiasm; she was a campaigner for social reform and a mother who delighted in, and recorded, the activities of her own five children. She may well have taken part in penny readings for the poor and visited the slums of London, but she was also a Victorian middle-class woman who wrote initially for pleasure and, later, from necessity. Paradoxically, while her categorisation as a street arab writer has served to preserve her name in reference books, it has simultaneously proved detrimental to her reputation overall and to her identity as an individual. She remains, in perpetuity, a worthy creature.

This enduring image of Georgina appears to emanate directly from the nineteenth-century preoccupation with idealised womanhood – a preoccupation that has ultimately obscured our understanding of the past. The Victorian predilection for the worthy woman author, evidenced in the reviews of Georgina's early work and in the letters from Lord Arran,[1] has distorted our perception of nineteenth-century women's writing. As Elaine Showalter points out, 'The Victorians expected women's novels to reflect the feminine values they exalted' (Showalter: 1977: 7), and they privileged those that did, presumably disregarding less 'appropriate' offerings. Homeless waifs and benevolent philanthropists were ideal subject matter for women writers, and a number of female children's authors, including

Georgina, found immortality in street arab tales. But this categorisation and implicit censorship of women's writing was a potent phenomenon and its consequences have been far-reaching. Today, our impressions of Victorian life and culture are gleaned from the works of a selected, approved elite. Moreover, we have colluded in the perpetuation of myth by accepting these offerings as truly representative of the time. Instead of seeking access to the whole spectrum of popular literature, and striving to expand our knowledge of the Victorians, we have been satisfied with preconceptions and with the preferences of an ideological regime.

A Broader Perspective

Yet we *can* achieve a greater, more accurate understanding of the Victorians and their world by recovering the works of once-popular women writers like Georgina. In doing so, we will inevitably expand our perspective. The inherent realism of many of Georgina's texts validates them as historical documents; it is probable that her portraits of Victorian life are more authentic than those of comparable, canonical works. But it is only by reviewing her forgotten books and those of her contemporaries that we can begin to create a more comprehensive insight into the Victorian world. And most importantly, perhaps, by relocating these texts within literary history, we can ensure their future survival.

Access to the past becomes increasingly more difficult as time passes, and while the popular fiction of a bygone age is a valuable research tool, it must be available in order to inform. During the my research I have learned much about Georgina and Victorian life, but I also became acutely aware of the fragility of history. The women writers of the Victorian age, whose work was subject to the vagaries of a male-dominated establishment, can easily be forgotten. Even those who have so far survived may be under threat; if *Froggy's Little Brother* disappears from academic reading lists, Georgina's tenuous place in the world of children's literature could eventually be lost. Publishers' records of Georgina were destroyed long ago; her personal writings have been mislaid or thrown away. The documents that have been entrusted to the care of her descendants will assuredly be cherished by the generations that follow, but the loss of memorabilia becomes ever more likely as the years progress. The reminiscences of Georgina's grandsons can only diminish, and the photographs will fade. Georgina, as a popular, prolific writer of the nineteenth-century and beyond, clearly deserves to be recorded before it is all too late – as do her forgotten contemporaries.

There are undoubtedly other women writers for children who have already vanished. Their survival was perhaps always in jeopardy; children's writers have rarely received just recognition for their efforts and so these women were doubly disadvantaged. It may be that their work was frankly mediocre and therefore unremarkable, but it may also be that their books failed to conform to the prescribed parameters of women's writing within the Victorian literary world. Georgina would appear to have survived because she *could* be satisfactorily categorised as a street arab novelist; she conformed entirely to ideological expectations. It may be that her forgotten contemporaries were perceived as less stereotypically worthy at the time and were thus subsequently deemed disposable. Whatever the explanation for their disappearance, they might prove to be as important to the study of children's literature – and to an understanding of Victorian life – as Georgina has shown herself to be.

There is, by implication, no specific source for these forgotten authors, but there is an abundance of available material that offers a clue to potential research projects. The final pages of Georgina's *The Pilot's House or The Five Little Patridges* feature titles by well-known authors of the time. Some of the names have survived the years; there are works by L.T. Meade and A.L.O.E., as well as further books by Brenda. However, and in close proximity, are titles by other 'favourite' authors who are now effectively unfamiliar. To explore their lives and works would necessitate detailed and lengthy study. But it is feasible that the children's tales of Catharine Shaw, Emily S. Holt and Emily Brodie, all vaunted as popular authors by publishers John F. Shaw and Co, will prove to be significant. Like Georgina and her books, these authors and their works may be well worth preserving.

Notes

1. See Chapter 9

Bibliography

Works by Brenda

There is some disagreement over the publication dates of Brenda's early texts. For example, although it is widely accepted that *Froggy's Little Brother* was published in 1875, Lennox-Boyd's evidence from the *Publishers' Circular*, which listed books published in the preceding fortnight, suggests that *Froggy* may have been published in late 1874 (Lennox-Boyd, 129). There are similar discrepancies with other texts. Consequently I have used British Library referencing for all of Georgina's undated books, other than *Nothing to Nobody*; Lennox-Boyd points out that this text featured in the *Publishers' Circular* of 1873, and it was reviewed by the *Hampshire Chronicle* in January 1874, which suggests that it may have been published at the close of 1873.

Nothing to Nobody (n.d.), London: John F. Shaw (first published 1873)

Froggy's Little Brother (n.d.), London: John F. Shaw (first published 1875)

Froggy's Little Brother (1968), London: Victor Gollancz (first published 1875)

Especially Those: A Story on the Prayer 'For All Conditions of Men`. (n.d.), London: John F. Shaw (first published 1875)

Lotty's Visit to Grandmama: A Story for the Little Ones (n.d.), London: John F. Shaw (first published 1877)

A Saturday's Bairn (n.d.), London: John F. Shaw (first published 1877)

Victoria-Bess: The Ups and Downs of a Doll's Life (n.d.), London: John F. Shaw (first published 1879)

Little Cousins or Georgie's Visit to Lotty (n.d.), London: John F. Shaw (first published 1880)

Fynie's Flower (n.d.), London: Hatchards (first published 1880)

Without a Reference: A Christmas Story (n.d.), London: Hatchards (first published 1882)

Old England's Story in Little Words for Little Children (n.d.), London: Hatchards (first published 1884)

The Pilot's House or The Five Little Partridges (n.d.), London: John F. Shaw (first published 1885)

Dinah Mite: A Story for Today (n.d.), London: Isbister (first published 1887)

The Shepherd's Darling (n.d.), London: John F. Shaw (first published 1888)

Uncle Steve's Locker (n.d.), London: John F.Shaw (first published 1888)

A Faithful Promise (n.d.), London: John F. Shaw (first published 1890)

The Earl's Granddaughter (n.d.), London: John F. Shaw (first published 1896)

Wonderful Mates (n.d.), London: John F. Shaw (first published 1900)

A Little Brown Tea-Pot (n.d.), (Also known as *Rosamond's Home*) London: John F. Shaw (first published 1902)

The Secret Terror (1909), London: Stanley Paul

Mary Pillenger: Supreme Factor (1912), London: Putnam

The Children of Windystreet, (n.d.), London: John F. Shaw (first published 1912)

Opened Doors: The Story of Sonny Baba (n.d.), London: Pickering and Inglis (first published 1932)

Brenda also provided the preface for *Five Minutes to Spare: Being Extracts on Various Subjects from The Everyday Book of the Late Rev. John Guard*. The book was published in 1879 by Hatchards of London.

Secondary Texts

Altick, Richard (1973) *Victorian People and Ideas*. London: Dent

Avery, Gillian (1975) *Childhood's Pattern: A Study of the Heroes and Heroines of Children's Fiction 1770 - 1950*. London: Hodder and Stoughton

Beetham, Margaret & Kay Boardman. (2001) *Victorian Women's Magazines: An Anthology*. Manchester: Manchester University Press

Bratton, Jacqueline (1981) *The Impact of Victorian Children's Fiction*. London: Croom Helm

Brontë, Charlotte (1985) *Villette*. London: Penguin (first published 1853)
Cunningham, Hugh (1991) *The Children of the Poor: Representations of Childhood Since*
The Seventeenth Century. Oxford: Blackwell

Cutt, Margaret (1979) *Ministering Angels: A Study of Nineteenth-century Evangelical Writing for Children*. Wormley: Five Owls Press

Davin, Anna (1996) *Growing Up Poor: Home, School and Street in London 1870 - 1914*. London: Rivers Oram

Dickens, Charles (n.d.) *The Personal History of David Copperfield*. London: Odhams (first published 1849)

Gilmour, Robin. (1993) *The Victorian Period: The Intellectual and Cultural Context of English Literature 1830-1890*. London: Longman

Hollingshead, John (1986) *Ragged London in 1861*. London: Dent (first published 1861)

Jalland, Pat (1999) *Death in the Victorian Family*. Oxford: Oxford University Press (first published 1996)

Mayhew, Henry (1968) *London Labour and the London Poor*. London: Constable (first published 1861-2)

Pool, Daniel (1993) *What Jane Austen Ate and Charles Dickens Knew*. New York: Touchstone

Reynolds, Kimberley & Nicola Humble. (1993) *Victorian Heroines: Representations of Femininity in Nineteenth-century Literature and Art*. London: Harvester Wheatsheaf

Showalter, Elaine (1995) *A Literature of Their Own: From Charlotte Brontë to Doris Lessing.*London: Virago (first published 1977)

Stretton, Hesba (n.d.) *Jessica's First Prayer.* London: R.T.S. (first published 1867)

Vallone, Lynne (2001) *Becoming Victoria.* London: Yale University Press

Walton, John K.(1983) *The English Seaside Resort: A Social History 1750 - 1914.* New York: Leicester University Press

Journals

Author Unknown. (1878) Books and What is Thought of Them: Nothing to Nobody. *The Ragged Schools Union Quarterly Record*, Winter 1878. (43)

Lennox-Boyd, Charlotte (1990) Brenda and Her Works. *Signal*, no. 62. (p14-130)

Electronic Sources

Churchyard, H. *Royal Genealogies.*
www.ftp.cac.psu.edu/~saw/royal/royalgen.
Accessed on 15.12.01

Intellectual Reserve. *Family Search.*
www.familysearch.org.
Accessed 12.10.01

Kaye Family. *Circus in Our Blood,*
www.members.tripod.com/herschy/circusblood3.
Accessed 12.01.02

Kolle, D. *Surname Index to Robson's 1839 Directory of Buckinghamshire Names.*
www.met.open.ac.uk/genuki/big/eng/BKM/Directories/bucksdirg.
Accessed 15.10.01

Maybole Community Services. *The History of Ragged Schools*
http://www.maybole.org/history/articles/historyofraggedschools.html
Accessed 14.01.02

Mullenger, L. *Classical Music Web*.
http://www.musicweb.uk.garlands/64.html.
Accessed 9.10.01

Research UK. *The Lost London Street Index*.
http:// www.members.aol.com/Whall95037/londonc.html.
Accessed 06.01.02

Sutherland Family. *Sutherland Family*.
http://www.pages. Prodigy.net/ptheroff/gotha/sutherland.html.
Accessed 08.12.01

Tomsett, B. *Gore, Arthur Jocelyn Charles, Earl of Arran 6th*,
http://www.tardis.ed.ac.uk/cgi/bct/gedlkup/n=royal?royal16038.
Accessed 18.12.01

Letters

Because several letters are undated, I have based their order on internal evidence.

Gore, A. 6th Earl of Arran.

To Georgina Castle Smith, October 4

To Georgina Castle Smith, October 11. From 3 Grosvenor Place, SW

To Georgina Castle Smith, August 9

To Georgina Castle Smith, January 2, 1920. From Thoby Priory

To Georgina Castle Smith, January 12. From the Royal Westminster Opthalmic Hospital, Broad Street, WC2

To Georgina Castle Smith, January 16. From The Alexandra Hotel, Hyde Park Corner, SW1

To Castle Smith, January 3, 1934

Princess Victoria of Hesse. Letter to Georgina Castle Smith, May 9. From Schloss Darmstadt

Rochdale, Beatrice. Letter to Castle Smith, January 5, 1934. From Lingholm, Keswick

Shaftesbury, Lord. Letter to Miss Eyre, January 30, 1875. From St.Giles House

Miscellaneous

BBC Radio Dorchester

BBC Radio Solent, Southampton

Bridport News, Bridport

Castle-Smith, P. (2001) Notes: 'Castle Smith (1849-1936). His Family by Colonel P.M.

Castle-Smith, MC.'

Castle-Smith, R. (2002) Notes on CD-ROM: 'Castle Smith Photos and Index.'

Debrett's, London

Dorset Records Office, Dorchester

Northamptonshire County Records Office, Northampton

Rose, J. Random House Archives

The Children's Country Holiday Fund, London

The Shaftesbury Society, London

Thiel, L. (2001) Interview with Dudley Rouse, Devon, November 22

Windsor Castle Archive

'Good, and lovely, and true'

A consideration of the contribution & legacy of Flora Shaw's fiction for children

Bridget Carrington

Flora Louisa Shaw (Lady Lugard) 1852-1929

'Good and lovely, and true': John Ruskin, of *Castle Blair*, in 'Letter LXXXVII', in *Fors Clavigera*, March1878

The Case for the Rediscovery of Flora Shaw's Fiction for Children

In 1998 I made an impulsive second-hand purchase which led to my discovery of Flora Shaw and her writing, the nine-volume *Masterworks of Children's Literature* edited in the 1980s by Jonathan Cott. Here in the second part of the fifth volume I found *Castle Blair*, edited by Robert Lee Wolff. Wolff's championship of the text appeared fully justified and I determined to investigate further the background to the text itself, her other writing, and the life of Flora Shaw, which emerged as a fascinating insight into what the twenty-first century frequently regards as the universal repression of Victorian women.

As I began to research Flora Shaw and her work it became clear that she was an exceptional woman, whose considerable and varied achievements in the male-oriented society which dominated Britain and its Empire during her lifetime (1852-1929) had, to date, been almost totally ignored. Her work fell into several quite distinct phases, of which her writing for children was the first and briefest, encompassing only the nine years from 1877 to 1886. During this period she wrote merely five books: *Castle Blair* (1877), *Hector* (1882), *Phyllis Browne* (1883), *A Sea Change* (1885) and *Colonel Cheswick's Campaign* (1886). No lesser authority than Ruskin had befriended her, encouraged her to write *Castle Blair,* and praised it highly in *Fors Clavigera*: *Letters to the Workmen and Labourers of Great Britain*, 1871-84, one of Ruskin's many contributions to the education of the lower classes. He considered the author's talents to be equal to Maria Edgeworth's, and to surpass those of Harriet Martineau. From writing fiction for the young, Shaw had then turned to reporting fact for an adult readership, and commenced a career in journalism which culminated in her appointment in 1892 as the first Editor in the new Colonial department of *The Times*. This position held considerable covert political influence, and its occupation by a woman was remarkable; it therefore seemed incredible that the incumbent had received no subsequent recognition other than an inaccurate biography by a friend (Bell, 1947), until a century after the *Times* post (Callaway and Helly, 1991). Equally unconventionally, Shaw had maintained her single status until the age of forty-nine, when she embarked on the final phase of her life, as wife to a colonial Governor General. Thence her literary talents were employed in producing substantial historio-cultural accounts of these colonies. Returning to England in 1912, during the First World War she had helped found the War Refugees Committee, her achievements for the dispossessed Belgians gaining her the award, in 1918, of Dame of the British Empire. An extraordinary woman in so many different spheres, yet scarcely remembered in most of them, and meriting no mention in any recent survey of children's literature; nor were there any current editions of her writing.

Flora Shaw's earlier works, and in particular *Castle Blair* and *Hector,* have considerable significance in the study of the development of later children's writing from its Victorian roots. The material of her later novels became increasingly aimed at a readership of older children and young adults, and by the fifth, the readership itself had dwindled. *Castle Blair* had been approved and recommended not only by Ruskin, but also by that unquestionably prolific and popular author, Charlotte M. Yonge, whose publication in 1887, *What Books to Lend and What to Give*, sought, much like Ruskin's *Fors*, to guide readers to the best available literature. That writers and critics of Ruskin's and Yonge's status, such formulators of public taste, should endorse Shaw's early work, must make these novels important in any historical survey or thematic investigation of the ideology of Victorian children's literature. In addition, the novels, particularly her first, repay examination when charting the development of the independent child, free from adult interference, in children's literature. Subsequent Victorian and Edwardian writers such as Nesbit, Crockett and Grahame are often regarded as the originators of this genre, but were expanding an already established theme to which Shaw made a considerably under acknowledged earlier contribution.

As a Victorian and from an established and influential Anglo-Irish family, Shaw's inherent ideologies are embodied within the themes of *Castle Blair* and *Hector*. The historical background to *Castle Blair* is that of Ireland in the 1860-70s: a legacy of centuries of deliberate Anglo-Irish neglect and misuse of the indigenous population which erupted in sporadic violence and, ultimately, rebellion. Although *Castle Blair* is essentially concerned with the adventures of a lively family of Anglo-Irish children, readers cannot escape the overtly colonial opinions of the adults, nor can they fail to recognize these opinions in the attitudes of the children themselves. Both in *Castle Blair,* where it is viewed as an inextricable aspect of colonial paternalism, and in *Hector,* where the perceived cultural differences between the English and the French characters are of considerable importance, the concept of the 'gentleman', and especially the *English* gentleman, is crucial. As an early example of colonial literature, as a rare expression by a representative of the colonizers in Ireland, the earliest of the English settler colonies, *Castle Blair* deserves recognition within this subsection of the genre. Because of its historical setting it also provides a particularly interesting text for analysis within the critical approach of new historicism.

These, then, are the arguments for a long overdue rediscovery of Flora Shaw's writing for children. It is possible to argue a case for reading her work in order to further our knowledge of the body of Victorian literature considered by contemporaries to be of value, to investigate its contribution to later authors in the development of independence in child characters, as an insight into seminal Victorian ideologies, and as an expression of a period of Irish history which continues to influence modern events. It is equally important to celebrate the achievement in the sphere of children's literature of a remarkable woman, and, hopefully, to introduce modern readers to her novels.

Because Shaw's life and fiction are now virtually unknown, it has been necessary to consider in some depth both the publishing history of her novels and her early life. These chapters therefore precede the consideration of *Castle Blair*, for modern readers the most significant of her novels. For my purposes this, and to a lesser extent *Hector*, are the most deserving of critical examination. Shaw's subsequent fiction became increasingly adult-oriented, and does not merit lengthy consideration in this discussion.

Chapter 14

The Publishing History of Flora Shaw's Fiction for Children

'The Legions of Story Books' (Avery, in *Nineteenth Century Children*, 1965)

Britain

One of the few twentieth century critical surveys of children's literature which considers Flora Shaw's books is Gillian Avery's 1965 volume for Hodder and Stoughton, *Nineteenth Century Children*, which Avery subtitles *Heroes and Heroines of English Children's Stories 1780-1900*. In the final paragraph of her introduction she acknowledges the publication of 'The legions of story books of the last three decades of the nineteenth century' (1965: 8), and states that 'their names may still be dear to an older generation, and their authors better known' (8), recognizing the enormous boom in publication of literature, and particularly fiction, which marked the second half of Victoria's reign. That a considerable proportion of this was for children was a direct result of the 1870 Education Act, in which W. E. Forster, vice-president of the Liberal government's education committee, ordained that, for the first time, a school should be placed within the reach of every English child under the age of thirteen. The initial goal of these 'Board' schools should be to remedy, at an early age, the almost universal illiteracy amongst the working classes whereby British education compared so badly with that of many of her European neighbours. Twenty years earlier, the Public Libraries Act had allowed for the establishment of public reading facilities in larger urban areas. Publishers, ever astute to sense a market opportunity, saw that vast quantities of literature of all kinds would be necessary to meet the needs of the pupils. Furthermore the newly literate class, whose tastes might increasingly be for more realism than provided by the overtly moral tales which had hitherto predominated in their lists, could emerge as a profitable source of revenue for purveyors of domestic fiction.

By briefly surveying the trends and forms of publication in the mid to late Victorian literary world, it is possible to consider, in context, the popularity and importance of Flora Shaw's fiction for children. Avery identifies the enormous and ever growing flood of stories with which Shaw's had to compete when she completed her first novel in 1877. The writing of *Castle Blair* had been encouraged by John Ruskin, and, once published, he endorsed it enthusiastically, an endorsement which continued to be quoted by publishers of subsequent editions. As Ruskin was revered both in popular and academic circles as a formulator and critic of literary style and content for children, this championship of her first novel, together with an equally influential recommendation by that indefatigable writer of children's stories and arbiter of literary taste for the masses, Charlotte Mary Yonge, ensured that the acknowledged high quality of Shaw's work remained in publishers' minds when considering republication. Darton (third edition reprinted with corrections 1999) considers the format of Victorian publication in general in some detail, but makes no mention of Shaw's work. At this time, lengthier works were commonly published in multiple volumes, and copies in the British Library show that *Castle Blair: A story of youthful days* was first published by Charles Kegan Paul in two volumes, continuing to be published by Kegan Paul & Co. with further editions in 1878, 79 and 82. It had reached its eighth British edition in 1907 (published by George Routledge & Sons), changes in reading fashion having reduced it to a single volume. *Colonel Cheswick's Campaign* was sufficiently long to warrant three volumes when published in 1886, a 'triple-decker', but already by this date there was a growing market for the publication of fiction in single volumes, cheaper, more easily portable and easier to read for the increasing number of railway travellers (Routledge had been one of the first to recognize the need for cheap, light 'railway novels' to sell in W.H. Smith's conveniently placed railway bookstalls).

Quite why Flora Shaw offered her first piece of fiction to Charles Kegan Paul is a mystery. George Meredith, to whom a family friend had shown *Castle Blair,* although himself about to publish a new cheap edition of *The Ordeal of Richard Feverel* with Paul, felt that Shaw's work was not yet sufficiently polished for publication.[1] It is unlikely, therefore, that his was the recommendation. Nor did Ruskin use Charles Kegan Paul's services; perhaps the reputation of Kegan Paul as publisher of the works of Hesba Stretton, Robert Louis Stevenson and George Meredith attracted Flora. Unfortunately any correspondence between author and publisher may have perished in the fire at of 1883 which destroyed the publisher's warehouse. No letters remain in the Kegan Paul archive at University College London[2], nor does the National Register of Archives have any record that a further collection at Reading holds pertinent correspondence: Helen Callaway confirms that the Shaw papers held elsewhere 'are still not properly archived'.[3] Howsam (1998), in her history of Kegan Paul makes no mention of Shaw, although her overview of the publishing policy in the last thirty years of the nineteenth century throws interesting light on the condition of the publishing world into which Flora Shaw was placing her writing. Howsam (135) tabulates by genre the proportion of men to women whose work was being published: 53.8% of authors of novels were female, but this rose to 82.6% of the authors of books of juvenile interest; exactly what the latter category covered is not clear, and it may include both fiction and non-fiction. However, when overall totals are compared, (136), more than 80% of all authors on Kegan Paul's list were male, fewer than 20% female; Shaw, therefore, was entering into a rarefied atmosphere. Howsam (108) confirms the boom in children's literature, but states that this led to the development of specialized publishers of this genre. Kegan Paul, with a general list, apparently found it difficult to compete with the specialists, and 'juvenilia' never accounted for more than 1% of their total production.

It is therefore not surprising that, although Kegan Paul continued to publish until the fourth edition (1882), by the eighth (1907), *Castle Blair* was being published by George Routledge, a company who were specifically targeting the fiction-reading public; certainly Shaw's fourth novel, *A Sea Change* was published in 1885 by George Routledge and Sons. The earliest copy of Shaw's second book, *Hector: A Story for Young People*, in the national catalogue of the Consortium of Research Libraries (COPAC), dates from 1883, and this was published by G. Bell and Sons, so it seems that she had changed publishers by this point. Almost certainly this is because it was Bell who published *Aunt Judy's Magazine*, for which, following the success of *Castle Blair*, Shaw had been commissioned by Scott Gatty, one of the editors, to write *Hector*. *Aunt Judy's Magazine*, issued monthly, had begun publication in 1866, edited by Mrs. (Margaret) Gatty, herself a well known author. It took its title from the family nickname for her story telling daughter, Juliana, who, as Mrs. Ewing, became one of the best loved of the Victorian children's writers, publishing some of her stories first, in serial instalments in *Aunt Judy*, then as books, by Bell. In the middle years of the century there arose a multitude of such magazines, at a price to suit the ever-increasing numbers of newly literate households, providing material in the most popular genres.[4] The major authors wrote for them, whether, like Dickens and Thackeray, for an adult audience, or like Kingsley and MacDonald, for children. Many 'classics', which are now only known in single-volume format, first appeared in print as separate chapters, in monthly serial form, within the pages of these magazines. That Shaw was invited to write for one of the most prestigious, her work appearing beside that of established and respected authors, is an indication of the informed critical reception of *Castle Blair*; this will be examined in a later chapter.

No copy of her next novel, *Phyllis Browne* (1883), appears in any British academic library, nor is there any record of a publisher for it; however, it seems likely that, as this was another commission from the Gattys, Bell again published it in a single volume. It is clear, therefore, that Flora Shaw's work was now appearing in the imprint of a major publisher of popular children's fiction. No further novels were serialized prior to their appearance in book form. *Aunt Judy's Magazine* ceased publication in 1885, on the death of Juliana Ewing, thereby denying Shaw the opportunity to introduce her last two novels to the wide audience *Aunt Judy* had provided. Undoubtedly such serial publication created a large market for the eventual single-volume versions, and the loss of this opportunity may be a significant factor in the subsequent decline in popularity of Shaw's last fiction, and her decision to turn instead to journalism. Although produced as part of their 'Young Lady's Library' by George Routledge and Sons, it seems from COPAC records that *A Sea Change* (1885) went no further than a single edition in Britain. Darton recognizes 'the change which…came upon books for girls' (288). He identifies '[t]hat class of reader, hitherto sparsely provided for when it grew out of short frocks – for between *Aunt Judy* and the milder sort of adult fiction there was a considerable gap – seems almost to have appeared suddenly' (288). It was to fill this gap that the ever entrepreneurial Routledge collected authors for their 'Young Lady's Library', authors whose writing, like Shaw's *A Sea Change*, introduced increasingly young-adult oriented subject matter in which platonic adolescent love became increasingly sexually driven. However, of the seven books and writers 'Uniform with this Volume' named on the reverse of the title page, none merits an entry in any reference work. Unfortunately, although details of this series and information about Flora Shaw's George Routledge connection were sought of the multinational publishing successors to Routledge, no reply was received, nor could an archive be traced. This is a fascinating area, and a thorough examination of the history of the development of material specifically for an adolescent/young adult, to which Charlotte Yonge, herself an admirer of *Castle Blair*, made such a considerable contribution, would prove of great interest. *Colonel Cheswick's Campaign* (1886), the 'triple-decker', its sentimental, romantic content indicating Flora's increasing temptation into what later became the province of 'Mills and Boon' publishing, was a failure, and no cheap, single volume edition appeared. Only three copies remain in academic libraries: probably few more survive in private possession. Shaw had a new publisher for this final novel, Longmans,

Illustration 15: A Sea Change: detail of cover, George Routledge and Sons 1886, Illustrator: M.E. Edwards

Green & Co. The reason for this is unknown, but perhaps even Routledge were uncertain of the popular taste of *Colonel Cheswick*'s content.

It seems that of all five novels, only *Castle Blair* continued publication into the twentieth century in Britain, and the British Library catalogue indicates that there were only two further editions after the eighth in 1907. A 1929 republication by Oxford was possibly triggered by the author's death in that year, and a subsequent, if short-lived, reawakening of interest in her books. Following the obituary which appeared in *The Times* on January 28th 1929, in which no mention was made of Shaw's career as a novelist, a letter from a 'Mrs. Creighton' appeared which reproved the Editor for this omission, describing how she had been recommended to *Castle Blair* by Walter Pater (and 'his sisters'), that it was 'an admirable book', and 'a favourite with children'. However, although *Hector* is described by another correspondent as 'a treasured possession of mine', this was obviously not sufficient to encourage a new edition of that book. Oxford (under the imprint 'Humphrey Milford') was still reprinting *Castle Blair* in 1938, the 'new edition' which contained a Preface by Mrs. (Louise) Creighton, in which she expands the remarks in her letter to *The Times*, and appends a short overview of Shaw's life.

Prior to a 2007 reprint of the 1877 original text, the only more recent edition of *Castle Blair* was that published in 1966 by Rupert Hart-Davis. This indicates a declining interest in Victorian subject matter by twentieth-century readers of children's novels (although Marryat, Stevenson, Sewell and others have never disappeared from the 'children's classics' school of publication on cheap paper with lurid illustration). This makes the Hart-Davis edition all the more interesting, as the rationale behind the publication of the series in which it appeared, *The Keepsake Library*, is given on the dustwrapper, that it is 'made up of books from the past which deserve to be better known by children of today'. Also in the series are Mrs C. V. Jamison's *Lady Jane*, (an American book of the 1890s), Frances E. Crompton's *The Gentle Heritage* (1893), and a lesser-known story by Louisa M. Alcott, *Eight Cousins.* This publisher clearly took seriously the idea of introducing forgotten books to a new generation, as an attempt at a short, though not totally accurate, biography was made on the rear flyleaf, together with a historical background to the story's setting, emphasizing the Irish interest in the light of the ensuing Troubles. It also provides, again slightly inaccurately, details of its original publication information. Ruskin's recommendation continues to be quoted, almost a century after its first appearance. On the front flyleaf Charlotte Yonge's description of it as 'a wild Irish story, very attractive

Illustration 16: *Castle Blair*: Rupert Hart-Davis 1966 dustwrapper, Jacket design: Carol Edwards

and exciting' no doubt further influenced Rupert Hart-Davis' decision to include this in *The Keepsake Library*. Moreover, Hart-Davis clearly wished to emphasize *Castle Blair's* stylistic merits, as a passage quoted from Anne Eaton's essay in Meigs (1953) indicates; the substance of this is examined in the general consideration of critical comment on Shaw's fiction in Chapter 18. This edition is exuberantly illustrated with typically romantic 1960s interpretations of Victorian life, and provides an attractive copy for modern readers. There appears, however, to have followed no further reawakening of interest in Flora Shaw's fiction: the last forty years have seen no further editions, other than the inclusion of *Castle Blair* in the second of the two Victorian volumes (Vii) of *Masterworks of Children's Literature*, under the general editorship of Cott, with the Victorian works edited by the American, Robert L. Wolff, and jointly published in the UK and USA by The Stonehill Publishing Company/Chelsea House Publishers, and Allen Lane. It was this edition which first brought Shaw's fiction to my notice, and to which all page numbers refer. The *Masterworks*, originally edited between 1983-86 and subsequently republished, reproduces in their entirety nearly one hundred texts from 1550 to 1900, describing its contents as

> ...the best and most representative English literature read and loved by children from the middle of the sixteenth century to the flowering of children's literature during the Victorian age. (Wolff, 1985: rear of dustwrapper)

As an example of what Wolff describes as 'the fiction of real life' (Wolff, 1985, front dustwrapper), amongst such familiar stories as *Countess Kate, Jessica's First Prayer* and *Jackanapes*, is '*Castle Blair: a Story of Youthful Days* By FLORA L. SHAW' [*sic*]. Wolff's edition, reproduced from the 1878 American first publication by Roberts Brothers of Boston, prefaced *Castle Blair* with a general survey of Shaw's life and a brief appreciation of the novel within its literary context.

America

It is now very difficult even to find second-hand British published copies of any of Shaw's novels. However, on the American continent, there remain many more, principally American editions, but occasionally those from the British publishing houses. The first American edition of *Castle Blair*, which Roberts Brothers produced a year after its first publication in Britain, is identical with the C. Kegan Paul edition. When searching internet booksellers' sites for copies of Shaw's books, there are few available in the UK, but from American sources there were usually several copies of *Castle Blair*, one or two of *Hector*, and single copies of all her other novels, except *Colonel Cheswick's Campaign*, of which I have never found a copy for sale. As will be seen in Chapter 16, there seems to have been a greater recognition of Flora Shaw as an author in the USA, which may reflect her greater popularity in that country, and may therefore account for the greater numbers of her books surviving on the American continent. Another possible explanation may be that, in a country such as the USA, with a much shorter non-indigenous history than Britain, Victorian books have been valued more as historical artefacts, and not thrown away with such careless abandon as in the UK. Alternatively, it may merely be an indication of the size of original print runs, which may have been smaller in the USA: the sale of a complete run would therefore have necessitated a reprint or a new edition. Whatever the combination of causes, editions of *Castle Blair* appeared regularly, in a variety of imprints, and therefore clearly fulfilled the needs of the American adolescent and young adult as well as those in Britain. Evidence from the bookplates pasted into them shows that they found their way into libraries as well as homes in both the United States and Canada. These editions advertise Shaw's other novels: an undated edition published by Little, Brown & Co. in Boston adds beneath her name on the title page 'author of "Hector", "Phyllis Browne" and "A Sea Change"' [*sic*], which places this copy after 1885. The text is identical with earlier publishings in Britain and America, quotes the Ruskin commendation, and is followed by lists of a further twenty-nine titles available in 'The Boys' and Girls' Bookshelf', which includes American authors such as Alcott and Coolidge as well as such British writers as Ewing, Ingelow and Stevenson. Little, Brown were still publishing *Castle Blair* in 1931, a reprint of a new edition issued in 1923 with illustrations, and a delightfully colourful dustwrapper which shows both 'noble child' and noble dog', the Ruskin quotation appearing yet again on this cover, and inside. No mention is made of other books by Shaw, which may indicate that no others were in print by this date. As well as a resumé of the story, the rear of the wrapper explains that this is an 'improved edition, printed from new type and with new illustrations...issued at the request of a large number of librarians who have wished for young readers a more attractive edition than has heretofore been available'. There are, in addition, reviews from newspapers which heartily recommend the book for young American readers. This may give a further clue to the continuing popularity of Shaw's first novel in America. The emigration of a large number of despairing Irish to America in order to escape from the poverty and unfair tenancy regulations imposed by their Anglo-Irish colonizers would have provided a vast audience for any book with Irish interest. A text which was suited to explaining the causes of emigration to the children of those migrants would have had a considerable audience. The explicitly Fenian content of *Castle Blair* would certainly have recommended it to an American audience; the Fenians, or Irish Republican movement, had been simultaneously founded in Dublin and New York in 1858. It appears that no more recent edition of *Castle Blair* has been published. In 1902 D.C. Heath of Boston produced an abridged edition although no admission of abridgement is made. The title page names Flora Shaw as author of all her other titles except *Colonel Cheswick's Campaign*, which is not surprising as this is a novel more intended for young adults than children, and this three-decker would certainly not be suited to an audience requiring an abridged edition of a children's book. Heath's edition reduces the 1877 text by some 20%, omitting phrases of inessential description and elaboration, an editorial policy which, whilst altering Shaw's style to a certain extent, does not seriously affect the tone of the work. More radical, however, is the omission of sentences and whole paragraphs which describe aspects of personality or background. In Chapter 1 Murtagh's character is modified by the omission of a passage in which he treats the remarks of his sister and the housekeeper 'with silent contempt' (Wolff, 1985: 435), while a comparison of the younger brother Bobbo, who is a 'pleasant, strong-looking boy, with clear eyes, rosy cheeks, and a turned-up nose, *in contrast to Murtagh's sallow face and dark deep-set eyes*' [italics mine] omits the passage in italics, thereby removing subtle visual aspects of Shaw's depiction of Murtagh. The original conclusion of that chapter provides, in some detail, a key to the French cousin, Adrienne's, background and first impressions of her young cousins and the country in which they live. The 1902 D. C. Heath edition omits the entire passage. The assumption must be that the author of the introduction, Mary A. Livermore was the abridger; the effect of her abridgement is to render the novel more suitable to a lower interest age for her readers, increasing the pace and accentuating action over analysis of character and situation. These are all perfectly acceptable methods of simplifying the novel for a younger audience, but unquestionably Livermore thereby reduces the ideological impact of Shaw's writing. In her introduction (discussed in greater detail in Chapter 18), in addition to making compliments about style and content, she considers that 'the young people who read "*Castle Blair*" [*sic*] will not only be charmed by it, but will be made happier and better for having read it'. This is clearly the editorial intention of this abridgement.

Although originally published by Roberts Brothers in 1881, *Hector* was also published in the USA by Little, Brown & Co., possibly as early as

1883, but the reason for this additional publisher is not known. The title page of this copy (by its cover and format clearly early), only mentions *Castle Blair*, and therefore presumably predates any further novels. Following the success of *Castle Blair*, Ruskin's comments are again used to recommend Shaw's latest book. Roberts Brothers first published *Phyllis Browne* in 1886; by 1907 Little, Brown & Co. had produced an edition, which is identical with that serialized in *Aunt Judy's Magazine*, using the same illustrations. It is obvious that, as in Britain, when Shaw's serialized work appeared in single-volume format, no changes (other than Americanized spellings) were made. Phyllis Browne names "'Hector", "*Castle Blair*" and "A Sea Change"' [*sic*] as the author's other works, thereby confirming the likelihood that Shaw's last novel was not considered suitable for children, although a contemporary review in *The Nation* (July 1st 1886) shows that it had been published in the U.S. by Roberts Brothers in that year. *A Sea Change* was published by Roberts Brothers, in 1887, but this was to be the last of Shaw's fiction to achieve success on both continents. As was the case in Britain, the appeal of Flora Shaw's novels, with their pervasive Victorian genteel colonial ideology, waned in the early years of the twentieth century; no more recent editions of these later works appear to have been published in America.

Foreign Language editions

At least one of Flora Shaw's novels was translated into French: *Castel-Blair: histoire d'une famille irlandaise*, was published in 1889 by Alfred Mame et Fils, who also produced another, undated edition, with a different frontispiece, and re-titled *Une Cousine de France*. The Bibliotheque Nationale gives a publication date of 1911 for this, and also holds editions of *Castel-Blair* republished in 1894 and 1897. Perhaps the changed emphasis in the title, from Ireland to a French connection, was seen as a means of improving sales. The translation of *Castle Blair* is unabridged. It is a lavish octavo production, larger than the quarto volumes which appeared in the UK and USA (the latter themselves generally more highly decorated than their British originals), with a scarlet cover elaborately embossed with a stylish border of lilies and leaves in pale blue, green and gold, the page edges gilded, and elegant, though unattributed, illustrations within. Although Shaw herself was fluent in French and would have been perfectly able to translate her work for publication Alfred Mame et Fils obviously preferred to publish it 'traduit de l'anglais par A. Chevalier'[5]; it is likely that by the time of the French edition, Shaw was too occupied with her developing career in journalism to enable her to undertake the task of translation. It is possible that this was an unauthorized publication. This, however, seems highly unlikely, as Mame was a major French publisher, established in 1766, famous for its varied list, which included much juvenilia and texts in translation. Mame was particularly noted for their religious publishing, and the explicit religious and moral philosophy of Shaw's works would have proved attractive. To date, there is no evidence that *Hector* was published in France, although it might be thought that its piety and French setting, would have particularly recommended it as an appropriate addition to their list. No information about the author or her other work is given in *Castel-Blair* or *Une Cousine de France*, nor apparently, was it thought necessary to encourage French readers by including Ruskin's comments; although no indication of copyright is given in English language editions, the French book states that the copyright belongs to the publishers. Although nowhere is there any indication that Shaw's close French acquaintances, family or friends, had any connection or influence in literary or publishing circles it is possible that her intimate knowledge of, and prolonged visits to, France encouraged her to seek a publisher there. However whether the translation and publication of her books was at Flora's request, or initiated by Mame, that so eminent a French publisher should have added Flora Shaw to his list is an important indication of the popularity and renown of her early novels. There is no information available about any subsequent editions of these or others of Shaw's books in France, although Dorothy O. Helly, who is researching Shaw for a modern, scholarly biography, believes that a publisher called Verrier brought out a French translation of *Phyllis Browne* and *Colonel Chiswick's Campaign*. She also believes Shaw sought out the French publishers for her books. (email 05/08/2005).

An abridged edition translated into Norwegian was published in Kristiania (now Oslo) in 1909, with the title *Barnene paa Castle Blair: En fortaelling for barn* (*The Children from Castle Blair: A story for children*). Curiously, some of the names have been altered, for example from Murtagh to Edwin, Donnie (Mrs. Donegan) to Betsy, Winnie to Annie, Rosie to Mary, Marion to Klara, Plunkett to Brown and the dog Royal to Leo. Others have been turned into the Norwegian form of the same name (for example Ellie to Elly), while Adrienne (and the children's version of her name, 'Nessa') and Theresa remain unchanged. The usual quotation from Ruskin, translated into Norwegian, and with the reference therein to 'Winnie' changed to 'Annie', prefaces the novel. The text is very substantially reduced, amounting to a mere 163 pages, compared with the American abridgement of 1902, which has 306 pages of smaller print. On the rear cover are advertisements for Norwegian translations of

Illustration 17: *Barnene paa Castle Blair*: cover of 1909 H. Aschehoug & Co. (W. Nygaard) Norwegian edition, Illustrator unknown

other English or German language children's books including Louisa M. Alcott's *Little Women* and *Little Women Grown Up* (the original title of *Good Wives*), John William Nylander's German version of a Finnish story: *Die Jungen auf Metsola* (*The Children from Metsola*), Edgar Jepson's detective stories for children collected as *Lady Noggs, Peeress*, and Evelyn Sharp's *The Youngest Girl in the School*. Shaw's first novel was obviously well enough known to have been considered worthy of translation as part of the eminent publisher H. Aschehoug & Co (W. Nygaard)'s list of classic and recent children's fiction.[6] The choice of *Castle Blair* might also have been prompted by the political background to its story, as Norway itself had finally achieved independence from Sweden in 1905, and Shaw's depiction of the Irish Nationalist movement would have resonated with Norwegian readers.

Notes

1. Bell (1947), p. 40

2. Lewis, K. *Re C. Kegan Paul and Flora Shaw* (26/11/02)

3. Callaway, H. *Re Flora Shaw and John Ruskin* (26/11/2002)

4. Others included Charlotte M. Yonge's *The Monthly Packet*

5. Identified on the Bibliotheque Francais catalogue as Amélie Chevalier

6. The Norwegian publishers H. Aschetoug themselves were keenly nationalistic. As booksellers in Kristiania, they set up the first Norwegian publishing house in 1872, almost all previous books in Norwegian having been published in Denmark (with whom Norway was united until 1814). Aschetoug were (and remain) particularly involved in publishing for children and schools.

Chapter 15

The life of Flora Louisa Shaw, Lady Lugard: biography versus accuracy

'Author, journalist'
(Entry under 'Lady Lugard' in an unattributed, undated cutting surviving as a photocopy in the Alice Marshall Collection, Special Collections, Penn State Harrisburg Library, USA)

Biography

The description of Flora Shaw as 'author, journalist' in a cutting in the Alice Marshall Collection in Pennsylvania, USA, is one of only two printed references which place her non-journalistic writing before her newspaper commissions, and indeed one of the very few instances in which her authorship is acknowledged equally with her later diplomatic career. The cutting is undated, nor is any attribution made, but it seems likely, by its format and content, that it appeared in an English biographical yearbook in the years between 1907 and 1912. There is little recognition of Flora Louisa Shaw, Lady Lugard in any contemporary reference work: despite her renown as a journalist, and the award, in 1918, of DBE for her work for Belgian refugees, she does not warrant her own entry in the *Supplement to the Dictionary of National Biography* (Williams, 1975). Her life after her marriage in 1902 to Sir Frederick John Dealtry Lugard is recorded in eleven lines within his entry in that volume, which is in excess of seven hundred lines. Here Flora Shaw is clearly regarded as a useful adjunct to Lugard's own outstanding contribution to Empire as a colonial administrator. The writer of the entry, 'Hailey' (no further detail is provided but it is acknowledged that he writes from 'personal knowledge' amongst other sources, so is likely to have been a friend of Lugard's) concedes that she was 'a gifted lady who had become widely known as the head of the colonial department of *The Times*'. What holds far more significance for Hailey in this context, however, is that 'Lady Lugard identified herself closely with her husband's work'; mention is therefore made of her 1905 history of Nigeria, but no other books. Other than her DBE no further comment on her achievements in her own right is made; clearly, in Hailey's opinion, she had finally achieved the ultimate goal of any sensible woman of that era: a good marriage. What need, therefore, to record details of an earlier existence which could not be used to improve readers' impressions of her husband? This omission has been rectified by the lengthy and accurate entry by

Dorothy O. Helly and Helen Callaway to the *Oxford Dictionary of National Biography* (2004). The reference to her within her husband's entry has also been revised and expanded, recognizing that she was 'the brilliant colonial editor of *The Times*', and that his later life and career were far more significantly reliant on Shaw.[2]

As has been observed in Chapter 14, Shaw's fiction has apparently been better served by American publishers, who both responded to and created a larger, more loyal readership than in Britain; it is therefore not surprising to find an entry in Kunitz and Hancraft's 1936 New York published *British Authors of the Nineteenth Century* which lists Flora Shaw's fiction as well as her journalism, and mentions Ruskin's opinion of *Castle Blair*. No reference to Shaw is made in any equivalent British publication. It is also interesting to note that, whereas Shaw's three-column obituary in *The Times* on January 28th 1929 completely ignores her authorship of fiction of any kind, the brief obituary in the *New York Times*, with the same date, begins 'authoress, journalist', adding near its conclusion that '[s]he wrote *'Castle Blair'* and Hector' [*sic*], the latter a story for young readers'. This emphasizes the far greater interest in her fiction which survived on the American continent; it seems that in Britain this was viewed more as a slightly unfortunate but mercifully short episode in the otherwise laudable public career of a journalist and wife of an eminent colonialist.

It is astonishing that so little has been written about a woman whose achievements in amazingly diverse fields would be notable in our own day, and which should be recognized as exceptional, indeed pioneering, in the context of late nineteenth and early twentieth century women's expectations of their role in society, and in particular, society's expectations of them. Much of what had been written until Callaway and Helly (1992, 2000 & 2004) was biased and uncritical, written by admirers who sought to emphasize some aspects of her life at the expense of completeness and accuracy. As part of her role at the Centre for Cross-Cultural Research on Women within the University of Oxford, the late Helen Callaway collaborated with Dorothy O. Helly to write an academic biography of Flora Shaw and this will provide, for the first time, a complete and critical account of her life and achievements. The three articles written by Helly and Callaway so far, which concentrate on Shaw's 'passion for Empire'[3] and political journalism, include brief but accurate biographical detail, supported by their own research, which corrects errors which have been perpetuated in earlier writers' biographical accounts.[4] Callaway and Helly's biography will include a chapter on her fiction, recognizing that this phase of her life, though relatively short, is vitally important to a full and reasoned understanding of Shaw's life.

Elsewhere Shaw is poorly served biographically. The internet, an increasingly prolific source of the insignificant and ephemeral, but by its transitory and immediate nature an easier medium in which to publish indulgent asides, confines its content to listings of her journalistic life and publications, and matters relating to her refugee work. An exception is a short passage in a compilation of notable Irish lives, the Princess Grace Irish Library (Monaco) (2001) which contains several incorrect dates and statements, including both year (1851 instead of 52) and place (Dublin instead of Woolwich) of birth; in fact it is likely that, if the correct place of birth were given, this biography would no longer appear, as its inclusion in the 'Irish Library' might be in doubt. However, the remaining information is reasonably accurate, and places its emphasis on the fiction writing, listing title and publication dates (the latter not entirely correct) of all her novels except *Phyllis Browne*, and including a précis of Ruskin's comments on *Castle Blair*. Interestingly the anonymous writer of this biography describes the succeeding fiction as 'lively romances'. If for no other reason, this brief acknowledgement of Flora Shaw's life and work deserves commendation for concentrating on her early, non- journalistic work. Access to source material for E. Moberly Bell's 1947 biography was carefully controlled by Flora Shaw's widower, Lord Lugard; in her 'Foreword' Bell records that Lugard had wished that a biography should be written, and that, soon after her death in 1929:

> he set to work to collect and arrange the material...torn between a strong desire to see some published record of his wife's remarkable achievements and a violent unwillingness to allow anyone to look at her private papers, [he]undertook the immense labour of summarizing the diaries, adding a narrative of her early life, as she had related it to him.(9)

As Flora Shaw's fiction was written in this relatively early period in her life, any record of it (and of Shaw's childhood upon which some events were based) within Bell's biography is filtered not only through Bell's own opinions, but through Shaw's memory when relating events to her husband at a distance of at least fifty years. When it is realized that, in addition, Shaw probably considered her fiction to be of lesser value and importance than her later journalistic writing, and therefore withheld important information concerning it, and that her widower may have been even less inclined to consider the relevance of mere stories to his wife's (and his own) achievements, readers of Bell can appreciate why the period 1852-1885 occupies only one tenth of the book, whilst the seventeen years of colonial journalism merit a full two-thirds. The Lugards had no children, and a surviving great-niece has apparently inherited the family reluctance to allow access to family papers or even disclose what is in her possession.[5] Added to the loss of nineteenth-century publishers' records consequent upon the twentieth-century amalgamation of publishing houses, it is not surprising that accurate recording of Flora Shaw's early life and writing remains no inconsiderable challenge.

Flora Shaw's biographer, E[nid] Moberly Bell was the daughter of C.F. Moberly Bell, who was a fellow correspondent on *The Times*, later the paper's Managing Director, and subsequently one of Flora's closest friends; as such, the publisher recommends on the endpaper of *Flora Shaw* (1947) that Bell 'is ideally qualified to write the life'. It is, however, these seemingly impeccable qualifications which are the source of many of the inaccuracies and for the variation in chapter length and depth of detail when Bell is writing about the different phases in Shaw's life and work. Once Bell's parentage and consequent particularity of interest is appreciated, her concentration on the period 1885-1902, when her subject was pursuing her career as a journalist, is understandable, if not excusable. She provides considerably more background detail for Shaw's newspaper work prior to and for *The Times* and although her citation of source material is imprecise, the 'Foreword' mentions access to 'diaries for the years 1885-1898...and for the South African journey of 1901, supplemented by...private letters...and the correspondence with Moberly Bell' (9), a far firmer foundation upon which to base her survey of this part of Flora's life than the 'narrative' and 'summarising' to which Lugard had restricted Bell for the early years of childhood and fiction-writing. Lugard's 'violent unwillingness to allow anyone to look at her private papers' (9), compared with the apparently unrestricted access Bell had to a considerable quantity of later 'correspondence...unpublished letters and memoranda' (9) would appear to indicate a deliberate attempt on his part to prevent the publication of information about Flora's early life and friendships. The recollection of some of these friendships, as will become apparent, was not what a former soldier-diplomat elevated to the peerage would welcome in a panegyric on his dead wife; worse, it might also reflect adversely on his own marital decisions. Bell's first chapters are a comfortably non-controversial episodic account of Flora's life up to the age of twenty, which concentrates on anecdotal material, descriptive passages of her attractive physical appearance and her religious sensitivities; Helen Callaway, in the letter mentioned above, characterized Bell's work as 'Victorian', despite a publication date in the mid twentieth-century. Nevertheless that detail which Lugard permitted is reasonably accurate and reveals an early life which deeply influenced her later career and attitudes, and which is implicit in the setting, events, characterization and ideology of Shaw's writing for children and young adults.

Bell devotes two pages to a discussion of Flora Shaw's fiction, concentrating on the resultant pecuniary advantages for Flora's housekeeping. She notes John Ruskin's involvement in the initial ideas for *Castle Blair*, and quotes his comments in 1874 as 'I am delighted with the idea of your tale, and do not doubt your power of making it quite entrancing to children' (30). Where this quotation originates is a matter of conjecture as, despite enquiries of both publishers' and Ruskin archives, no letter containing it has been traced; perhaps it survived (or was created or adapted) as part of the 'narrative' Lugard had concocted from his wife's memories of her early life. Curiously Bell makes no reference to Ruskin's commendation of *Castle Blair* in *Fors Clavigera* (c.1895: 59: 'Letter LXXXVII', March 1878, quoted in the heading to my chapters on Flora Shaw), which would, had she known of it, admirably suited her description of *Castle Blair* and *Hector* as 'entrancing' (30), 'charming' (31) and 'vividly written' (32). It is tempting to see in this omission further evidence of Lugard's controlling influence in the biography. Bell commends the setting of *Castle Blair* as accurately descriptive of Kimmage, the Shaw grandfather's estate near Dublin, where Flora and her siblings spent their summers, and states that the child characters represent some of those siblings, their behaviour reflecting 'a revelation of Flora's own character...her joy in all the beauty of nature, her sensitive understanding of children and the virtues she chiefly valued - honesty, generosity, above all courage' (31). Bell goes on to describe *Hector* as 'based on her experience in France' (31): this appears irrefutable. She further enthuses about Shaw's 'vivid and delightful picture of the Gascon countryside' (32). While little of this comment is controversial, Bell makes a statement in the course of her passage about *Hector* in which she asserts that it was 'the only one of her works of fiction, except *Castle Blair*, which she herself regarded with some favour' (31). The veracity of this remark cannot be proved, but if this is an accurate record of Shaw's opinion it may reflect the gradual change in plot and characterization, and apparently, the intended audience, for her fiction, which took place in the last three novels. *Phyllis Browne,* with its adolescent heroine, continues the series of exciting adventures, and has its origin in Shaw's time in Waltham Abbey where she accompanied the Colonel Charles

Brackenburys when he (brother to her brother-in law) became head of the munitions factory there in 1880. She had undertaken to be in charge of the household for his wife while they were stationed at Aldershot, where her sister Mimi was living with her husband, Edward Brackenbury. *A Sea Change* and *Colonel Cheswick's Campaign* show significantly less originality, and aim at an increasingly newly adult readership, the former being a sentimental tale with a repressed undercurrent of incestuous sensuality, while the latter novel is more overtly suited to publication by a Victorian precursor of Mills and Boon. Given that Shaw received, and refused, several offers of marriage at this time, and that she was infatuated with another noted figure of colonial history immediately prior to marrying Lugard, it is hard to avoid speculation that these novels may reflect her own (actual or desired) emotional experiences. Whether or not Bell's assertion is true, Shaw's dissatisfaction with her later fiction is largely justified, and *Colonel Cheswick's Campaign* found insufficient favour with the contemporary readership to encourage Flora to persevere with fiction rather than pursue journalism. There is also, of course, the possibility that this comment was made *for* rather than *by* Flora, and that in 'summarizing' this period of her life, Lord Lugard preferred not to remind Bell or her readers of his wife's later, more sensational, and possibly more questionable fiction. It would, after all, not reflect well on a hero of the Empire to have chosen as wife a former writer of novelettes for young ladies.

Given the dominance of Frederick Lugard on biographical accounts of Flora Shaw, it is unsurprising to find that the only other major published source of information on her life is the massive two-volume account of her husband's achievements by his acolyte, Margery Perham. These, *Lugard: The Years of Adventure 1858-1898*, published in 1956 and followed four years later by *The Years of Authority 1898-1945*, catalogue in considerable detail, and with enormous reverence, the military career and subsequent rewards of a man whose life can be considered the epitome of imperialistic endeavour. Modern academic commentary on the divisive methods Lugard used in the period 1890-1906 first to colonize and then rule the recently acquired lands of Nigeria recognizes that, since Flora's death, Perham had became his greatest admirer and her biography is a model of effusive and uncritical hero-worship. With this clearly defined rationale for her biography, therefore, in Perham's work once again Flora Shaw is regarded not in her own right but as an (albeit extremely useful) adjunct to her husband's renown. Perham acknowledges that:

> Flora Shaw has a place of her own in the colonial history of the nineteenth century: indeed the change into Lady Lugard was in a sense the end of a remarkable public career. (1960: 55)

but is content to regurgitate an edited though partly verbatim, three-page version of Bell's account of Shaw's life before she began in journalism. It maintains Bell's tone, and emphatically states that:

> Her life has now been written and all those who wish to see the full length portrait of the most unusual woman whom Lugard married should turn to the biography by Miss Moberly Bell, the daughter of Flora's friend and colleague on *The Times*. This is the official life, for which both Lugard and his brother helped to prepare the materials. (55)

Not only is Shaw 'the most unusual woman whom Lugard married', but 'both Lugard and his brother helped to prepare the materials': an impartial consideration of Shaw's achievements is still denied, nor is there recognition of any need for a fresh appraisal of her life. Helly states that 'Perham may call the marriage an end to Shaw's public career, but in fact Flora's assiduous backing of her husband's work, her continued writing, and then her backing of the Ulster movement and her undertaking of Belgian relief suggest that though directed to other aims, she did not stop trying to affect public policy.'[6] Perham mentions only *Castle Blair*, in a single sentence in which she considers that its success 'led to further writing for journals' (57), presumably the serializations of *Hector* and *Phyllis Browne*. It is clear that Perham's interest is in the journalism, which would eventually lead to Flora's encounters with her future husband.

Accuracy

Until the anticipated publication of the Callaway and Helly biography of Flora Shaw, in which she will be placed firmly within the context of women's achievement, she will remain in her present ignominious position, viewed as a colonialist, diplomat and journalist, whose major importance is as Lady Lugard, a suitably qualified wife for a great soldier turned colonial governor, whose life both before and after marriage should be viewed more as a feature of her husband's good judgement in marrying her than a recognition of her own ability and achievements. Her previous biographers have ensured that her earlier life and writing will remain in carefully controlled obscurity, her readers largely ignorant of her full talent.

A brief survey of the major events of Flora Shaw's life reveals much about the formation of the ideologies which are as evident in her fiction as in her colonially inspired journalism. Flora Louisa Shaw was born in Woolwich in December 1852 into a family firmly entrenched in a socially advantaged, militaristic hierarchy. There is, despite Bell's claims, no evidence that her maternal grandfather was the Governor of Mauritius, nor that he was a French aristocrat who had retained his post even on the transfer of the island into British control forty years earlier. Nevertheless, the (unverifiable) family story proclaims them to have been defiantly aristocratic, and to have survived the French Revolution. Legend told how Flora's great grandmother had refused to leave Paris and displayed, according to Bell (1947: 13) her central belief that '[c]ourage …should be the distinguishing trait of the nobility'. Flora evidently believed this story and inherited the attitude, and this clearly informs her pervasive ideology of the 'gentleman', a constant theme in her writing, fiction and non-fiction, and one which is particularly at the core of both *Castle Blair* and *Hector*. Flora's father, Major General George Shaw, was the second son of Sir Frederick Shaw, an eminent member of Dublin's gentry, and came from an impeccable lineage of Anglo-Irish landowners.[7] He was a career soldier, primarily seconded to Woolwich and the manufacturing department for the bases of the cannons there. He rose to become third in charge at Woolwich by 1868. His young family spent long periods in the summers on their grandfather's estate in Ireland. These were to provide both the geographical, political and social setting for Flora's first book, *Castle Blair* (1877), published when she was twenty-five. Prolonged residence with Sir Frederick provided Flora and her twelve siblings with periods of idyllic childhood in which they were allowed great freedom, but during which the overtly paternalistic role of the Anglo-Irish landlord pervaded every aspect of life on the estate, and which became a further influence in the formation of the ideologies as implicit in Flora's fiction as her colonial journalism. Bell (12), presumably paraphrasing Lord Lugard's recollections of his wife's retelling of her early memories, comments that Flora's grandfather instilled in his young visitors, 'a high sense of the responsibility which belongs to the privileged, of the duty of generous service'. Central to Flora's theme of the 'gentleman', seen particularly in the characterization of Murtagh in *Castle Blair*, and the eponymous hero Hector, is a statement that was apparently made by Sir Frederick which Bell quotes (12): 'It's the privilege of a gentleman…to get the worst of any bargain throughout life'.

The young Flora, therefore, was, from both maternal and paternal backgrounds, the recipient of ideologies ingrained in imperialism and privilege, elevated social positions which both families considered imposed a considerable degree of responsibility and required lifelong devotion to the perceived duty of a 'gentleman'.

Having first visited them when a baby, Flora returned to meet her French relatives at the age of fifteen, and made an extended visit after the remarriage of her father. She became particularly close to her maternal aunt who lived in Gascony, becoming fluent in the language. *Hector* embodies many of her experiences and perceptions of life in this area. Hector himself, as an English child sent on the death of his mother to live with French relatives, becoming involved in the adult machinations of French provincial life, represents and expresses the ideologies not only derived from Flora's (possibly apocryphal) aristocratic French great grandmother, but from her Anglo-Irish paternal grandfather, ideologies which concentrate on the *Englishness* of the concept of the gentleman.

After her mother's death Flora, aged eighteen and the third of the fourteen children, assumed all domestic responsibilities, a duty which she only relinquished when her father remarried, and relations became strained with her stepmother (a situation which forms a basis for her final novel, *Colonel Cheswick's Campaign*). Duty for her, as a young Victorian woman, was to ensure the continuation of the smooth running of household life: she would not have contemplated otherwise. Despite offers of marriage, Flora remained single: for whatever reason, her own story did not end in happy marriage to the subaltern of her dreams, as it did for her heroine in *Colonel Cheswick's Campaign*. Many years later, after a lifetime of contribution in the fields of journalism and devotion to colonial and social duty, Shaw commented that, whilst she was anxious that a biography of her husband should be written, she did not consider herself a suitable subject, because she had had no children.[8] To twenty-first century eyes it may also appear surprising that such a pioneer of political journalism, who was deeply aware of the restrictions and inequalities her gender inflicted upon her, was nevertheless opposed to the movement for women's suffrage, believing that women should not be entitled to influence political decisions until such time as they were prepared and able to carry arms for their country.[9] This attitude, however was totally in keeping with the imperialist constructions of gender, which sought to maintain the status quo in which women fulfilled their traditional roles by supporting and promoting the male perpetuation of the apparently unquestionably superior levels of civilization and justice which the British Empire offered its colonies. Imperialist women made no claims to equality of gender, and sought to shield their sex from the greater dangers and stresses which, in their perception, an active political or military life would exert, being content with their role as wives, mothers and backroom assistants - a 'tea and sympathy' support. Flora Shaw, as Colonial Editor of *The Times*, simultaneously defied convention, in her journalistic role, and encouraged it, by actively promoting imperialism with its rigid gender stereotyping. Her belief in her great grandmother's aristocratic doctrine that women, though unable to fight, could at least die at their posts[10], appears to have further informed Flora's ideology.

As the daughter of a senior officer at Woolwich, Flora had access not only to the Royal Military Academy Library, but also to the series of lectures by eminent men which took place each winter. In 1869, as a new debutante, she attended her first lecture, given by John Ruskin, and entered into a friendship which provided intellectual stimulation, advice and support in both domestic and literary spheres. As his friend she was also introduced to the aging Thomas Carlyle, himself a supporter of colonialist policies. From these men she found encouragement with her fiction, and developed further the passion for the ideologies of colonialism which informed this writing, and which encouraged her move into journalism. The importance of Ruskin's theories on a multiplicity of social, political and artistic subjects, which were becoming widely available to the general public through the publication of his lectures and letters of instruction to the working classes, was very considerable.[11] Public opinion was much influenced by his conviction that poverty at home could be remedied by harnessing the riches to be found in the colonies, a view possibly expressed in the lecture given on December 14th. 1869 at the Royal Institution, Woolwich,[12] and espoused thereafter by Flora Shaw, who saw in it a further justification for the ideology inherited from her aristocratic imperialist ancestors. She was confirmed in her support of Ruskin's theory by the poverty she had witnessed in Ireland (often made worse by the absentee landlords Murtagh criticizes so vehemently in *Castle Blair*) and the condition of the women and children she met when undertaking charitable works in the east end of London after she had left the family home in Woolwich. *Phyllis Browne* (1883) testifies to her concern about conditions for workers and their families, a concern born of the perceived paternalist responsibilities which were central to the ideologies of her class and background as much as to Ruskin's theories.

The evidence for the ideologies implicit in Flora Shaw's writing will be examined in greater detail within the discussion of *Castle Blair* and *Hector*. It is clear, however, that her early life had considerable influence on the choice and treatment of the subjects of her fiction. Within these novels she expressed her belief in a paternalistic imperialism, which accepted the responsibilities as much as the rights of the gentleman, as clearly as in her journalism. When considering why, then, this aspect of her writing has been so ignored (whereas writers such as Charles Dickens are viewed as weighty chroniclers of social conditions), the inevitable conclusion must be that Flora Shaw was writing fiction for a young audience, and that, to the critics, this reduces the importance of her work.

The success of *Castle Blair*, and a subsequent invitation to serialize her next two novels in *Aunt Judy's Magazine,* one of the most prestigious of the monthly publications so popular in Victorian households, encouraged Flora, in 1883, to rent (and eventually purchase as her own home) rooms in a cottage at Abinger in Surrey. Here she was close to the novelist and literary critic George Meredith, a friend of a distant relative, who had admired her novels, and, in turn introduced her to another novelist and essayist, Robert Louis Stevenson. With such eminent writers of fiction to encourage and support her, it might be expected that Shaw would have continued her fiction and developed her increasingly adult-oriented subject matter. However she interviewed Meredith in 1886 for an article she wrote about him and his work that was published in the US with the help of Norton. At this time she probably broached with him the question of switching to journalism in order to earn a dependable living. Accordingly, when later that year Flora was invited to accompany family friends on a trip to Gibraltar, and was in need of extra funds, Meredith also introduced her to W.T. Stead, Editor of the *Pall Mall Gazette*, who suggested the possibilities for publication of any letters which she might send him about the political situation in the area. When Shaw fortuitously gained an interview with Zebehr Pasha, a notorious figure from General Gordon's Egyptian campaigns, and began to supply the *Gazette* with lucid and well-researched articles, both the *Manchester Guardian* and *The Times* solicited work from her. The same distant relative who had introduced Flora to Meredith had previously combined his military career with writing for *The Times*, so such a change of direction provided her with no qualms, and at this juncture, Flora Louisa Shaw moved from 'author' to journalist', a move which resulted in her commissions to travel and research the situations in Europe from1889, and then to concentrate on the development of the colonies: South Africa (1892), Australia (1893)[13], Canada (1893 and 1898), and West Africa (1902).

Illustration: 18: A portrait of the author in later life by the Belgian artist André Cluysenaar (1872-1939), reproduced in Bell (1947) *Flora Shaw*

In 1893, her work clearly superior to that of any previous colonial correspondent, she was invited to become the Colonial Editor of *The Times*, a post which had hitherto not existed. In a letter to *The Times*, after Shaw's death, Lady Jersey writes that the change from fiction to factual writing was because Shaw had realized 'the absolute necessity of making the Empire better known to the ever-growing population of the Homeland'. The letter continues, '[t]herefore she relinquished other literary ambitions, feeling that the Press was the one medium through which she might convey the knowledge to the people.' Flora Shaw clearly possessed a crusading zeal to spread and explain the colonial ideology which underpinned her fiction, a zeal which sought a wider audience than that for children' literature.

During the course of these journalistic commissions she met, and, in 1902 married, Sir Frederick Lugard. At this point *Flora Louisa Shaw* retired, apparently content to undertake the role which the expectations of late Victorian/early Edwardian society demanded of its married women: she became *Lady Lugard.* Her life as wife to the Governor, together with her extensive journalistic and diplomatic experience encouraged her to write one final book.[14] This was the first substantial history of those parts of West Africa which had now become a British colony, Nigeria (the new country's name suggested by Shaw herself), a book which is, in Callaway and Helly's words 'told with sweeping panache' (1992: 90), has become reviled among those in modern Nigeria who ascribe that country's problems to its Imperialist past, embodying as it does Shaw's central philosophy of racial superiority which underlies the paternalistic attitudes of her fiction. This philosophy, based on colour as well as class, informs a book which reflects contemporary colonial attitudes and favours the Islamic northern area of the new country, largely ignoring the history and culture of the peoples of the African south. From then until her death in January 1929 she supported her husband in his work, undertook charity work and wrote letters to benefactors and to the press. Some of these letters reveal that her deep-rooted ideology remains unchanged: letters to *The Times* during 1914 show her continuing interest in the Irish question, and consider the demands of Ulster to maintain self-determination, and freedom of religion, while others examine various aspects of the imminent war with Germany. Shaw's view of the rights of the gentry, social position and class is reiterated in a letter of thanks in April 1915 to the Ottawa Women's Canadian Club, who had raised money for the Lady Lugard Hospitality Committee (for Belgian Refugees), in which she explains that '[t]he problem of dealing with working class Refugees is almost entirely in the hands of the Government, but the large numbers of better class

Refugees cannot be dealt with on the strict lines of Government relief'. She continues '[w]e …organize large houses on the footing of an economical gentleman's establishment…we…use Belgian Refugees of the lower classes as cooks and domestic servants and to organize life on a moderately comfortable and dignified scale for upper class Refugees.'

Clearly Flora Shaw maintained her concept of hierarchical stratification throughout her life. The degree to which her ideology pervades her dialogue in her first two novels for children will be considered in greater depth in the next chapter.

Notes

1. Helly, O. D. and H. Callaway (2004), 'Lugard , Dame Flora Louise, Lady Lugard (1852–1929)', in the *Oxford Dictionary of National Biography*, Oxford: University Press

2. Kirk-Greene, A. H. M. (2004) 'Lugard, Frederick John Dealtry, Baron Lugard (1858–1945)', in the *Oxford Dictionary of National Biography*, Oxford: University Press

3. letter from Helen Callaway, March 11th. 2002

4. Wolff (1985), in the biographical notes included in his introduction to *Castle Blair,* acknowledges Bell as his source, though, unlike her, he mentions *Phyllis Browne*; he places Shaw's death ten years too late, however

5. Callaway, H. *Re: Flora Shaw & John Ruskin* (26/11/02)

6. Helly email (5/08/05)

7. The author George Bernard Shaw was a distant cousin.

8. Bell, p301

9. Obituary in *The Times*, January 28th 1929

10. Bell, p3

11. for example *Lectures on Art* (1880), delivered 1870, *Fors Clavigera* (1871)

12. Bradley (1997), p 77

13. Using her experiences there to write, in 1898, *The Story of Australia*, a volume in a popular series, *The Story of the Empire*, widely used in schools as well as becoming an indispensable item in every aspiring Victorian's home library. Shaw writes with clarity, accuracy and dispassion.

14. *A Tropical Dependency* (1905)

Chapter 16

Castle Blair: a story of youthful days

> 'The proper way of managing Irish people':
> (John Ruskin, in 'Letter LXXXVII', in *Fors Clavigera*, March 1878)

Castle Blair is universally acknowledged as Flora Shaw's best piece of writing for young readers. Chapter 18 examines in detail the critical reaction to her fiction expressed during Shaw's lifetime, and in modern times. Of Shaw's five novels only *Castle Blair* achieved and maintained even a short lived popularity. Although regrettable, this cannot be condemned, as it is only *Castle Blair* which possesses those unique qualities which should entitle it to be regarded as an important text in the development of fiction for children. It holds considerable interest for a modern audience not only because of its setting, the political situation in Ireland in the middle years of the nineteenth century, but also because it voices the archetypical Victorian ideological convictions which instigated and maintained this political situation. This situation has been a significant factor in the escalation of the 'Troubles' in Ireland which continue into the twenty-first century. *Castle Blair* is also an important text in any survey of the development of the 'emancipated child' in children's literature. In it the child characters represent a significant, though little recognized, step in this movement towards the modern children's novel, in which the young protagonists operate with an autonomy largely denied to child characters before Shaw. Because of the nature of its socio-political concern, *Castle Blair* is an interesting text to consider in terms both of post-colonial critical theory and new historicism.

The story of *Castle Blair* reflects Flora Shaw's early life in Ireland in the years between 1852 and 1870 (considered in greater detail in Chapter 15). The five Blair children, sent by their parents from India to live with their uncle on his estate in Ireland, are allowed, by his lack of interest and the indulgence of his housekeeper, to run wild. In so doing they not only appreciate the natural world, but also become actively involved in local events resultant upon the larger political picture. Mr. Blair is in effect an absentee landlord; as he ignores the children, leaving their upbringing to his housekeeper, so he ignores his responsibilities as a landowner, leaving the running of his estate and the management of his Irish tenants to his agent, Mr. Plunkett. The children befriend Theresa Curran, the step-daughter of one of these tenants, a violent drunkard who terrifies his wife and children to the extent that Theresa, having lost the money entrusted to her to pay the rent, fears for her life. With the best of intentions, they hide her whilst they attempt to solve the problem of the rent, but delays caused by Mr. Plunkett being shot at by local political activists result not in their resolving Theresa's family problems, but in unwittingly exacerbating them. A further attack by the Fenian activists results in accusations by the agent against Murtagh, the oldest Blair boy, whose position as a 'gentleman', although still a child, requires him to behave according to a strictly honourable code. Through the modifying influence of their French cousin, Adrienne, whose sympathetically civilizing influence is unencumbered by the ideologies of the Anglo-Irish colonizers, all is finally resolved, and the children realize that Mr. Plunkett's intentions towards the tenants are, in fact, just and benevolent, whilst the agent accepts that a greater degree of understanding and tolerance would improve his administration of the estate. Readers are also left with the hope that Mr. Blair will, in future, take a more active role as landlord.

In order to assess Shaw's ideology, evident in her portrayal of the particular form of paternalistic colonialism which had created the Ireland of the mid-nineteenth century, it is necessary briefly to review that island's history. The Anglo-Norman ruling classes, the crown and aristocracy, had begun to create settlements in Ireland after the Norman conquest of England in 1066. The extent of this colonization of Ireland, undertaken in order to control the island which was seen as a threat to English security because of the possibility of its use by hostile forces as a mustering place for a threat to England itself, is still evident, if the prevalence in modern Irish surnames of the Norman prefix 'Fitz' is appreciated. Ireland already possessed its own Gaelic ruling class, which posed its own threat to the colonizers; subsequent English policy was, therefore, to keep the newly established Anglo-Irish and the indigenous Gaelic Irish apart. This was the root of the widely different cultural and political conditions which emerged for colonizer and colonized, a difference which the successive English administrations sought to increase in order to reduce the status and credibility of the native Irish, who became increasingly resentful of the imposed Anglo-Irish landowners. By the sixteenth century, as a result of the Reformation and the suppression of Catholicism in England, the rights of the Catholic Irish had been seriously restricted, and the indigenous population effectively lost all control of their land, being forced to hold it as tenants of the ruling Anglo-Irish gentry. The abolition of the English monarchy worsened this situation, Cromwell's republic providing nothing for the common wealth of Ireland except considerable further colonization and draconian suppression of the Irish tenantry. This policy was continued with vigour by the restored crown, particularly under William III. At this point those Irish who could began to emigrate to the newly colonized lands in North America, still under the control of the English crown, but vast enough to allow settlers a reasonable living without direct intervention by the colonizers. Thus began the sympathy, which exists to this day, between North America and Ireland. An explosion in population amongst the native Irish further worsened their conditions at home and led to widespread starvation. Through the writings of observers such as Jonathan Swift[1] who had bitterly attacked the society which tolerated the terrible condition of the poor, and Arthur Young[2] who toured Ireland and recorded the wretched state of great numbers of the rural population at the time, eighteenth century England became aware of the abominable policies of the Anglo-Irish landlords and their agents. Gradually writers of fiction began to ridicule the despised Anglo-Irish ruling gentry class. Maria Edgeworth, already well known for her books for children, used her own Anglo-Irish background in her first adult novel, *Castle Rackrent* (1800), in which she portrayed the decline of a family of debauched absentee landlords, pursuing the theme in *The Absentee* (1812) and *Ormond* (1817), and powerfully describing the effect of 'the tyranny of a bad agent' on tenants (1994: 221). Flora Shaw would have known Edgeworth's work: it is interesting that Edgeworth had already created a 'Murtagh' in the Rackrent dynasty, but hers was a 'gentleman' whose sole desire, to dominate his tenants by litigation, is utterly opposed to Shaw's impulsively compassionate young Blair.

Conditions for the Irish tenantry continued to worsen during the early years of the nineteenth century, with famine caused by crop failure and resultant food shortages. Flora would have witnessed scenes of great poverty amongst her grandfather's tenants, a considerable contrast to the privileged life of the Shaws, in their elegant country house. Increasing social unrest amongst the poor led to their greater political activity, with the rise of a number of republican organizations seeking land reform and the removal of Ireland from direct British government (in 1801 it had ceased to be a mere colony and been 'united' with mainland Britain). The Irish Republican Brotherhood - the Fenians - with their American wing, were particularly dangerous and recruited almost entirely from the working classes. Flora's grandfather, Sir Frederick Shaw, had been a prominent figure in Anglo-Irish politics, had defeated the republican Daniel O'Connell and entered parliament. It was, therefore, with an intimate knowledge of the causes and consequences of civil unrest, that Flora Shaw wrote her first novel.

Critically, therefore it is particularly valid to consider *Castle Blair* in the light of 'new historicism'. Informed, like post-colonial theory, by the writings of Michel Foucault in the 1970s, which acknowledge the complex multiplicity of social, political and economic factors influencing texts, developed and expanded in 1980 by Stephen Greenblatt, new historicism considers that equal importance should be given to contemporaneous literary and non-literary texts, as the relationship between history and the literary text is seen as a dialectic: they 'constantly inform and interrogate each other'.[3] As the historical survey above indicates, in this instance the colonial context of Ireland is also implicit within the new historicist approach, as it has dictated that country's history and fortunes for a millennium. Post-colonial critical theories are therefore equally valid in a consideration of *Castle Blair*. Text is a representation of the culture from which it came and reveals its ideology; both analytical techniques will reveal the ideologies which drove the Victorian Anglo-Irish landlords to manage the affairs of their life, their estate and their tenants as they did, and which underlie Shaw's narrative.

Although Arthur Young's account was written almost a century before Shaw's, it serves to confirm the accuracy of her description of the appalling living conditions of the Curran family. Shaw describes their cottage:

> The cottage was much like many another, but bare and neglected-looking. It felt cold like an uninhabited place. A mud floor; at one end a cupboard; at the other a bed; a table, a couple of broken chairs;...she had nothing to eat, and there was no fire, and the door was open, and the pig had got in and the chickens were pecking her oatmeal, and oh! Everything was so miserably uncomfortable...a cup and plate and spoon had to be found and washed. (1985: 481)

Young writes:

> The cottages of the Irish, which are called cabbins *[sic]*, are the most miserable- looking hovels which can well be conceived...The furniture of the cabbins is as bad as the architecture; in very many consisting only of a pot for boiling their potatoes, a bit of a table, and one or two brokenstools; beds are not found universally, the family lying on straw...(quoted in Moody & Martin, 1780: 221)

A comparison of these passages reveals a remarkable correlation between fact in 1780 and fiction in 1877, and each serves as confirmation of the accuracy of the other. It is also apparent that the ideals driving colonial policy in Ireland had remained unchanged in the intervening century.

Arthur Young's observations on the 'middlemen' or agents employed by the Anglo-Irish landlords to run their estates when absent, or, as in the case of Mr. Blair, choosing not to involve themselves directly in the management of their land, agents who often 'took the land at a reasonable rent and sub-let at the highest price [t]he[y] could get, a procedure which caused untold misery'[4], are equally apposite:

> Living upon the spot, surrounded by their little under-tenants, they prove the most oppressive species of tyrant that ever lent assistance to the destruction of the country. They re-let the land, at short tenures, to occupiers of small farms; and often give no leases at all. Not satisfied with screwing up the rent to the uttermost farthing, they are rapacious and relentless in the collection of it. (quoted in the introduction to Edgeworth *Castle Rackrent*, 1995: xv)

This comment reveals that many agents were corrupt in the extreme. Shaw, however, gradually allows readers to see that the children's opinion of Mr. Blair's agent is ill informed. Although Murtagh calls him 'that brute Plunkett' (1985: 448), he admits, 'I don't know exactly what agents are, but it's something very bad. They're tyrants, and they oppress everybody' (474). The children's hatred of him, which encourages them to demand that their friends should swear an oath to 'hate the "Agents"' (530), is actually based on his disapproval of, and attempts to correct, their wildness, not his treatment of the tenants.

Shaw shows that Plunkett is not oppressing the tenants, but trying to encourage them to improve their own conditions. Mr. Blair tells Adrienne that the agent, 'has succeeded in making the cottagers round about keep roofs on their houses, and conform to a few other customs of civilization, unpicturesque perhaps, but very desirable' (505). She, in turn, attempts to correct the children's pro-Irish interpretation of the agent's actions:

> Mr. Plunkett is not tyrannizing over these people...[h]e's trying all he can to make things better for the people, only they are so unreasonable they expect to have everything done for them, and they don't want to give anything in exchange. It's quite fair when a lot of expensive improvements have been made that the rent be raised; and then when people are drunken and worthless and won't take care of their land of course they have to be turned out. (596)

Such behaviour is, nevertheless, wilfully interpreted by tenant and children alike as cruelty. The mother of the young republican activist, Pat O'Toole, complains, '[h]e's been a blight an' a curse upon the country since the day he first set foot in it' (549), whilst Pat declares '[i]sn't he oppressin' every one of us, and changin' all the old ways that was good enough for them as was better than him!' (587). Justifying his own hatred of Plunkett, Murtagh cites Pat's opinion that, 'Ireland will never be free till all the agents [are] killed' (474), for 'he turns the people out of their houses, and sends them to prison for nothing, and sees them starving in the winter-time and doesn't care. No wonder they hate him' (596). Mr. Blair's statement that his agent has enforced the improvements 'at the risk of his own life' (596), and that, '[m]ore than one of the men about here would think it a praiseworthy action to shoot him from behind a hedge some dark night' (596), anticipates Pat's attempt to do just that. This action is thwarted by Murtagh's intervention when he overhears Marion's loving fears for her father's life and realizes the error of his assessment of Plunkett's behaviour, and the true awfulness of Pat's intended assassination of the agent. Shaw uses her description of Plunkett's physical appearance to represent the dichotomy of his position. He is a 'correct-looking person…there was a certain severe dignity in his bearing that commanded respect' and beneath this outward appearance 'was something deeper…a strength of some kind, the presence of which was felt at once through all the superficial accidents of his nature' (447). Mr. Blair holds a high opinion of his agent, who has doubled the estate's income and 'saves me more trouble than twenty other men would do in his place' (505), without the landlord having to leave the 'musty old parchments' (561) of his library. Mr. Blair considers that the Irish who are reluctant to change their ways, preferring to 'leave things to take care of themselves' (568), need an agent such as Plunkett to galvanize them into acting in their own best interests.

This, of course, does not include political self-determination, and so the Blair children, who, left by their neglectful adult guardians to run wild with the local children, espouse everything Irish (although, true to the ideological influence of their social position, they select for themselves the parts of Irish Kings and Queens, not peasants), and wholeheartedly enter into the tenants' demands for separation from British rule. Murtagh tells his French cousin, Adrienne, '[I]f you can't understand Irishmen, you can't understand me' (491). Enflamed with the iniquity of Pat O'Toole's situation whilst he is in hiding, they are, '[w]ild fierce little things…they were up in arms directly and stormed like staunch little Home Rulers, as they were, at anything they considered unjust' (565). Shaw continues to modify readers' opinions of Plunkett with scenes of his domestic life with his small daughter, Marion, to whom he is her devoted and indulgent 'Fardie' (452). Gradually this modification also affects Murtagh's opinion. Following the cathartic illness brought on by saving both Plunkett and Pat, an illness used by Shaw as a metaphor to show that Murtagh has emerged from his total immersion in the republican cause, which prompted wild assertions such as 'I believe that everything's all wrong together, and nothing can ever be right' (596), Murtagh realizes how wrong his original assumptions had been. He accepts the colonialists' ideals being put into action by the agent, and apologizes, 'I am very, very sorry I was so…dreadfully wicked' (604) When the error of their judgement is revealed, Shaw allows all sides to retreat with dignity: Mr. Blair, emerging from his absenteeism, undertakes the duties of a landlord for the first time, ensuring that Pat is removed to worthwhile employment which will hopefully wean him from his republican tendencies, and, knowing that his agent is, in fact, a scrupulously fair man, resting content in the certainty that Mr. Plunkett will seek no retribution from O'Toole or his family. Plunkett himself, having unjustly accused Murtagh of setting fire to his house, is assailed with self-doubt, 'the revelation of his injustice to Murtagh had strangely shaken his trust in himself. He had been wrong with him, perhaps he had often been wrong with other people too' (602). He admits to Murtagh that 'perhaps there were faults on both sides' (604). A conviction in the immovable correctness of colonialism is here tempered by the best manifestation of paternalism: the ideals of the gentleman, who in the words of Murtagh, 'don't tell lies' (448), have also informed the actions of the gentleman's agent. This was then, like Maria Edgeworth's arguments against the perils of absenteeism, in Ruskin's opinion, 'the proper way of managing Irish people' (*Fors Clavigera*, Letter LXXXVII: 259).

Flora Shaw's unquestioning acceptance of the justification for colonizing would have been confirmed by her friendship with Ruskin, whose Inaugural Lecture as Slade Professor of Art in 1870 had a profound effect on the new generation of enthusiastic colonizers typified by Cecil Rhodes. Ruskin maintained that Britain's burgeoning population could only be supported by active partition of other lands. He advocated an enlightened rule, but one which demanded absolute loyalty from those colonists; he wrote:

> And this is what [England] must do, or perish: she must found
> colonies as fast and as far as she is able, formed of her most
> energetic and worthiest men;-seizing every piece of fruitful waste

ground she can set her foot on, and there teaching her colonists that their chief virtue is to be fidelity to their country, and that their first aim to advance the power of England by land and sea, and that, though they live on a distant plot of ground, they are no[t to]consider themselves disenfranchised from their native land...
(1880: 29)

He expects those colonists to 'plough and sow' for England, 'behave kindly and righteously for her...bring up their children to love her', and foresees that they will then be enabled to 'gladden themselves in the brightness of her glory'. An adherent to this ideal, Flora Shaw, in *Castle Blair*, shows the transformation, through the unwitting offices of the Blair children, of an unsatisfactorily managed Irish estate towards the epitome of enlightened colonial rule described by Ruskin. In the eyes of the new historicist critic, therefore, Shaw's book is both informed by, and (by its publication and dissemination in England), approves, cements and perpetuates the ideologies from which sprang the colonization of Ireland. In addition, although ultimately not supporting a slavish adherence to a republican cause, it reveals the social inequalities a colonial regime may engender. The popularity of *Castle Blair* amongst American readers ensured that Shaw's writing added to the corpus of literature of all genres which influenced their opinions on the Irish question.

Whilst such a policy is expressed in both Ruskin and Shaw in terms of great desirability, it is a policy born of unquestioning national pride, laden with self-interest and disregard for the lives and culture of the indigenous peoples of these colonies. Although Shaw shows the Blair family all to fail in their duty to some degree, this, she asserts, can be rectified by a return to truly genteel ideals: this is an inborn quality which those of lower social status cannot achieve. Shaw's championship of this ideology forms the principal theme of *Hector*; her depiction of its importance in the upbringing of a true Englishman in *Castle Blair* will therefore be examined in the next chapter.

It is however, appropriate here to examine briefly, with reference to postcolonial theory, the implications of Shaw's attitude in *Castle Blair* towards the ordinary Irish people. Shaw's book belongs to a distinctive colonial genre, writing as she does about a long established rule of one white race over another, whose aspirations and culture have been eroded by what was viewed by the colonizers as the dominant superiority of their ideology. Postcolonial writers as distinct from critics seek to free their work from characteristically colonial attitudes and expressions. As has been discussed above, Shaw emerges as a champion of colonialism and it is therefore surprising to realize that, to a certain extent, Shaw's writing shows a characteristically postcolonial attitude. This can be seen in the degree to which the Blair children accept and integrate with all that is typically Irish, particularly its apparent free-thinking, its myths and music. It is precisely because the young Blairs are portrayed so sensitively and sympathetically that readers empathize with the Irish whom the children desire to emulate. Shaw allows this empathy to extend to those who suffer because of their social position, but she is careful to ensure that readers appreciate true innocence and justifiable action against oppression, rejecting what in her particular ideological convictions, is biased, ill-judged and violent behaviour. However, although readers are permitted to share the unrestricted freedom from adult interference which the young Blairs enjoy with the local Irish children, Shaw's depiction of the adults reveals that her writing is firmly entrenched in the ideology of upper class English supremacy. Implicit in Shaw's novel is the understanding that, although Mr. Blair and his extended family live in comfort, that comfort is gained at the expense of the indigenous Irish tenants. An improving agent Mr. Plunkett may be, yet the tenants are, nevertheless, primarily a source of income, 'I have twenty pounds now for every ten I used to have', says Mr. Blair (505), who regards them as 'barbarians' (471). The expenses of the Blair children, sent from India to Ireland by their parents, are presumably met by the income from those Indian colonial interests, an income produced by a native Indian workforce whose conditions would have compared unfavourably even with the Irish.

Shaw's descriptions imply that Irish appearance and speech are inferior to those of the English. Although Murtagh is passionate in his love of all that is Irish, and uses Irish phrases, he also criticizes the idiosyncrasies of that speech, '[i]t's wonderful we are entirely' (501) he says 'for a last mock' at the housekeeper, Mrs. Donegan. Shaw writes Irish speech as she hears it, which emphasizes its lack of sophistication in contrast with the carefully composed correctness of the Anglo-Irish speakers. Mrs. Donegan is 'uneducated', the Irish children 'little beggars and vagabonds' (536), the tenants, in the eyes of Adrienne, often 'unreasonable... drunken... worthless' (596). The difference in physical stature between the English and the Irish appears more a function of the innate superiority of the former than the result of the inferior diet of the latter:

> Pat O'Toole...older than Murtagh by some three or four years. But perhaps by reason of his small stature-perhaps because of a certain capacity for admiration he possessed, he always seemed to the

> children younger than Murtagh, and far from attempting to lead, he
> was one of their most devoted servitors. (524)

This implication, that Pat's deference results from his inherent admiration for Murtagh and all he represents, confirms Flora Shaw as a colonial writer whose obvious love for Ireland and the Irish could only exist within the ideology of a society in which the Anglo-Irish would have sole responsibility for 'the proper way of managing Irish people'.

Notes

1. whose savage satire *A Modest Proposal* (1729) had proposed killing, cooking and eating year-old Irish children as a solution to the over-population.

2. who wrote in the late eighteenth century of the viciousness of the tenancy agreements enforced by the landlords and their 'rapacious and relentless' agents who together 'screw[ed] up the rent to the uttermost farthing', which resulted in their living in 'the most miserable looking hovels'. (Young (1780) *A Tour in Ireland*, quoted in Moody and Martin (1967))

3. Barry (2002; 72)

4. Maria Edgeworth, in *The Black Book of Edgeworthstown*, an ongoing family document, begun by her grandfather in the eighteenth century, quoted in the Introduction to *Castle Rackrent* (1995: xiv)

Chapter 17

The role of the gentleman in *Castle Blair* and *Hector*: a story for young people

'...as a gentleman should'
(Hector, in Flora L. Shaw, *Hector*)

Published four years after *Castle Blair*, *Hector*, like her first book, relies on Flora Shaw's youthful memories for source material. It is a far less innovative work, its interest lying largely in its examination of the role of a 'gentleman', and especially an *English* gentleman. Gillian Avery, in *Nineteenth Century Children* (1965), in comments examined more thoroughly in Chapter 18, cites a quotation from Captain Marryat which she considers to be a sentiment typical of Victorian ideology. A gentleman, Marryat asserts, 'holds a position in which he has the least temptation to do wrong, and the most opportunities of doing good'.[1] This is in accord with the principle which Bell alleges that Flora Shaw's grandfather expounded to her during childhood visits to Ireland, that '[i]t's the privilege of a gentleman to get the worst of any bargain throughout life' (12), a statement which emphasized the perceived responsibilities of a gentlemen to the lower classes over the rights which were due to his position. Avery summarizes the code of conduct to which a Victorian 'gentleman' conformed:

> Gentlemen never told lies, were never dishonourable...They were brave and fearless, considerate of their inferiors. They were also rather high-handed, in an engaging sort of way, and did all manner of things that would have been regarded as crime in books for the poorer classes. (197)

Avery selects Shaw as a writer whose work epitomizes the gentlemanly ideal, and she considers that in *Castle Blair* and *Hector*, Shaw is making many explicit references which other mid- and late-nineteenth century writers prefer to endorse implicitly.

The role of the gentleman was, as discussed in Chapter 16, fundamental to the colonial ideology within which Shaw sets the action of *Castle Blair*; the perceived superiority of the Anglo-Irish ruling class arises from that class's societal position as 'gentlemen'. Murtagh, although at first a rebellious adherent to the cause of Irish nationalism, never forgets that he is by birth a gentleman. With such a birthright, he feels, it is impossible for him to behave as anything but a gentleman, *'[g]entlemen* never tell lies' he says (1985: 448). Hector, in that novel, is equally incensed when similarly accused. This conviction about the superiority of class and the impossibility of behaving badly extends to the Blair girls: Winnie, accused of stealing apples from the estate orchards, protests, '[w]e're not stealing!...[w]e're ladies and gentlemen' (438). Mr. Plunkett cannot conceive that the abduction of Theresa could have been carried out by anyone other than 'members of the lowest class of society' (471). The children are so convinced of that their position is unimpeachable that Winnie 'didn't believe ladies and gentlemen were ever put in prison' (483). That this is considered a genetic inheritance as much as a learnt behaviour is shown by Mrs. Donegan's assertion that, 'if they've got the good blood in them they'll never go far wrong; it's only the half-an-half folks take such a deal o' looking after' (455). Ladies may be as deserving of the lower classes' reverence as gentlemen, but their role is clearly defined by the gentleman as a domestic and maternal one, '"It's always women who look after the babies," said Murtagh' (459), as well as speaking of 'a sneaking woman's way' (479), and 'hop[ing] to goodness there are no women in heaven' (490). A microcosm of English society exists in the children's play world: Murtagh elevates Winnie to 'my Lady Winifreda', consigning the younger Bobbo 'in a grandiloquent tone' to the humble position of 'varlet' (464). Whilst Mr. Plunkett reminds the children of the example they should give as 'young ladies and gentlemen' (496), Winnie considers that, not being a gentleman, '[h]ow could [the agent] know why gentlemen do things?'(496). Murtagh is confused by what is expected of them, '[i]f things are kind or brave or anything, then they talk about young ladies and gentlemen' (497), and retreats from these expectations if they conflict with his wishes. Reprimanded as 'Mr. Murtagh' by Mrs. Donegan, he replies 'gravely', 'I've been to Mr. Murtagh ... and he says he can't give any opinion on the matter' (514). However, when he feels secure in the unassailable position of a gentleman, Murtagh is contemptuous of the servants who attempt to curb his excesses, and addresses them rudely, '[s]hut up your impudence' (513). In fact, through Murtagh, Shaw is revealing that there is a lot to be learnt about the role even if gentlemen are born and not made.

Adrienne, the French cousin, who stands in a position between the children and the expectations of a fully formed adult world, acts as intermediary between them. It is she who, in *Castle Blair*, speaks to the children of *honour*, which is another fundamental aspect of the idealized gentleman, '[y]ou are doing something that will not be honourable', she says to them, '[i]t does not matter if a gentleman loses his rights, but it does matter very much if he stoops to get them back by deceit' (519). She phrases the duty of a gentleman in terms of their play roles amongst the Irish children when she says, 'the chief ought to watch over his followers, oughtn't he? He ought to see that they keep their promises, and he ought to keep them out of trouble' (542). It is this duty which Murtagh thinks requires him to act on the tenants' behalf against Plunkett, '[t]he people looked to him to help them' (588). Adrienne herself fulfils the duty of the lady when she visits the sick, bereft Mrs. Curran, to care for and comfort her. Furthermore, being, like Winnie, a lady, Adrienne cannot conceive that a gentleman could commit a crime. Accordingly, she dismisses the accusations against Murtagh because, '[o]nly one of those people [i.e. the Irish republicans] would have done a thing so cowardly and so cruel' (547). It is also in exactly those terms that Winnie describes Mr. Plunkett's killing of her dog: clearly this compounds the children's opinion that he is unable to act as a gentleman because he was not born to that position. The agent, however, as if to emphasize both his duty, and what he views as his dereliction of it, constantly addresses Murtagh as 'young gentleman', and sarcastically describes the Blair brothers as 'charming young gentlemen'. He upbraids Murtagh for lacking 'sufficient gentlemanly feeling' (539) in failing to shield his sisters from the 'rabble of the village' (539) he chooses as his friends, maintaining that 'the society that you have chosen is not likely to fit you for the career of gentleman' (540). Later he urges Murtagh to 'make a manly confession' (545), and upbraids him for being 'not only revengeful, but cowardly and dishonourable' (557), demanding his 'word of honour' (560). Murtagh, mindful of his own code as a gentleman, tries to extend it to others, and upbraids the renegade Pat O'Toole, not for his plan to kill Mr. Plunkett, but for the proposed method, 'you mustn't do it that cowardly way' (592). The attribution of gentility is even extended to Winnie's dog, which behaves 'like a perfect gentleman' (535), and which, as the pet of gentlemen and ladies, is addressed by the Irish children as 'Master Royal' (536).

In *Castle Blair*, therefore, Shaw has explored, endorsed and perpetuated the ideal of the gentleman, an ideology whose societal expectations, firmly rooted in the historical demands of aspirant rulers, maintained the class distinctions Victorian children's authors sought to instil, and justify to their readers. Shaw succeeded in promulgating this ideology far better in *Castle Blair*, by placing it at the heart of a stylishly written, exciting plot, peopled by believable and lively children, than she did in the overtly genteel *Hector*: *Hector* lacks virtually all those features which make its predecessor such an outstanding novel. Whereas, in *Castle Blair*, Shaw creates realistic characters, children whose independent lives lead them into engrossing adventures which continually engage and involve readers, thereby recommending its ideology almost subliminally, the characterization and plot of *Hector* are distinguished by the constant emphasis on the role of the gentleman. Although it provides a clear statement of the ideal, to a large extent it fails to express it in a form which engages, and therefore influences its readers. Even to a nineteenth-century audience, accustomed to a diet of far worthier fiction than modern readers experience, after the excitement of *Castle Blair*, *Hector* must have proved something of a disappointment. As the discussion on contemporary criticism in Chapter 18 reveals, *Hector* received praise for avoiding 'that didactic schoolroom flavour' (*The Times*, October 18th 1882), but that critic's admiration for its 'high and pure' tone identifies the very feature which reduces its literary impact .

In *Hector*, Flora Shaw follows the eponymous hero, a young member of the English gentility, living in France with his French relatives. Like the young Blairs, he has been sent away from his own family, but unlike their situation, in which readers feel that, however misguided the action, the Blair parents acted in their children's best interests, Hector's is a banishment, by uncles who act only in their own self interest. Shaw wreaks vengeance on the uncles, in best Victorian tradition, by killing them off at the end of the book, enabling Hector to return home as heir to the estate, to a grandfather who, whilst displaying love for Hector in a manner Mr. Blair never could, is depicted to be as weak as that character, having allowed his sons to overrule his wishes and send the boy to France. Hector and his younger French cousin, Zélie, involve themselves in the machinations of a village love affair, seeking to ensure that the impoverished lovers marry each other, and are not forced into the financially prudent, but romantically unpalatable, union urged on them by others. Conveniently, through the unwitting efforts of the children, the young lover also achieves a fortune and is able to claim his bride. The children's adventures, although allowing an abundance of Shaw's characteristically vivid descriptions of the countryside, have nothing of the genuine drama of *Castle Blair*, their extremes (such as Hector and Zélie's near starvation on their journey to warn the young soldier of his fiancée's imminent marriage to the elderly miller) tending far more to melodrama. Despite some perceptive and amusing images, (such as when Hector describes Soeur Amélie, the elderly nun who visits to give the children daily lessons, who, he thinks, has a face 'like an india-rubber cracker in a cornette') (n.d.: 24), these passages are not integrated into the text as a whole with the vigour which so distinguishes and drives the

Illustration 19: Hector: frontispiece to Little, Brown, and Company edition, c1882, Illustrator unknown

action of *Castle Blair*. Hector displays a recklessness and disregard for authority more than equal to Murtagh's, yet he rarely emerges from his place as a cipher for Shaw's portrait of an English gentleman, a two-dimensional character lacking in any of the complexity she achieves by occasionally permitting Murtagh to entertain doubts about his behaviour. Hector has no doubts: he is a gentleman; that is his birthright, it both dictates and excuses his behaviour.

As a younger child, French, and female, (in Victorian eyes surely a triple misfortune), the narrator, Zélie, provides the most receptive of audiences, to whom can be expounded the ideals of gentility; Shaw ensures that this is done, at length and in detail. The reputable French characters in *Hector* serve as a commentary on Hector's ideology. When they have been frightened by the unscrupulous tramp, Grand'-mère tells the children that 'he who abandons his duty is not only wicked, he is a very great fool, for he abandons happiness too...the dishonest are unhappy, while the honest and industrious, and those who know they must not meddle with what they do not understand, are happy' (92). She is justifying class distinction, and warning against any attempt to improve social position - this will only bring unhappiness. Hector's conviction of right in his role as a gentleman is, in his opinion, unassailable. Questioned by the blacksmith, he replies, as a 'proud little monsieur', merely that he will spend his money 'as a gentleman should' (298). The local French aristocrat ignores his duty as did Mr. Blair in Ireland. His neglect provides an opportunity for the blacksmith and doctor, representatives, like the Blair agent, Mr. Plunkett, of a class of respected and respectable professionals and master craftsmen, to expound on the perceived duties of the true gentleman:

> In England...the old aristocracy have not abandoned the people so, they have kept their rightful place; they work for the people and with the people; they are leaders; they employ their leisure in gaining knowledge, and their knowledge is at the service of the country....You still have in the great English families gentlemen who would hold themselves disgraced if they did not work harder for their country than any of the labourers they daily see work for themselves... (86)

The blacksmith voices sentiments which might more appropriately have been found in a manual of correct behaviour for gentlemen than in a book for children. He follows this with a condemnation of what he sees as a wilful abdication by the French aristocracy. Shaw presumably inherited this view from her indomitable French great-grandmother, who had allegedly refused to leave Paris during the Revolution, preferring to face the mob, and professing that courage was the distinguishing trait of the nobility, and staunchly certain of the justice of class distinction. The blacksmith, scornfully dismissing a newspaper claim that 'the people is above the law' (85), continues:

> Each class does its own work. Those who have instruction lead, those who know little follow…here our aristocracy has failed us. We…have been forced to put ourselves forward. Ambition was soon mixed in it… when the personal ends to be gained are too great…his hand [may] be turned aside to grasp power for himself. (86-87)

This warns of the dangers which will follow the removal of the natural leaders of the country, the gentlemen, and the enforced rise of those who are not born to that position.

It is the doctor whose catalogue of the iniquities of a 'selfish gentleman' spurs Hector into encouraging Zélie to join his expedition to help the young lovers, 'because you and I are a gentleman and a lady, we ought to work for Irma' (260). The doctor considers that the selfish gentleman is:

> perhaps what there is of worst in the human species, for the same position which gives him privileges for himself makes him necessarily an example and a leader to many other people. The power of the cultivated man is great. If he teaches nothing but selfishness he betrays his trust, and probably does…
> a great deal more harm than a ruffian who cuts his neighbor's throat forth sake of a few gold coins. (169)

The doctor continues his thesis for three pages, praising the diligent artisan above the selfish gentleman, but always maintaining the desirability of the gentleman industriously carrying out his duty. Zélie, whose youth and race permit Shaw a tone of innocent observation when the French girl speaks of her English cousin, comments that '[t]here was something in Hector…which made people talk to him in this way' (71). Hector himself, despite his youth, has already formulated his opinions about his role. Objecting to his grandmother's asking him to work for his dinner, he protests '[g]entlemen are different' (10), and proceeds to expound another of Shaw's textbook speeches, 'clearly and steadily':

> Gentlemen ought to work for something better than dinner. There is no shame in a poor man, because if he didn't gain food he'd have to die. Gentlemen have everything they need, and they ought not to

work for themselves at all. They ought to work for other people…
(111)

Grand'-mère agrees that this is a laudable ideal: 'your idea of the difference between a gentleman and a plebian is that a gentleman works for others, and the plebian for himself. Well, keep that idea, it will do you no harm if you act up to it' (111). When he and Zélie have no food at the end of the journey, however, he *is* prepared to work for their supper, because, like Murtagh, when he tries to help his uncle's Irish tenants, Hector believes that 'a gentleman must not fail the people who trust him' (327).

Shaw allows Hector to expand Murtagh's scathing comments about women, discussed in the previous chapter. Clearly, to a boy of gentle birth, the behaviour which that ideology expected of 'ladies' made them uninteresting in the extreme. Having carefully observed the French peasant girl, Irma, he tells Zélie, who he feels is a 'wishy-washy girl' (260):

> I don't intend to marry a lady…a girl like Irma is much better. Ladies scream and wring their fair white hands and think it is grand to pretend they don't care about you a bit when you are making love to them. Now Irma was nice and kind to Georges, and then she went on spinning all the time, and that's so much more useful. Ladies can read and write a little more than Irma, but they don't know anything much, and they can't do any work, and I don't see any good of having a wife unless she can be of some use to you. (80)

Here Shaw presents a picture of the ideal Victorian gentlewoman, a creature, according to Murtagh, of such total uselessness that he would prefer a more practical, less socially elevated wife. Whether such views would have survived into adulthood may be doubted; marriage to a woman of Irma's position would have made him unacceptable as a gentleman. This is matched by Hector's scorn of gentleman lovers. Luckily, in his opinion, Georges, *not* being a gentleman, is free from the restrictions that station in life places upon their behaviour as lovers. These passages are similar in tone to many in later Victorian and Edwardian writers, such as Edith Nesbit, who refined the tradition which Shaw expanded so successfully in *Castle Blair*, and whose emancipated child characters, discussing the qualities necessary when engaged in role play as ladies and gentlemen, also express their contempt for anything other than the most practical of girls.

A review of Shaw's last novel, *Colonel Cheswick's Campaign*, in the edition of the US journal *The Nation*, for July 1st 1886, speaks of the 'simple perfection' of *Hector*. In the twenty-first century, we can see that *Hector*, with its statements of overt genteel ideology, was a continuation of what had gone before it in literature. In *Castle Blair* Shaw integrated this ideology far more successfully; it is ever present, but never obscures or slows the action, and it is expressed through adventures in which she skilfully retains true realism.

Notes

1. Marryat (1844), *The Settlers in Canada*, quoted in Avery (1965)

Chapter 18

Shaw in the eyes of the critics

'Wholesome and amusing literature'
(Charlotte M. Yonge, in the introduction to *What Books to Lend and What to Give,* 1887)

Contemporary criticism

For a writer to receive the initial review of a first book from one of the country's most influential literary critics and formulators of contemporary public taste, and for that review to express uncompromising admiration for the work, is an undeniably favourable start to an authorial career. Flora Louisa Shaw achieved just this, and John Ruskin's recommendation of her first novel for children, *Castle Blair*, was an endorsement which publishers would continue to quote whenever a new edition of one of her books was proposed. Bell quotes (as usual without any bibliographical reference) George Meredith's comments, having apparently been sent the manuscript of *Castle Blair*: 'I say earnestly it will be better to put the work by; read, meditate and wait to produce another. She will in time do good work... she is too good to produce the popular rubbish; too young to hit the higher moods' (1947: 40). It seems that, though later to become an ardent friend, at this point Meredith considered Shaw's first effort to be 'popular rubbish'. Luckily, however, Ruskin's was not the only approving comment, and, in addition to complimentary newspaper reviews, Shaw was commended by Charlotte Yonge, herself a prolific and highly respected children's author. Such commendations were of very considerable importance for the Victorians, whose response to culture in general was firmly founded upon the informed opinions of revered and energetic proselytizers such as Ruskin and Yonge. The eighteenth and early nineteenth century espousal of Romanticism advocated by writers such as Rousseau and Wordsworth had, by the 1840s, been tempered by the incorporation of Christian teachings about sin and redemption. An often uneasy coexistence grew up within children's literature, a coexistence which resulted in a mass of well-intentioned but stylistically barren stories, about which Ruskin, a firm believer in the power of imagination to develop virtue, protested vehemently.

By 1869, when Shaw first gained the friendship of Ruskin, his had been a formidable influence for more than thirty years. Not only had he written at length and with the passion engendered by the deepest understanding about art and its interconnection with morality, but also about religion, politics, economic and social subjects. In 1851 he had written an original fairy tale for children, *The King of the Golden River*, to please the twelve year old Euphemia Gray (Effie), the first of the many female children and adolescents he befriended and desired during his lifetime. Darton is in no doubt about Ruskin's influence on academic as well as popular opinion. Considering the development of the Victorian fairy tale he insists, 'John Ruskin declared the national mind upon the subject in a preface (1868) to John Camden Hotton's edition of *German Popular Stories*' (1999: 241), and quotes from Ruskin who, Darton states, says 'pontifically' that a child 'should not need to choose between right and wrong. It should not be capable of wrong; it should not conceive of wrong...[it should become] obedient...true...gentle through daily entreatings of gentleness ...good... strong...self-commanding'. 'Children so trained', Ruskin continues, 'have no need of moral fairy tales' (242). Once Ruskin had made such a pronouncement, Darton considers, '[he] exalted the fact into doctrine. His voice was thunderous in those days' (243). Ruskin was not alone in his opinion: nine years earlier Diana Craik, author of *John Halifax, Gentleman*, had expressed very similar views.[1] In his lectures *Of King's Treasuries*, and *Of Queen's Gardens*, published together in 1865 as *Sesame and Lilies*, Ruskin had attacked those who desired an education only to achieve 'a "position in life"' (1907: 12); he complains that, 'it never seems to occur to the parents that there may be an education which, in itself, *is* advancement in Life' (12). These pronouncements on what was appropriate for children, their moral upbringing and education, were, therefore, freshly delivered to the public when Shaw and Ruskin first met, and, according to Bell (1947), he encouraged her to write *Castle Blair*.

Bell states that Ruskin's reply to Flora's proposal for her story was 'I am delighted with the idea of your tale, and do not doubt your power of making it quite entrancing to children' (30). Although no evidence is available to support Bell's statement [2], it does not seem unreasonable that Ruskin should have supported his protegee's plans, as he so obviously delighted with the book, once published. A major effort in his drive to raise the cultural and educational aspirations of the working classes was the publication of *Fors Clavigera: Letters to the Workmen and Labourers of Great Britain. Fors* is a 'vast miscellany, a profound reading of life, an urgent, sometimes incoherent, outburst at the wrongness of things and an impassioned expression of how they may be righted' (Bradley, 1997: 81). Within it, criticism of the state of contemporary children's literature featured more than once; in 'Letter L' he attacked the physical appearance and content of one of the popular magazines for children, finding it to be 'dreadful doggerel' and wholly inappropriate for young readers (quoted in Darton, 1999: 270), although, luckily, *Aunt Judy's Magazine* seems to have escaped his wrath. In the final letter of the first period of writing, 'Letter LXXXVII', published in March 1878, very soon after *Castle Blair*, Ruskin specifically considers 'the matter of choice of books', and the advisability of providing for *Fors* readers a 'list of the books I want them to read constantly, and with such casual recommendations as I may be able to give of current literature'. In fact, no such list is given, although individual authors are approved. Ruskin follows this statement with the comments on *Castle Blair* which were to remain her publishers' favourite quotation when recommending to the public both that and Shaw's later novels. The passage is never quoted in full, but, in its entirety, it provides a further gloss on the ideologies which dictated the predominant subject of Shaw's first book, and pervade the attitudes of the characters of the other four. In full, Ruskin's criticism reads:

> For instance, there is a quite lovely little book just come out about Irish children, *Castle Blair*, - (which, let me state at once, I have strong personal, though stronger impersonal, reasons for recommending, the writer being a very dear personal friend; and some Irish children, for many and many a year, much more than that). But the impersonal reasons are - first , that the book is good and lovely and true; having the best description of a noble child in it (Winny,) that I ever read; and nearly the best description of the next best thing - a noble dog; and second reason is that, after Miss Edgeworth's *Ormond* and *Absentee*, this little book will give more true insight into the proper way of managing Irish people than any other I know. (259)

That Ruskin thoroughly admired and approved the book is undoubted. His description of *Castle Blair* as 'a quite lovely little book…good and lovely, and true' elevates it to a position where it is the embodiment of the sentiments he expressed in the preface to Hutton's book, written ten years earlier. In Ruskin's opinion, Shaw has fulfilled all that he requires for the education of children. She has provided in the book, through characterization such as that of 'a noble child…(Winny,) [*sic*], and through the subject matter, exactly the material which will allow the child audience reading, or being read, the story to assimilate the 'entreaties of gentleness' (Ruskin, in his preface to Hotton) contained therein. The words used in the preface, 'good' and 'true', are echoed, of *Castle Blair*, in 'Letter LXXXVII', with the addition of 'lovely', and leave no doubt that this book, with its independent children, free from moralizing adult intervention to conduct their own lives and discover their own truths, provided within it the opportunities for readers to obtain Ruskin's goal, that they should achieve obedience 'in the freedom of its bright course of constant life' and in 'fields and woods' (Ruskin, in his preface to Hotton).

The statements which publishers removed from Ruskin's comments on this novel, though not suitable for their purposes, illuminate other aspects of *Castle Blair* and Shaw's later works. Ruskin's 'strong personal…reasons' confirm not only that Flora Shaw was 'a very dear friend' (although he never names her), but that a principal attraction of the story for him was that it concerned Irish children. He continues, intriguingly, 'some Irish children, for many and many a year, much more than that' (very dear friends). This is a reference to the continuing infatuation with and courtship of Rose La Touche, the psychologically unstable Irish nine-year-old with whom Ruskin had fallen in love with twenty years earlier. This disastrous infatuation was coming to its crux when Ruskin first met Flora Shaw. Some Victorian adult males seem to have been particularly drawn to female children and adolescents, who appear to have held for them a distinct sexual frisson. While Lewis Carroll entertained them with picnics and stories, and photographed them in what popular taste then considered to be 'sentimental' attitudes (the twenty-first century sees them rather differently), Ruskin pursued them with a view to marriage. It is possible he saw an attraction of this kind in Shaw; at any rate they engaged in protracted correspondence about the Rose débacle at this time, and Ruskin deeply valued Flora's advice on his unhappy situation. Shaw's books, from *Hector* onwards, include confused romantic themes, with, in *Phyllis Browne*, what Wolff (1985) describes as passion 'sublimated by innocence' (430). The English publishers of *A Sea Change*, with its implicit sexually oriented juvenile relationships, clearly recognized the market potential of a cover advertising such covertly salacious material.[3] The American cover, however, is congruent with Shaw's earlier titles published by Little, Brown: a floral frame for the title and author's name.

The final sentence of Ruskin's critique of *Castle Blair* congratulates Shaw on being only second to Maria Edgeworth in giving 'more true insight into the proper way of managing Irish people than any other I know'. Edgeworth, much of whose early writing was also for children, and who was like Shaw, a descendent of Anglo-Irish landowners, witnessed at first hand the evils which absent landlords and thoughtless agents could bring to Ireland and its population, which she revealed in the two novels Ruskin names, and in *Castle Rackrent* (1800), the first of her novels for adults. On the subject of colonial policy Ruskin and Shaw agreed, and it is not, therefore, surprising to find him advocating *Castle Blair*'s paternalistic conclusions as a remedy for the Irish situation.

Charlotte Mary Yonge was no less influential than John Ruskin, although she confined her authorship to writing over one hundred novels, to editing her own magazine, *The Monthly Packet*, and to assessing the suitability of both classic and contemporary texts for the increasing body of young and impressionable readers. As an author who anticipated and filled the gap between young children's stories and adult novels, providing 'an unwonted element of chivalry …happily grafted on the realism of contemporary English life' (an unattributed criticism quoted in Darton, 289), Yonge was well suited to judge the work of other writers such as Flora Shaw for a similar audience. In 1887 she assembled *What Books to Lend and What to Give*, a small volume of advice for those involved in the selection and administration of parish and Board and Sunday school libraries, which suggested suitable titles under a variety of headings, encompassing the needs of readers of all ages. In addition to several categories of Biblical and adult non-fiction recommendations Yonge included 'Fairy Tales', 'Novelettes', and 'Penny Readings' (but warns against 'penny dreadfuls' on page 6) which might have supplied some suitable titles for the younger reader or listener, but specifically caters for their needs in evaluated lists of books for:

> Little Ones - Fit to be read or given to children from four to eight.

> Junior Classes - Children from seven or eight to ten or eleven.

> Senior Classes - From ten upwards.

> Boys - The books may be read by girls also, but most boys will not read girls' books, therefore their literature is put separately.

> Drawing Room Stories - The best are mentioned here, but all, though excellent, are, on experience, out of the ken of the schoolchild. (13)

It is within this last category that Yonge recommends *Castle Blair* , one of sixty-six titles 'chosen for their unusual excellence', describing it as '[a] wild Irish story, very attractive and exciting' (39). In her introduction to this list of 'Drawing Room Stories', Yonge considers the subject matter to be beyond the understanding of most parish library readers; she writes:

...they deal in general with a way of life, with pursuits, allusions, and temptations, so much out of the line of the ordinary clients of the parish library that we do not recommend them for that purpose, although they do no harm but decidedly good, so far as they are understood, and where readers of a superior degree are included, would be excellent. (35)

The mention of readers of 'superior degree', it is to be feared, probably refers to social class rather than reading ability. Other books recommended include titles by Mrs. Molesworth, Mrs. Ewing, Mrs. Gatty, together with many of Yonge's own books and SPCK stories; an even greater number of titles and authors have now disappeared from all but the national deposit libraries. Nevertheless, Yonge is placing Shaw's first book on equal terms with some of the most respected and loved authors available in late Victorian England. *Castle Blair,* being in Yonge's opinion 'wild...attractive and exciting', may have proved more accessible to 'ordinary clients of the parish library' than some of the other suggestions in this category. In her eleven-page general introduction to *What Books*, Charlotte Yonge expresses her wish to ensure that those books which children are lent to read, or given as prizes, should be of the highest quality. Here she is at one with Ruskin, who had, in his 1868 preface to Hotton, also complained at the proliferation of cheaply produced, moralistic yet morally barren, and intellectually worthless 'reward' books. Yonge recognizes that:

Wholesome and amusing literature has become almost a necessity among the appliances of parish work. The power of reading leads, in most cases, to the craving for books. If good be not provided, evil will be only too easily found, and it is absolutely necessary to raise the taste so as to lead a voluntary avoidance of the profane and disgusting. Books of a superior class are the only means of such cultivation. (unnumbered first page)

Yonge continues with entreaties to adults to ensure that young readers should have only books accurate in detail, be they fiction or non-fiction, and should never encourage activities such as birds-nesting. This is something that Shaw's Hector unthinkingly does, only to regret his actions when his cruelty is pointed out to him. Moreover '[b]oys especially should not have childish tales with weak morality or 'washy' piety; but should have heroism and nobleness kept before their eyes; and learn to despise all that is untruthful or cowardly and to respect womanhood' (6). This view fits very well with Shaw's ideological convictions about the role of the gentleman, and with many of the sentiments expressed through Hector himself in Shaw's second novel. It is interesting to speculate why Yonge excludes *Hector*. That she had no knowledge of subsequent novels by an author whose first work she clearly admired is highly unlikely, particularly as, in the advertisements at the end of Yonge's book, one of the titles named in George Bell and Sons' 'Shilling Series' is 'Miss Shaw's Hector [*sic*]: a Story for Young People'. Expressing, as it does, exactly the gentlemanly virtues Yonge wishes to instil, the absence of *Hector* in Yonge's recommendations is puzzling. Although Shaw's last three novels might not have suited Yonge's purposes, *Hector*, admittedly not as exciting as *Castle Blair*, was no less so than others of Yonge's recommended titles, and certainly expounds, as well as any, the virtues of true nobility, courage and truthfulness. Nevertheless, Yonge's inclusion of *Castle Blair* in *What Books to Lend and What to Give* may have been a significant factor in its achieving eight editions in the next thirty years.

When *Castle Blair* had been published in 1877, an unnamed reviewer in *The Times* had considered that it was 'one of the few first works by a young author which is worth keeping' (December 6th 1877: 3). It was praised for 'lead[ing] us straight into that world of imagination, of heroism, and unconscious, unblushing selfishness, of mirth and tenderness, of mingled tears and laughter – the world of childhood'. The article continues by asserting that, because of its Irish subject matter, adults as much as children would benefit from reading it, and 'Irish landlords, agents, and tenants would be better for a course of study and examination in "Castle Blair" [*sic*]'. The reason for this is, the writer feels, that the majority of adults have no clearer understanding of the Irish situation, particularly the relationship between agent and tenant, than do the Blair children; accordingly, adults make the same mistaken judgements about the apparent harshness with which the tenants are treated. The writer likens *Castle Blair* to a fairy tale, 'for all lives of children are but fairy tales partly explained', with Mr. Plunkett the giant and Adrienne the Good Fairy. The characters are described as 'both natural and original', and 'we think of them when the book is closed as of people we have known, and some of whom we have loved'. The children themselves, the reviewer confirms 'stand... out distinctly from the mob of witty but ignorant Irish men and women, girls and boys, whom the children sway by virtue of their old blood and high spirit'. The prevailing imperialist ideology espoused by Shaw herself and voiced in *Castle Blair* is here confirmed and recommended as the best way for Anglo-Irish relations. Shaw's style is praised because it is 'very simple and unaffected', that when 'children and peasants are not speaking' it is 'elevated in tone, and clad in pure English', but 'avoids the abomination of fine writing'. Having acknowledged that '[f]rom beginning to end the book is full of life and movement', the reviewer concludes, 'few writers have the power of expressing such infectious merriment or such pathos'. Whereas we feel that the readability of Shaw's book is, for the *Times* reviewer, principally a means of promulgating the ideological message of the book, for children and adults, twenty-first century readers may reflect that it is the liveliness of the novel, and the clarity of writing which extended its life in print, and its attraction for subsequent audiences.

On October 18th 1882, a year after the first publication of *Hector*, another unnamed *Times* reviewer was even more effusive, complimenting Shaw on her 'uncommonly good and even charming' English, recommending the book 'to all young or old who are not out of sympathy with the life of children'. More significantly, within a lengthy and thorough overview of the storyline, the critic gives some consideration to the ideology underlying the action and characterization. He praises *Hector* '[l]ike Miss Shaw's earlier work, "Castle Blair"' [*sic*] as 'rather an interpretation of childhood than a book written for children alone', and castigates the majority for 'being too apt to regard the life of children from a superficial point of view, and to miss that strange double life which they lead - on one side graceful and playful, but on the other full of depth, imagination and pathos'. The writer goes on to elaborate on the elements which distinguish Shaw's characterization of children. The review continues:

> It does not follow that children of fine temper and high imagination die young, any more than that healthy children are stupid and insensitive; and the peculiar gift of Miss Shaw enables her to draw the portraits of boys and girls who, while being perfectly simple, sweet, and inexperienced, show *such fine breeding that we know they must run well forward in the race of life.* [italics mine] (*The Times*, 18/10/1882: 4, col. d)

The italicized phrase is an extremely interesting observation, indicating how firmly Shaw's ideological conviction, that of the superiority of the upper class and the attitudes their upbringing instilled, was within the generally accepted ideologies constantly expressed in the pages of similarly upper class commentators such as *The Times*. The review further praises Shaw's descriptions of the natural surroundings as they allow readers to 'picture...the life of the woods which exercises so great an influence on children *fine bred enough to appreciate* [italics mine] its teaching'. Again the italicized phrase places Shaw firmly within the mainstream of upper-class opinion, no extreme right-wing maverick. The critic states that Shaw's children make mistakes which are 'those of noble natures', and then considers, in some detail, Hector's characterization as a developing 'gentleman'. He says that the English boy 'endeavours to do what he considers the duty of a gentleman by helping the weak and innocent... the protecting duty of a gentleman'. The review concurs with Shaw's emphasis on this duty, which she found missing amongst absentee Anglo-Irish landlords and French aristocrats alike. The article also confirms that the attitude of a society which saw its women's main duty to be supportive of the men; nevertheless did not prevent them from being critical of those men. The critic admires Shaw's characterization of Marie Anna, whose commentary on the inability for men to fend without the help of women, is applauded as 'some vigorous opinions'. The review concludes with a recommendation of *Hector* as 'a book of high and pure tone, yet without a tinge of that didactic schoolroom flavour about it which is so inappropriate'. This article is particularly important as an indication of the opinions of professional journalists, whose writing, though not perhaps as intellectually informed as that of Ruskin or Yonge, is nevertheless aimed specifically at the section of society which Flora Shaw represented. They also were influential on society in general: only the most revolutionary were prepared to challenge the accepted codes of class stratification and its implicit expectations. Flora Shaw's ideologies were clearly those of her intended audience.

Most contemporary commentators on Flora Shaw's fiction are not named, and their remarks are used on covers or within editions as endorsements recommending Shaw's work. Their independence or, in the case of quotations from critiques published in other journals, accuracy in quotation, cannot therefore be guaranteed any more than the plaudits of modern works which are emblazoned on twenty-first century advertisements. Nevertheless they provide a valuable light on what was considered valuable within Shaw's writing. In the undated Little Brown & Company edition (probably published about 1886) the *Christian Union* commends *Castle Blair* for the author's 'genuine sympathy with children', the *New York Times* considers *Hector* 'more than a story for children...we pass in review the status of the peasant, the small proprietor, the smith, gamekeeper, physician, and noble in a French country neighbourhood. Yet all is brought in naturally and without effort'. The *Worcester Star* confirms Shaw's gradual drift towards an adult audience, delighting in *Phyllis Browne*'s 'tender and loving things' which 'bring back the splendid dreams of one's youth', as well as 'mak[ing] the heart grow larger'. The *Congregationalist* approves *A Sea Change* for being 'full of most valuable suggestions for the young' which encourages the writer of this comment to 'commend it heartily for the Sunday-school library and for the home'. This review, possibly almost exactly contemporaneous with *What Books to Lend and What to Give*, recommending books for exactly the same market, obviously overlooks the underlying sexual content which may have influenced Yonge's omission of both this and *Phyllis Browne*. In an article on 'Children's Books' in *The Nation*, on October 23rd 1884, *A Sea Change* receives a mixed review, described as 'charming', Marina's character as 'very sweet and noble, in striking contrast to the persistent selfishness of the young girls with whom she is compelled to associate'. Whilst recommending it as 'pure and wholesome', and particularly suitable for girls, the reviewer does, however, acknowledge that 'the action drags in the middle, and is hurried toward the end'. This s/he feels, 'mak[es] the denouement, which is not too probable, seem sudden and confused' (357). The review of *Colonel Cheswick's Campaign* in *The Nation* in July 1886, which describes that novel as 'not a great book', singles out *Hector* for particular praise, and Shaw's final novel clearly suffers by comparison. The reviewer begins by stating that '[a] novel by the author of 'Hector' [*sic*] has been a pleasant anticipation'. It is obvious that *Phyllis Browne* and *A Sea Change* are held in lesser regard than *Hector*, which is described as possessing 'simple perfection'. In the opinion of the writer, Ailsa, the central character of Shaw's last work of fiction, is 'only Zélie (from 'Hector' [*sic*]) or Phyllis Browne (from the story of that name) grown up'.

Mary Livermore's 1902 introduction to her *Castle Blair* abridgement values the qualities earlier critics had identified; she finds it 'a bright, breezy story for children, most entertainingly told'. Like *The Times* review of *Hector*, she admires the characterization of children who are 'utterly untrained, high-spirited, and lawless, but who are good-hearted, very capable and *innately noble*' (vii); the distance of the Atlantic and twenty years had clearly made few inroads on the prevalence of this ideology. She concludes that such an example of 'uplifting' story will make the readers 'happier and better for having read it' (vii). A note by 'C.W.' at the conclusion of the book, (C.W. is nowhere further identified), whilst acknowledging the 'very fair picture' given by Shaw of 'both sides of the question which has led to Ireland's troubles', and regretting the lack of 'a sympathetic acquaintance with the people on the part of agents and landowners' which could have 'prevented many distressing outbreaks such as are related in this story' ('note', on unnumbered final page), nevertheless names '*the peasant farming classes*' [italics mine], indicating C.W's attitude to be identical with that of Shaw's own social class and time. The Preface by Louise Creighton to the Oxford edition of 1929 commends its picture of Irish life, and Shaw's characterization, as 'each of the children in her book has an individuality of its own' (v). She describes *Castle Blair* as 'one of the most delightful of the many delightful books for children in the English language' (iii).

The newspaper comments which are quoted on the dustwrapper of Little, Brown's 1931 edition of *Castle Blair*, a story which the publishers describe as 'of alert, red-blooded, likeable boys and girls' show that little had changed in criteria by which the critics were judging children's books. *The New York Tribune* found that it was 'so wholesome and breezy and tender [it could] hardly be too heartily recommended', *The St. Louis Post-Dispatch* considered that 'no young person or any other can read it without being benefited by it', whilst *The Providence Journal* found it a 'thoroughly well-written and ennobling book for children from 10 to 15'. These are not all journals of the greatest reputation, perhaps, but arbiters of popular taste and ideology, which clearly had not changed significantly in the fifty years since Flora Shaw had begun writing novels. Flora Shaw's fiction was obviously viewed by her contemporaries as an embodiment of those attitudes and sentiments which parents and guardians of her social class should instil into their children.

Modern criticism

Very little critical comment has appeared about Flora Shaw's fiction since that last American edition of 1931; the 1966 Rupert Hart-Davis reprint of *Castle Blair*, discussed in Chapter 14, refrains from repeating any of the earlier comments other than those of Ruskin and Yonge, presumably on the grounds that the effusively sentimental earlier commendations were more likely to repel than attract 1960s readers. The inner flap of the dust-wrapper justifies the purpose of the new edition but also acknowledges that the story is 'invincibly Victorian in upholding the Anglo-Irish Ascendancy', thereby warning readers that the opinions expressed in Shaw's text may be unfamiliar and unpalatable. This emphasizes the change in critical ideology which had taken place in the thirty-five years between these two editions; this shift in critical ideology itself reflected popular attitudes, a breaking down of both the rigid social class structure and the espousal of paternalistic colonialism, largely as a result of the Second World War. The first scholarly criticism of the twentieth century appeared in 1954, its American origin suggesting a continued knowledge of Shaw's writing on that continent, in contrast with the apparent total lack of interest in Britain. Anne Eaton, considering a 'Broader Field' of the 'Widening Horizons 1840-1890' in Meigs (et al) *Critical History of Children's Literature* (1954), writing of *Castle Blair*, asserts, '[i]t reads as well today as when it was published in 1878'...[it] reaches a climax of feeling and excitement which few books of the period have been able to achieve. The strength of this climax lies in its complete freedom from sentimentality' (189). Eaton considers that the 'fact that the Irish Revolutionary Movement plays a part in the story puts it on a larger stage than that of the nursery, schoolroom or village tales which formed most of the reading matter for boys and girls of the 70s' (90); the Irish political content clearly retains its interest for Eaton.

Eleven years later Gillian Avery is the first British critic to reappraise Shaw's work. In *Nineteenth Century Children: Heroes and Heroines in English Children's Stories 1780-1900* (1965), she considers *Castle Blair* and *Hector* in five pages of highly-informed and perceptive discussion, honouring Shaw as 'one of the very few writers who succeeded' in exploring 'adults' as well as children's motives and present[ing] them both acceptably to a child reader' (180). Avery considers *Castle Blair* to be 'still unique' and 'impossible to fit into the pattern of the nineteenth-century story book', as 'the tone of the book is anarchical, utterly destructive of authority'. She praises Shaw for her detachment, allowing the children's point of view, and concludes that '[o]n the whole her sympathies are with the children...but she does not imply commendation of their conduct as she does in...*Hector*' (181). The latter story, Avery contends, 'sentimentalizes a child's contempt for authority' and is stylistically inferior to *Castle Blair*, in addition to glorifying 'that rather unpleasant manifestation of the Victorian age...a gentleman' (181). She examines the Victorian ideology of the gentleman at some length, and places Shaw's two earliest books centrally within fiction epitomizing the spirit of this ideal. Although Avery presents a typically mid-twentieth-century, negative, opinion of the justification for this ideology, she nevertheless acknowledges Shaw's considerable skill in writing so vividly (in *Castle Blair* at least), and acknowledges the importance of Shaw's characters in the development of the juvenile novel. Avery considers that her characters reach the furthest extent of child emancipation from adult control prior to 1895, when Kenneth Grahame wrote *The Golden Age*. She maintains that Shaw and Grahame were unsurpassed in this respect, and that subsequent authors did not permit their child characters to flout adult rules to the same extent.

Although Gillian Avery returned Flora Shaw's work to the canon of modern British critical writing, and elevated it to a position of considerable influence and importance within the development of children's literature, few subsequently mention her books. In the same year as Avery, Roger Lancelyn Green, in the third of his many editions of *Tellers of Tales* (1965), quotes part of Eaton's essay, using it to reflect that Shaw has been 'rescued from oblivion in America, though apparently still unknown here' (95). Since then only brief references have been made, in 1975, by Margery Fisher in her *Who's Who in Children's Books*, and in 1984, in Carpenter and Prichard's *Oxford Companion to Children's Literature*; both of these confine themselves to listing characters and outlining plot in *Castle Blair*. Avery's remained the only serious critical consideration of Flora Shaw's fiction in the last forty years, until the paper by Robert Dunbar in 2004 which considered *Castle Blair* as part of an Irish tradition of children's literature. In 'Rebuilding Castle Blair: A Reading of Flora Shaw's 1878 Children's Novel' Dunbar foregrounds Shaw's attention to political complexities, and reads the book as a children's literature version of the Irish big house novel. Acknowledging the number of children's historical novels which examine the Irish famine, Dunbar praises Shaw's unusual willingness to confront contemporary political events, 'deal[ing] with a period that has remained virtually untouched since then in any children's literature'.[4] It is surprising that a book as thorough and scholarly as Victor Watson's recent *Cambridge Guide to Children's Books in English* (2001) continues to ignore her. *The Oxford Encyclopedia of Children's Literature* (2006) has rectified this neglect, and returns Shaw and her work to brief but public notice.

Notes

1. In *Macmillan's Magazine*, volume 1 (November 1859), Mrs Craik (author of *John Halifax, Gentleman*, felt that, 'there may be some little mistake in the flood of moral and religious literature with which our hapless infants are now overwhelmed...[w]e honestly confess we should very much prefer "Jack the Giant-killer"' [*sic*}

2. Helen Callaway confirmed that she found no letter containing this quotation in any collection of Shaw papers, and that it may be in a family collection not made available for research (email 26/11/02)

3. See illustration

4. In Keenan, C. & Shine Thompson, M (eds.) (2004) *Studies in Children's Literature, 1500-2000*, Dublin: Four Courts Press

Chapter 19

Shaw's Legacy

'Unusual excellence'
(Charlotte M. Yonge, justifying her choice of 'Drawing-room stories' in *What Books to Lend and What to Give*, 1887)

A powerful case can therefore be made for the rediscovery of Flora Shaw's fiction. It can be argued that both *Castle Blair* and *Hector* are important, but neglected, texts in any overview of the role of the gentleman in fiction, and that the dialogue between text and history in *Castle Blair* is crucial to an understanding of the literature of colonial Ireland. However, it is Shaw's 'unique' (Avery, 1965: 180) contribution to a genre central to the 'golden age' of children's literature which should prompt her rediscovery for the most important critics: young readers.

The 'golden age' found its finest expression in the works of those writers to whom, as Carpenter (1987) says, childhood itself seemed a golden age. These writers sought to recapture the sensations of their childhood, and to express them free from the unsympathetic authoritarianism which they considered was inflicted by progression to adulthood. It was Kenneth Grahame who first applied this phrase to childhood, it being the title of his short stories about childhood published in 1895. Grahame, although he abhorred the interference of adults, (the 'Olympians'), in the affairs of children, was, nevertheless, writing for adults, and from an adult viewpoint. In his creation of five children whose contempt for authority encompasses an extreme anarchy which Shaw's characters, steeped in the gentlemanly ideal, would never emulate, Grahame is usually regarded as the inventor of the genre, which Avery terms 'the emancipated child', and which, continued in the work of writers such as S. R. Crockett, flowered in the writing of E. Nesbit. However, as has been seen, there is, in *Castle Blair*, evidence of an earlier date, and another creator for the genre.

Whilst no evidence exists which indicates that any of these authors knew Flora Shaw's books, there is an interesting coincidence between Shaw's last novel, *Colonel Cheswick's Campaign*, and two of Nesbit's. At the conclusion of Shaw's work, the heroine, mourning her father's death, says '[m]y Daddy, oh my Daddy goodbye' (1886, volume 3: 181), anticipating *The Railway Children* (first published in 1906), in which Bobbie's greeting to her father, who is returning from prison, is, '[o]h! My Daddy, my Daddy!' (1971: 239), a phrase which Nesbit altered only slightly for use in *The House of Arden* (1908), where the final words are '[o]h my daddy. Oh, my daddy, my daddy!' (1949: 371).[1] Nesbit's child characters are, like Shaw's Blair children, removed from direct adult supervision, and, like the Blairs, their exploits are well intentioned but have unfortunate repercussions; this is particularly true of the Bastable family in the *Wouldbgood* books (1897 onwards) and of the five children (both Grahame and Nesbit seem to have shared Shaw's attraction to this size of group), whose adventures are first chronicled in *Five Children and It* (1902). Carpenter (1987) considers that Nesbit's adults condescend to the errant children, but that Grahame permits his child characters freely to criticize the behaviour of adults. Shaw, however, ensures a reconciliation between what the Blair children interpret as just, and a justice which accords with the ideology of the adults. Both Shaw and Nesbit see the freedom enjoyed by emancipated children to have emotional repercussions. As Bobbie's greeting indicates, Nesbit's children, although never completely lacking parental love, welcome their return to a complete family. Shaw shows the Blair children to be emotionally, as well as physically, neglected. When Adrienne kisses Murtagh, '[I]t was nearly five years since any one had caressed him so' (Wolff, 1985: 492), '[I]t was new and pleasant to them to be loved' (508). For Shaw, emancipation born of an adult disinterest offered practical advantages but devastating emotional disadvantages. However, these are not the sole arguments in favour of the rediscovery of her work.

Castle Blair would also repay study in any discussion of the role of the emancipated female in children's literature. It is interesting that Ruskin's praise for the book particularly commented on the 'noble child (Winny)' [*sic*]. There is no mention of the main male protagonist, Murtagh; instead, for Ruskin, Shaw has provided 'the best description…that I have ever read' of a girl. Winnie is indeed a vivid creation, whom Shaw allows to act as an equal with her brother, despite Murtagh's expressions of sexual stereotyping. Flora Shaw, although a proven equal of men in the field of journalism, was no overt crusader for women's rights, and represented the relationship between brother and sister realistically, complete with gender-based sibling rivalry. Winnie is the practical foil to Murtagh's impulsive idealism, an inventive, courageous girl: it is she, not Murtagh, who is out with Bobbo in the dark, wet night of Adrienne's arrival, scrumping apples. Shaw's physical description of the girl, with its images of light and action, establishes our opinion of her; she is:

> a little elf-like thing…her scarlet cloak twisted all crooked with the
> wind, the skirt of her brown dress gathered up in both hands to hold

the apples…her hair beaten down over her forehead by the rain, her great dark eyes dancing, her cheeks glowing, the merry mouth ready to break into smiles, she seemed the very incarnation of life and brightness. (1985: 437)

Winnie is a tomboy, not merely an emancipated child, an early example of a character-type whose importance has increased immensely in the years since *Castle Blair* first appeared; through her, Shaw's legacy to modern children's literature is immeasurably richer.

There are, therefore, outstanding arguments in favour of an academic rediscovery of Flora Shaw's fiction, a rediscovery which would further inform our knowledge and understanding of the origins and development of children's literature. That such a rediscovery might provide access to *Castle Blair* for twenty-first century children would be a considerable bonus.

Notes

1. A more recent example occurs in M. Laski's (1949) *Little Boy Lost*, in which a father, searching for his son, finds the child's toy rabbit, and says, 'It's Binkie Binkie come back!'

Bibliography of Primary Sources

Editions of works by Flora Louisa Shaw, later Lady Lugard used (all published under her maiden name unless otherwise indicated)

Fiction

'Castle Blair' (ed.) (1878), Wolff, R.L., Boston: Roberts Brothers, in Cott, J. (ed.) (1985) *Masterworks of Children's Literature*, volume 5, part 2 1837-1900, London: Allen Lane

Castle Blair: A story of youthful days (n.d.), Boston: Little, Brown & Co. (first published London 1877)

Castle Blair: A story of youthful days (1882), London: Kegan, Paul, Trench & Co

Castel-Blair: Histoire d'une famille irlandaise, traduit de l'anglais par A. Chevalier (1889), unattributed illustrations, Tours: Alfred Mame et Fils

Une Cousine de France (n.d.), unattributed translation, Tours: Alfred Mame & Fils

Castle Blair: A story of youthful days (1902), introduction by M.S. Livermore, Boston: D.C. Heath

Castle Blair: A story of youthful days (1907), unattributed illustrations, London: George Routledge & Sons

Barnene paa Castle Blair: En fortælling for barn, oversat av M. Lysholm (1909), Kristiania: H. Aschetoug & Co (W. Nygaard)

Castle Blair: A story of youthful days (1931), illustrated by G. Varian, Boston: Little, Brown & Company

Castle Blair: A story of youthful days (1938), London: Oxford University Press, Humphrey Milford [published under the name 'Shaw, F. (Lady Lugard)']

Castle Blair: A story of youthful days (1966), illustrated by C. Everest, London: Rupert Hart-Davis

Castle Blair: A story of youthful days (2007), Whitefish: Kessinger

'Hector' in. Gatty, H. F. K. (ed.) (1881), *Aunt Judy's Magazine*, London: George Bell and Sons

Hector: A story [for young people] (nd), Boston: Little Brown and Company (first published in serial form 1881)

'Phyllis Browne' in Gatty, H. F. K. (ed.) (1882), *Aunt Judy's Magazine*, London: George Bell & Sons

Phyllis Browne (1907), unattributed illustrations, Boston: Little, Brown and Company (first published 1883)

A Sea Change (1885), illustrated by M. E. Edwards, London: George Routledge and Sons

A Sea Change (1913), illustrated by M. E. Edwards, Boston: Little, Brown & Co (first published 1885)

Captain Cheswick's Campaign (1886), London: Longmans, Green and Co.

Non-fiction

The Story of Australia (1898), London: Horace Marshall & Son

A Tropical Dependency: An outline of the ancient history of the Western Soudan with an account of the modern settlement of Northern Nigeria (1905), London: James Nisbet [under the name Lady Lugard]

Letters

Lugard, F. L. (1914) 'A Conference at Belfast' in *The Times*, March 31st. 1914, London: The Times

Lugard, F. L. (1915) Letter to the Secretary, Ottawa Women's Canadian Club, August 17th. 1915

Novels by other authors

Crockett, S.R. (1897) *The Surprising Adventures of Sir Toady Lion with those of General Napoleon Smith: An improving history for old boys, young boys, good boys, bad boys, big boys, little boys, cow boys and tomboys*, London: Gardner, Darton & Co

Edgeworth, M. (1995) *Castle Rackrent*, Oxford: University Press (first published 1800)

Edgeworth, M. (1994) *Castle Rackrent* and *The Absentee*, Ware: Wordsworth Editions Ltd (first published 1800 and 1812)

Edgeworth, M. (1990) *Ormond*, Gloucester: Alan Sutton Publishing Ltd (first published 1817)

Grahame, K. (1950) *The Kenneth Grahame Book: The Golden Age, Dream Days, The Wind in the Willows*, London: Methuen & Co. Ltd. (first published in this form 1932, individually 1895, 1898 and 1908)

Nesbit, E. (1949) *The House of Arden*, London: Ernest Benn Ltd. (first published 1908)

Nesbit, E. (1971) *The Railway Children*, Harmondsworth: Penguin Books Ltd first published 1906)

Magazines

Gatty, H.F.K. (ed.) (1881 and 1882) *Aunt Judy's Magazine*: Annual Volume[s], London: George Bell & Sons

Contemporary and earlier literary and political criticism

Anonymous reviewer (1877) 'Review of Castle Blair by Florence Shaw' *[sic]* in *The Times*, 6th December 1877, London: The Times

Anonymous reviewer (1882) 'Hector', in *The Times*, October 18th. 1882, London The Times

Anonymous reviewer (1884) 'Children's Books' in *The Nation*, October 23rd 1884, New York: The Nation

Anonymous reviewer (1886) 'Recent Novels' in *The Nation*, July 1st 1886, New York: The Nation

Ruskin, J. (1880) 'Inaugural' in *Lectures on Art: delivered before the University in Hilary Term, 1870*, Oxford: Clarendon Press

Ruskin, J. (nd) 'Letter LXXXVII' in *Fors Clavigera: Letters to the Workmen and Labourers of Great Britain*, Volume III, New York: Lovell, Coryell & Company (first published 1878)

Ruskin, J. (1907) 'Sesame and Lilies' in *Sesame and Lilies, Unto this Last, The Political Economy of Art*, London: Cassell ('Sesame and Lilies' first published 1864)

Swift, J. (1973) 'A Modest Proposal' in *The Writings of Jonathan Swift*, New York: Norton, (first published 1729)

Yonge, C. M. (1887) *What Books to Lend and What to Give*, London: National Society's Depository

Letters

Creighton, Mrs. 'Lady Lugard' in *The Times*, January 30th. 1929, London: The Times

Jersey, M. E. 'Lady Lugard' in *The Times*, February 5th. 1929, London: The Times

Garston, E. M. 'Lady Lugard' in *The Times*, February 6th. 1929, London: The Times

Obituaries and entries in biographical reference works

Anonymous (1929) 'Lady Lugard' in *The Times*, January 28th. 1929, London

Anonymous (1929) 'Lady Lugard Dead' in the *New York Times*, January 28th. 1929: New York

Anonymous (no date) 'Lady Lugard', clipping in the Alice Marshall Collection, Special Collections, Penn State Harrisburg Library, US

Hailey, ? (1975) 'Lugard, Frederick John Dealty' in Williams, E. (ed.) *Dictionary of National Biography (supplement)*, Oxford: University Press

Helly, D. O. and H. Callaway (2004), 'Lugard , Dame Flora Louise, Lady Lugard (1852–1929)', *Oxford Dictionary of National Biography*, Oxford: University Press

Kirk-Greene, A. H. M. (2004) 'Lugard, Frederick John Dealtry, Baron Lugard (1858–1945)', in the *Oxford Dictionary of National Biography*, Oxford: University Press

Kunitz, S. J. & H. Hancraft (1936) *British Authors of the Nineteenth Century*, New York: H. W. Wilson

Bibliography of Secondary Sources

Biography

Bell, E. H. C. M. (1947) *Flora Shaw – Lady Lugard DBE (with portraits)*, London: Constable

Bradley, J. L. (1997) *A Ruskin Chronology*, London: Macmillan

Callaway, H. *Letter to B. Carrington*, March 11th. 2002, in response to queries about Flora Shaw

Callaway, H. *Re: Flora Shaw*, message sent to
<abc20875@primex.co.uk>
(sent and accessed 14/3/02)

Callaway, H. *Re: Flora Shaw*, message sent to
<abc20875@primex.co.uk>
(sent and accessed 27/3/02)

Callaway, H. *Re: Flora Shaw*, message sent to
<abc20875@primex.co.uk>
(sent and accessed 26/11/02)

Callaway, H. & D. O. Helly (1992) 'Crusader for Empire: Flora Shaw/Lady Lugard' in Chauduri, N, and M. Strobel (eds.) *Western Women and Imperialism: Complicity and Resistance*, Bloomsbury: Indiana University Press

Helly, D. O. & H. Callaway (2000) 'Journalism in Active Politics: Flora Shaw, The Times and South Africa' in Lowry, D. (ed.) *The South African War Reappraised*, Manchester: University Press

McClay, K. *obit for Lady Lugard*, message sent to
<abc20875@primex.co.uk>

(sent and accessed on 26/11/02)
National Archive of Canada,
http://www.archives.ca
(accessed 13/12/02)

National Register of Archives,
http://www.hmc.gov.uk/nra
(accessed throughout research)

Palmer's Index to The Times, accessed via EDINA
http://edina.ed.ac.uk
(accessed throughout research)

Perham, M. (1956) *Lugard: The Years of Adventure 1868-1898*, London: Collins

Perham, M. (1960) *Lugard: The Years of Authority 1898-1945*, London: Collins

Princess Grace Irish Library (Monaco) 2001 *Flora L[ouisa] Shaw*, http://www.pgil-eirdata.org/
(accessed 18/04/02)

Sachs, M. *Re: Flora Shaw,* message sent to
<abc20875@primex.co.uk>
(sent and accessed26/11/02)

Stray, C. *Fiona* [sic] *Shaw*, message sent to
<abc20875@primex.co.uk>
(sent and accessed 28/6/02)

The Times newspaper 1790-1980, microfilm held at the British Library, London, and on CDROM at the Millenium Library, Norwich

Wolff, R. L. (1985) introduction to 'Castle Blair' in *Masterworks of Children's Literature, volume 5, part 2 1837-1900*, London: Allen Lane

Histories

Political and Social

Dodd, L. (2002) 'After the Famine' in *The Guardian Weekend Magazine*, October 5th 2002

Ensor, R. (2nd. Edition, 1962) *England 1870-1914*, volume 15 in *The Oxford History of England*, Oxford: University Press (first published 1936)

Moody, T. W. & F. X. Martin (eds.) (1967) *The Course of Irish History*, Cork: The Mercier Press

Woodward, L. (2nd. Edition, 1962*) The Age of Reform 1815-1870*, volume 14 in *The Oxford History of England*, Oxford: University Press

Publishing

Abbots, J. *Flora Shaw-Castle Blair*, message sent to
<abc20875@primex.co.uk>
(sent and accessed 22/11/02)

Callaway, H. *Re: Flora Shaw*, message sent to
<abc20875@primex.co.uk>
(sent and accessed 23/05/02)

Feather, J. (1988) *A History of British Publishing*, London: Routledge

Howsam, L. (1998) *Kegan Paul: A Victorian Imprint*, London: Kegan Paul International

'Kegan Paul' *Re: Flora Shaw and Ruskin*, message sent to
<abc20875@primex.co.uk>
(sent and accessed 22/11/02)

Lewis, K. *Re: C. Kegan Paul and Flora Shaw*, message sent to
<abc20875@primex.co.uk>
(sent and accessed 26/11/02)

Patterson, R. *Ruskin and Flora Shaw*, message sent to
<abc20875@primex.co.uk>
(sent and accessed 22/11/02)

Routledge & Kegan Paul Ltd. Archive, accessed via AIM25,
http://www.aim25.ac.uk
(accessed 25/11/02)

Literature

Abebooks
http://www.abebooks.com
(accessed throughout research)

Avery, G. (1965) *Nineteenth Century Children: Heroes and Heroines in English Children's Stories 1780-1900*, London: Hodder & Stoughton

Bodleian Library Catalogue, accessed via COPAC
http://www.copac.ac.uk/copac
(accessed throughout research)

British Library Catalogue
http://blpc.bl.uk
(accessed throughout research)

Carpenter, H. & M. Prichard (1987) *The Oxford Companion to Children's Literature*, Oxford: University Press (first published 1984)

Carpenter, H. (1987) *Secret Gardens: A Study of the Golden Age of Children's Literature*, London: Unwin (first published 1985)

Darton, F. J. H., revised B. Alderson (3rd. edition, with corrections, 1999), *Children's Books in England*, London: The British Library (first published 1932)

Davidson, M. *Re: E. Nesbit intertextuality*, sent to
<abc20875@primex.co.uk>
(sent and accessed 30/6/02)

Dunbar, R. (2004) 'Rebuilding Castle Blair: A Reading of Flora Shaw's 1878 Children's Novel' in Keenan, C. & M. Shine Thompson (2004) *Studies in Children's Literature, 1500-2000*, Dublin: Four Courts Press

Eaton, A. T. (1953) 'A Broader Field' in 'Widening Horizons 1840-1890', part 2 in Meigs, C, A. T. Eaton, E. Nesbitt & R. H. Viguers *A Critical History of Children's Literature: A survey of children's books in English from earliest times to the present, prepared in four parts under the editorship of Cornelia Meigs*, New York: Macmillan

Fisher, M. (1975) *Who's Who in Children's Books? A Treasury of Familiar Characters of Childhood*, London: Weidenfield and Nicholson

Green, R. L. (3rd. edition 1965) *Tellers of Tales: Children's books and their authors from 1800-1964*, London: Edmund Ward (first published 1946)

Hunt, P. (1995) *Children's Literature: An illustrated history*, Oxford: University Press

Kirkpatrick, K. (1995) 'Introduction' to Edgeworth, M. *Castle Rackrent*, Oxford: University Press

Library of Congress Catalogue
http://www.catalog.loc.gov
(accessed 19/08/02)

Mackerness, E. D. (1966) 'The Voice of Prophecy: Carlyle and Ruskin' *in From Dickens to Hardy,* volume 6 of Ford, B (ed.) *The Pelican Guide to English Literature*, Harmondsworth: Penguin Books (first published 1958)

Moss, A. (1991) 'E. Nesbit's Romantic Child in Modern Dress' in McGavran, J. H. (ed.) *Romanticism and Children's Literature in England*, Athens, Georgia: University of Georgia Press

Reynolds, K. (1994) *Children's Literature in the 1890s and the 1990s*, Plymouth: Northcote House

Shakeshaft, M. *Letter* in response to query from B. Carrington, re C. M. Yonge (1887) *What Books to Lend and What to Give*, 23/06/02

Stemp, J. *Quotations on children's literature-
19C (long-ish)*, The UK list for academic discussion of all aspects of children's literature <children-literature-uk@JISCMAIL.AC.UK>
(sent and accessed 09/04/02)

Watson, V. (ed.) (2001) *The Cambridge Guide to Children's Books in English*, Cambridge: University Press

Wullschlager, J. (1995) *Inventing Wonderland: The lives and fantasies of Lewis Carroll, Edward Lear, J. M. Barrie, Kenneth Grahame and A. A. Milne*, New York: The Free Press

Zipes, J. (ed.) (2006) *The Oxford Encyclopedia of Children's Literature*, New York: Oxford University Press

Index

absent mothers – see maternal loss
Adam Bede 43
adolescent fiction 217, 271
adoption 97
adultery 53
Alcott, Louisa M. 219, 222, 227
Andersen, Hans Christian
    The Princess and the Pea 132
angel fiction 112-127
Anglo-Irish v, 212, 235, 244, 246, 268
  absentee landlords 247, 265
appearance 36, 39, 61, 63
Aschehoug, H. & Co. (W. Nygaard) (publisher) 225, 226(ill) 227n6
Aunt Judy's Magazine 216-217, 224, 238, 264
Avery, Gillian 214, 253, 261, 273

Barlee, E.M.
    Pantomime Waifs 41n10
Barnardo, Thomas 30, 31, 37, 39, 48, 42n14
    'A City Waif' 27, 30, 48
    ' "God's Little Girl" ' 36
    'Kidnapped' 32
    Taken Out of the Gutter 41n8
begging 60
behaviour 83, 84, 97, 100, 110, 113, 115, 117, 134, 137, 138, 182, 187, 192-193, 198-199, 267
  see also manners, etiquette
Bell, C.F. 231
Bell, G & Sons 216, 268
Bell, E Moberly 211, 230-232, 262
Besant, Annie 44, 46, 55n6
Blackwell, Elizabeth 123
Bleak House 22n15, 28
Booth, Charles 50
Borrow, George 66
Boucicault 18

'Boys' and Girls' Bookshelf' 222
Brenda (Mrs Castle Smith) i, iv, v, 16
  adult novels 149, 156
  as non de plume 169
  'Brenda's Box' 154-163, 168
  burial 172
  charity work 168,183
  childhood 164-167
  children 172, 187, 193-195
  family 151-153, 161, 167
  family vacations 170-171
  fan letters 156, 161
  last years 172
  marriage 153, 154, 169
  obituary 149, 161
  reviews 149, 155-156, 162
  social reformer 200
  titles
    A Little Brown Teapot 156
    Especially Those: A Story on the Prayer 'For all conditions of Men' 154, 170
    Froggy's Little Brother iv, 31, 40n2, 62, 149, 150, 154, 155, 157, 158, 159, 160, 169, 185, 170, 172, 175, 177-181, 180(ill), 201
    Film of 163
    Little Cousins or Georgie's Visit to Lotty 151, 188, 191-193, 196, 199
    Lotty's Visit to Grandmama: a Story for the Little Ones 151, 166, 188, 189-191, 192, 199
    Mary Pillenger Supreme Factor 162
    More about Froggy. A Sequel to Froggy's Little Brother 166

The Water-Babies 70n3
Kravchinsky, Sergei (Stepniak) 11, 22n10
Kropotkin, Prince Peter 11, 22n10

Lady Lugard *see* Flora Shaw
Langham Place Group, the 124
Little, Brown & Co (publisher) 222, 223, 270, 272
The Little Princess 132
Livermore, Mary A. 223, 271
London 18, 62
London Society for the Prevention of Cruelty to Children 10, 21n7, 183
Longmans, Green & Co (publisher) 217
Lugard, Sir Frederick John Dealtry 228, 232

MacDonald, George
    At the Back of the North Wind 40n3
The Making of a Marchioness 136
Mame, Alfred & Fils (publishers) 224-225
Manchester Guardian 238
manners 83, 84, 129-131, 137,
  see also behaviour, etiquette
marriage 43-44, 46, 54, 55n6, 121
Married Women's Property Acts 45, 121
Marryat, F. 253, 261n1
Martineau, Harriet 5, 211
Mary Barton 19, 20n2, 27, 40, 47-48
'Masterworks of Children's Literature' 211, 221
maternal loss 27, 28, 47-48, 50
maternal role 31, 65, 105
Mayhew, Henry 26, 32, 35, 39, 40n4
Meade, L. T,
    Atalanta 83
    Scamp & I 50, 63

Mearns, Andrew 41n4
Meredith, George 238, 262
middle class ii, iv, 84, 85-90, 96, 133, 138, 149, 150, 151, 187-199, 200
Mill, John Stuart 44, 45, 55n2, 55n5
The Mill on the Floss 115
Molesworth, Mrs i, ii-iii, v, 16, 82(ill), 139(ill), 267
  children 85
  family 85
  letters 124
  marriage 85-86
  reviews of her work 83-84
  titles
    Blanche 131-132
    Carrots: Just a Little Boy 91-92, 93
    The Carved Lions 127, 135
    A Charge Fulfilled 105-106
    The Children of the Castle 117
    The Cuckoo Clock 118-119
    Hermy 117, 119-120, 138
    Hoodie 93-95, 99, 117
    Jasper 113, 115-116, 117, 134
    My New Home 117, 122
    Mary 102 (ill), 112-113
    Nurse Heatherdale's Story 107, 135
    Philippa 108
    The Rectory Children 92, 100, 117, 134
    Rosy 98, 117
    The Ruby Ring 71n5, 117, 136
    Robin Redbreast 119, 120, 122
    Sheila's Mystery 71n5, 88(ill), 96-97,100, 117
    Sweet Content 99-100, 117
    The Story of a Spring Morning 106
    The Story of a Year 122
    That Girl in Black 123

marriage 211-212, 228, 233-4, 240

in Nigeria 240

obituary 229

parents 235-236

popularity in America 222

reviews of her work 224 261, 262, 270-273, 274

titles

Barnene paa Castle Blair 225, 226(ill), 227

Castel-Blair 224-225

Castle Blair 211, 212, 213, 214, 216, 217, 219, 221, 222, 223, 224, 226(ill), 227, 229, 230, 232, 234, 235, 237, 238, 243-252, 253-256, 260-267, 268, 275, 276, 277

abridged edition 223, 225, 271

critical comment 273-274, 275

in America 222-223, 250

in translation 224-227

publishing history 215-216, 219, 221,220 (ill), 222, 223, 224

reviews 262, 263-264, 266, 268-269, 270, 272

Colonel Cheswick's Campaign 211, 215, 217, 219, 222, 223, 225, 233, 236, 261, 271

publishing history 217-219

Hector 211, 212, 213, 216, 219, 222, 225, 232, 234, 235, 236, 237, 250, 253, 255-261, 257 (ill), 265, 267-268, 275

critical comment 273

in America 223-224

publishing history 216, 223-224

reviews 269-270, 271

Phyllis Browne 211, 217, 224, 225, 230, 232, 234, 237, 241n4, 265, 270, 271

A Sea Change 211, 216, 217, 218 (ill), 224, 233,265, 270-271

The Story of Australia 242n12

A Tropical Dependency 242n13

Une Cousine de France 224

in Waltham Abbey 232

in Woolwich 230, 235, 237

Sherwood, Mrs 5

Sims, George 18

slums 10, 61, 175, 176, 183, 184-185, 200

Smith, Barbara Leigh 124

Smith, Castle 153-154, 169-170

Smith, Georgina Castle *see* Brenda

Smith, Lizzie *see* Stretton, Hesba

Smith, Sarah *see* Stretton, Hesba

social deprivation ii, 26, 28, 33, 36, 49-50, 61, 63, 64, 175, 181

social education 14-15

social exclusion ii, 4, 57, 59-60, 62, 64

social history i-ii, iv

social mobility 58

social reform 10, 17, 34, 61, 157

spinsters 54, 99, 121

Stepniak *see* Kravchinsky, Sergei

Stead, W.T. 238

stereotypes 61, 64

Stevenson, Robert Louis 222, 238

street-arabs 3, 14, 30, 34, 35, 36, 37, 39, 42n12, 68, 149, 150, 151, 175-181, 185, 200

street children *see* street-arabs

Stretton, Hesba (Sarah Smith) i, ii, v, 6(ill), 149, 150, 183, 200

adult novels 12, 16

diaries 7, 8, 9, 11, 12, 30-31, 53, 57-58, 66

family 5-8

magazine stories 20

obituary ii

popularity 14, 15-16

religion 10, 17, 19, 32

short stories 63, 65
sister (Lizzie Smith) 8
as social reformer 10, 17, 69-70
titles

Biographies

Bridget Carrington is researching the development of fiction for Young Adult girls 1750-1890 for a doctorate at Roehampton University, following her MA work on Flora Shaw. Formerly a teacher, her previously published work includes articles on historical and literary topics for popular and academic journals, and contributions to the *Oxford Encyclopedia of Children's Literature* and the *Oxford Dictionary of National Biography*. She currently reviews literature for young people for a number of organisations including *Book Trust* and writes educational material.

Elaine Lomax completed a PhD on Hesba Stretton at De Montfort University in 2003, and is currently a part-time lecturer in English at the University of Bedfordshire. She is the author of articles and essays on Stretton, including 'Telling the Other Side: Hesba Stretton's "Outcast" Stories' in *Popular Children's Literature in Britain*, (eds) Briggs, Butts and Grenby (Ashgate, 2008). Her full-length study, *The Writings of Hesba Stretton: Reclaiming the Outcast* (2009), is published by Ashgate.

Mary Sebag-Montefiore was called to the Bar, and also holds an MA in Children's Literature from Roehampton University, researching class and culture in the works of Mrs Molesworth. She has published *Women Writers of Children's Classics*, Northcote House, 2008. Women Writers of Children's Classics*, Northcote House, 2008;* for Usborne Young Reading, *Black Beauty* (2005)*, Heidi* (2006), *Little Women* (2006), *Oliver Twist* (2006), *The Secret Garden* (2007), *The Railway Children* (2007), *Great Expectations* (2007), *A Tale of Two Cities* (2008), *David Copperfield* (2008).

Liz Thiel is a lecturer in Children's Literature at Roehampton University where she teaches at both undergraduate and MA level. A former journalist, her research focuses on both contemporary and historical texts for children. Her most recent publications include *The Fantasy of Family: Nineteenth-century Children's Literature and the Myth of the Domestic Ideal* (Routledge, 2008) and the co-edited *An Invitation to Explore: New International Perspectives on Children's Literature* (Pied Piper Publishing, 2009).